Mingquan Zhou
Guohua Geng
Zhongke Wu

Digital Preservation Technology for Cultural Heritage

Mingquan Zhou
Guohua Geng
Zhongke Wu

Digital Preservation Technology for Cultural Heritage

With 149 figures, 27 of them in color

高等教育出版社
HIGHER EDUCATION PRESS

Springer

Authors
Mingquan Zhou
College of Information Science and Technology, Beijing Normal University, Beijing 100875, P.R. China
E-mail: mqzhou@bnu.edu.cn

Zhongke Wu
College of Information Science and Technology, Beijing Normal University, Beijing 100875, P.R. China
E-mail: zwu@bnu.edu.cn

Guohua Geng
College of Information Science and Technology, Northwest University
Xi'an 710069, P.R. China
E-mail: ghgeng@nwu.edu.cn

ISBN 978-7-04-031879-1
Higher Education Press, Beijing

ISBN 978-3-642-28098-6 ISBN 978-3-642-28099-3 (eBook)
Springer Heidelberg New York Dordrecht London

Library of Congress Control Number: 2011945840

Printed on acid-free paper

Springer is part of Springer Science+Business Media (www.springer.com)

Preface

As a great nation with a profound civilization of more than five thousand years, China has a rich resource base cultural heritage. However, due to wars and other negative impacts, much of the cultural heritage has been damaged and corroded. A new era of information richness is coming after the Stone Age, the Bronze Age, the Agricultural age, and the Industrial age. This new era presents us as Chinese researchers and global citizens the responsibility and mission to use information technologies to protect and save cultural heritage for future generations.

We want to be responsible to history. The Chinese cultural heritage is the witness of the history of Chinese civilization and has an impact to over 1 billion people's identity. We want to be responsible for human civilization to make Chinese culture seen no less favorable than any other world civilization, because the Chinese cultural heritage is an important part of the world's cultural heritage. We desire for the future responsibility in the protection and preservation of cultural heritage as a continuation of civilization for all the citizens of the world to explore. We have to be fair to the future generations.

Based on the above basic principles and mission of our work, we have been carrying out the digital protection of cultural heritage for more than fifteen years. With the joint efforts of many computer scientists, archeologists and digital art experts participating in the research field, we have made some important breakthroughs. With the support from the National Natural Science Foundation of China, the State Administration of Cultural Heritage, and the Key Project of the National Research Program of China, this book presents readers a detailed knowledge about the research and practice of digital protection and preservation methods of cultural heritage. It combines information technologies with digitization procedures for cultural heritage, such as data acquisition, model representation and operation, virtual restoration, digital management, web based retrieval, and digital museum exhibition techniques. This book also gives some practical applications in at the end.

With the goal of digital protection of cultural heritage, this book is organized in four parts:

The first part, Chapter 1, summarizes the topics covered in this book. This chapter introduces the basic concepts of digitization protection of cultural heritage, the objectives of protection, conservation status, protection strategies, protection requirements, and the contents of various research efforts.

The second part, Chapter 2, introduces the fundamental techniques in digital protection of cultural heritage including model representation, geometry processing, model rendering, and computer animation and simulation technologies.

The third part, which includes Chapter 3, Chapter 4, Chapter 5, Chapter 6, and Chapter 7, introduces the special techniques solving the bottleneck issues in the process of digital protection of cultural heritage. Chapter 3 focuses on digitization techniques of the cultural heritage containing overviews of various devices of data capture, 3D reconstruction of artifacts by range-imaging and sequence of images, and 3D reconstruction of cultural sites including terrain modeling. Chapter 4 describes digital management of cultural heritage protection based on digital archaeology and monitoring, which covers digital aided investigation, digital environment archeology and dynamic environment of monitoring systems. At the end of the chapter, an archeological site space information system is introduced. Chapter 5 centers on virtual restoration techniques for ancient artifacts. Fragments classification, digital artifacts representation and fracture-curve-based restoration method are adopted to achieve fragments restoration. This chapter also introduces hole-filling technology to repair incomplete artifacts with an arbitrary shape and estimation methods of symmetric and generatrixes to recover incomplete artifacts with a symmetry-shape. Chapter 6 focuses on virtual restoration techniques for incomplete calligraphy and painting, and demonstrates the use of technology to restore defective areas. Chapter 7 presents the fundamental concepts of digital museum and its major components, such as standards and specifications of the digital collections, display, retrieval, and copyright protection technology of digital collections.

The fourth part, Chapter 8, provides several examples of digital protection of cultural heritage such as the digitalization of the third excavation of Pit One of Terracotta Warriors and Horses of Qin Shihuang and the virtual presentation of Tang Paradise, which is the largest tourist program in Northwest China.

In addition, the book has two features. First, it presents the results of the cross-study of information techniques and artifacts protection, and has a relatively complete scientific interdisciplinary system. With the reference of achievements in domestic and foreign archeological findings, this book constructs the fundamental and application system of Preservation of Cultural Heritage through Digitization, presenting the forefront and progress of the interdisciplinary research. Second, the technologies presented in this book can be adopted with wide coverage and effective application. This book covers the entire process of digital preservation of cultural heritage, including digital capture, collection, representation, processing, restoration, and virtual display. All the technologies in this book are from empirical research and practice of many years in the digital protection of cultural heritage.

I would like to express my great and sincere thanks to the following people for their contributions to this book: Wuyang Shui, Ru Wang, Xuesong Wang, Qingqiong Deng, Xuan Zhu, Xiaodong Zhu, Jun Liu, Jing Zhang, and Yan Hu. I am also grateful to the Key Lab of the Ministry of Education on Cultural Heritage Research and Protection Techniques at Northwest University, Beijing Key Laboratory of Digital Protection, and Virtual Reality for Cultural Heritage in Beijing Normal University, the Palace Museum, Museum of Terracotta Warriors and Horses of Qin Shihuang, Archaeological Research Institute of Shanxi Province for their great support. We, the book authors, are grateful to Mr. Victor Morrison for his great help editing and providing revision of this english edition of the book. Specially thank to Mrs. Chen Hongying from Higher Education Press for her invaluable help.

This book is a good reference not only for researchers and graduates in the majors of computer graphics, image processing, virtual reality, et al. but also for those in archeology, heritage conservation, and museums fields. I hope this book can expand new ways of thought in the digital protection of cultural heritage as well as guidance for the preservation of cultural heritage as well.

Mingquan Zhou
Beijing Normal University
March 2012

Contents

1 Introduction

China is an ancient country with long history and profound civilization, which has numerous cultural remains and archaeological sites. These remains and sites, which are treasures of all people of the world, contain unique spiritual values and ways of thinking, and drive the imagination of the Chinese people and represent vitality and creativity. Protection of the cultural heritage and historical legacies is the key foundation to keep the cultural bonds between people, which is also the prerequisite to maintain the cultural pluralism and the creativeness in the world, and to promote development together. The traditional relocation and replication methods have showed difficulties to reproduce the complete, truthful, and vivid original look of the sites or the culture. The development of informational technology, such as artificial intelligence, virtual reality, multimedia, broadband network, and databases, has provided effective tools for heritage protection. How to apply these technologies to preserve history culture, propel culture protection, and accomplish digital protection, is a challenging problem for archaeologists and computer scientists focused on three-dimension (3D) imaging, and also an important task of contemporary science. contemporary contemporary contemporary

1.1 Review of Cultural Heritage Using Digital Protection

Definition of cultural heritage

The conception of cultural heritage was firstly put forward in the *Convention Concerning the Protection of the World Cultural and Natural Heritage* by the United Nations Educational, Scientific and Cultural Organization (UNESCO) in November 1972 [1]. The convention presented that the cultural property demonstrates the importance, for all the population of the world, of safeguarding this unique and irreplaceable property, to whatever people it belongs. The following shall be considered as cultural heritage: Monuments, Groups of Buildings, Sites, Cultural Landscape, Human Beings Verbal, and Intangible Cultural Heritage.

Categories of the world cultural heritage

Figure 1.1 describes the category of the world cultural heritage. Among them, *material cultural heritage* is of outstanding universal value from the point of view of history, art, or science; *unmovable cultural heritage* is fixed, such as architectural space, natural space, which includes sites of ancient culture, ancient tombs, ancient architectural structures, cave temples, and stone carvings; *movable cultural heritage* includes important authentic objects, art works, historical documents, and manuscripts of different eras. *Intangible cultural Heritage* is represented by diverse traditional cultural expression and cultural aspects, which are closely related to the people's life and could be transmitted from generation to generation, such as oral traditions, performing arts, social practices, rituals, festive events, knowledge and practices concerning nature and the universe, or the knowledge and skills to produce traditional crafts. This book is mainly focused on *material cultural heritage*.

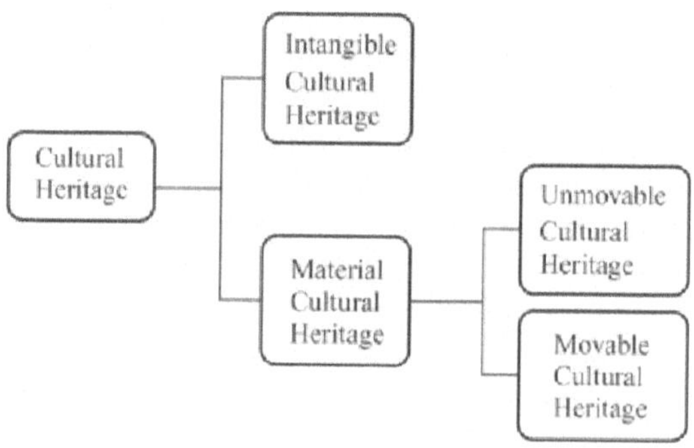

Fig. 1.1 Category of the world culture heritage.

Digitalization of cultural heritage

The digitalization of cultural heritage is the process of digitalizing the movable or unmovable cultural heritage using contemporary remote-sensing and virtual technologies to achieve 2D or 3D digital archiving, for the merits of protection, reparation, restoration, and archaeological research.

Application of digital cultural heritage

The application stratum to provide digitalization of the cultural heritage is summarized in Fig. 1.2.

(1) Digital archiving is a basis for cultural heritage preservation.

(2) Repair and restoration revives the cultural heritage.

(3) Archeological research provides basis for the intrinsic values of the cultural heritage.

(4) Cultural communication and transmission carries forward and develops national culture.

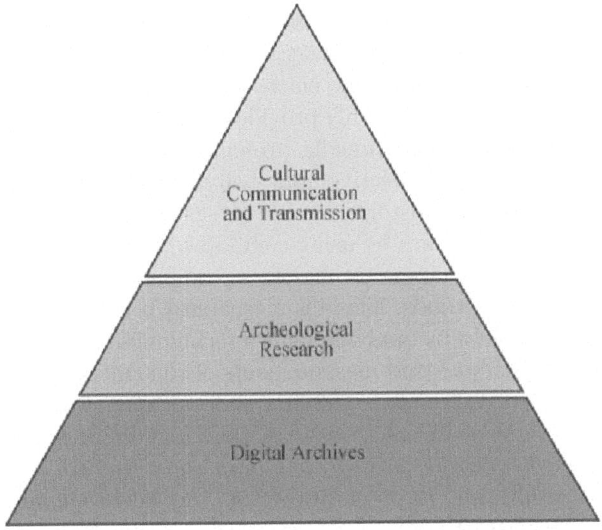

Fig. 1.2 Application stratum of the digital cultural heritage.

1.2 Meaning and Value of Cultural Heritages Digital Protection

Cultural heritage reflects human civilization and wisdom. Protecting cultural heritage is protecting the history and creations of human beings. China is a major world cultural heritage country, which has around 400,000 historic landmarks and sites under conservation. The Chinese government has listed 6,000 sites that are under the protection of state (1,271), province, autonomous region, or municipalities. Six Chinese heritage sites, including the Palace Museum, are approved on the World Heritage List by the Committee for World Heritage in 1987 [2]. Until the end of December 2011, forty-one culture heritages and natural landscapes are inscribed on the World Heritage List [2]. Among them, there are 29 cultural heritages, 8 natural heritages, 4 cultural and natural heritages, and 1 cultural landscape. Moreover, there are 35 additional applications in progress. The civilization's history of over 5,000 years has left us numerous precious heritage artifacts, which are mostly represented with porcelain, jade, and bronze objects. However, for thousands of years, these heritages have suffered unprecedented damage by weathering, war, and historical changes. In modern society with enormous economy development and human activities, a considerable number of heritages have become damaged or broken. Many of them are impossible to be repaired due to some factors, like artificial destruction. For example, many relics of Longmen Grottoes are scattered overseas, which makes the view of a whole Longmen Grottoes impossible. Another example is the Old Summer Palace, which has fallen into ruin after two disasters. Thus, how to protect these precious heritages using the contemporary science and technologies has become a challenging problem faced by the entire human race.

Information technology not only provides benefits like huge data volumes, high speed computation, multimedia presentation, and on-line access, but also gives an essential and effective approach to protect cultural heritage. It is the obligatory task and historic mission entrusted of computer scientists to restore these destroyed relics by using computer graphics, image processing, virtual reality, and other new technologies, combined with traditional protection and display methods. There is a technical revolution in the cultural heritage protection field by applying digital techniques to it. This will change the traditional techniques and measurements of the cultural heritage protection, and even change the way of thinking and working of the archaeologists.

According to the traditional ways of thinking, heritage should be displayed. However, once the heritage has been separated from their original environment, resulting in the separation from the view as a whole, the damages will be caused to the respective heritages. The museums and other protection organizations could utilize digital technologies and devices, such as multimedia and virtual reality, to rebuild the "Museum Experience", where the audiences could navigate to view the virtual cultural heritages and understand the meaning of cultural heritage as a whole. A comprehensive and complete space of meaning could be rehabilitate and reproduced thus the educational role of digital cultural heritage could be fully exploited.

Related digitalization technologies for cultural heritages are as follows:

(1) High-fidelity, integrated storage and access techniques.

(2) Categorization and digital archives of cultural heritage, and digital techniques to build cultural resource databases.

(3) Virtual museums, virtual reconstruction and rehabilitation of cultural relics, digital simulation and visualization technology of the cultural spaces and procedures.

(4) The technology to recreate the lifestyle, practice, consumption, currency, transmission, and continuity of the traditional craftsmanship.

(5) The pattern and technology to display and transmit the digital cultural heritage.

Currently, the applications of the computer technologies in archaeology are focused on exhibition while deeper and substantive systems in archaeology are rare. Although there are a lot of research and practice bases, the key technologies are still awaiting further research, such as follows:

(1) The modeling, simulation, and rendering technologies of the sites, scenes and heritages to support the original works, such as expert reasoning, forecasting, recognition, proposal, and confirmatory experiments.

(2) The technologies of registering, matching the rigid 3D models, and providing a restoration plan to help the restoration process for archaeologists.

(3) The technologies to exhibit precise antiques and scenes , measurement and transmission of the cultural heritages.

(4) The digital technologies of the cultural heritages' information, which could supply tools to generate flowcharts, profile and notation of archaeology so that the archaeological excavation reports and charts can be automatically generated.

1.3 Targets of Digital Cultural Heritage Protection

Targets of cultural heritage protection can be divided into material and intangible heritage.

The main extents and targets of material cultural heritage protection have been clearly defined by the United Nations Educational Scientific and Cultural Organization in the *Convention Concerning the Protection of the World Cultural and Natural Heritage* in 1972 [3], which including three main scopes:

(1) Culture relics: from historical, artistic or scientific aspect, including buildings, steel, and murals of outstanding universal values, as well as inscriptions, and whole union structures of archaeological significance.

(2) Architectural complexes: from historical, artistic, or scientific aspect, individual or joint architectural complexes with outstanding universal values in style, distribution, or surroundings.

(3) Ruins: from historical, esthetic, ethnological, or anthropological aspect, these outstanding including human constructions, human-nature combined works, and archaeological sites.

According to the *The Convention for the Safeguarding of the Intangible Cultural Heritage* [4] adopted in October of 2003, "intangible cultural heritage" means the practices, representations, expressions, knowledge, skills, including oral traditions and expressions, performing arts, social practices, rituals, festive events, knowledge and practices concerning nature and the universe, and traditional craftsmanship.

1.4 Status of Digital Cultural Heritage Protection

Since 1990s, digital technology has been under great development, for example, virtual reality technology has made remarkable achievements in cultural heritage protection. Centered on digital techniques, protection theories have been established, and work specialization have been formed, thus gives solid guarantee for cultural heritage protection, and provides new solutions in this area. Meanwhile, as cultural heritage has been a part of the world market as information productions, its digitization is delivering increase importance to governments and researchers.

1.4.1 Status of International Digital Cultural Heritage Protection

Digital cultural heritage protection in foreign countries has been under great development in recent years. With sound theories and technical support, many conferences have set up subjects on cultural protection, including areas of multimedia, virtual reality and computer graphics. Digital graphics or vision art conferences have accepted digital technology as sound methods of cultural protection. Many leading universities have started the research on digital protection related works. Universities worldwide are cooperating with cultural institutions of other countries and seeking better solutions for world cultural protection.

Europe

3D MURALE projection [5], which is funded by the European Union, has proposed a full set of methods on ancient sites protection and rebuilding, and is already applied to Turkish Sagalassos ruins. This projection contains acquisition and recording of cultural heritages, forming a multimedia database, virtual rebuilding, visualization, rebuilding ancient sites [6] according to database and excavations, providing many new media technologies on recording, classification, protection, and recovering ancient utensils, buildings and ruins.

In 2004, Belgium, the Fifth International Symposium on Virtual Reality, Archaeology, and Cultural Heritage (VAST) started special discussion on Avatar, considering human actions [7], group behaviors [8], and experiencing historical events [9] in virtual ancient scenes.

The United States

Digital Library

Indiana University built traditional music archives to protect historical files using digital technology [10]. The Digital Humanity Center of University of Nebraska built Whitman text digital library that started using digital methods in literature protection [11]. Visual Media Center of Columbia University started a series of teaching practices on cultural heritage collection and virtual artwork showcases [12]. Besides, Stanford University, the University of Washington, and the Cyberware Company are cooperating on Digital Michelangelo Project [13]. The University of Chicago and University of Western Ontario's Sulman Mummy Project are other examples [14].

Using ancient civilization to present state of art with the use of technologies

The most influential work in digital archaeology area is the "Digital Michelangelo Project" conducted by Stanford University in 1990 [13], followed by Forma Urbis Roma project of Stanford University [15], and the Digital Coliseum and Bema Project of University of California, Los Angeles [16], and as a final example the "Rome Regeneration" project of University of Virginia [17] that is progressing currently to digitalize the whole of Roma city. Digital Michelangelo Project uses 3D laser scanner to digitalize Michelangelo's works, including a 7.5 meter high of the David sculpture, which contains 2 billion points, with accuracy of 50 micrometer. Forma Urbis Roma Project uses Cyberware 3D scanner to digitalize 1,163 Marble fragments of the ruins to try to restructure ancient Roma's terrain mapping. Because fragments' shapes and thicknesses are random, this work is impossible to perform by manual operation, they take digital solutions to reduce the difficulties of traditional methods. IBM's Thomas J. Watson Lab applied the hologram technique that digitalized Michelangelo's Florentine Pieta sculpture by scanning more than 1,000 times, but the accuracy of this model is relatively low [18]. Princeton University and Akrotiri Excavation institution started work on Akrotiri ruin's fracture mural's digitalization and repair. They designed and implemented a set of mural fracture digitalization systems and splicing methods, finally accomplished fractures' virtual splicing and repair [19].

Other countries and areas

Canada's National Research Center developed a kind of high precision 3D scanning system to start the digitalization of libraries and ruins. They cooperated with Padova University to accomplished 3D digitalization of Virgin Mary and Christ Child. They also cooperated with Israel to start digitalization of ancient buildings and ruins of the Caesar era.

1.4.2 Status of Digital Cultural Heritage Protection in China

In China, many representative achievements in digital cultural heritage protection have also been made. The CAD & CG lab of Zhejiang University started Dunhuang arts' digital protection in 1997. They proposed fresco copying techniques and fresco colorific evolvement techniques, developed Mogao Caves' virtual travel system, Dunhuang fresco's copying aid and repairing system, and computer aided cave protection and repairing system [20]. Peking University started the Longmen Grottoes' digital protection work. According to different sizes and accuracy requirements, they used different types of scanners to build models of Longmen Grottoes drum sets facade area, cave, Buddha sculpture in the round big day, small Buddha sculpture, and other adornments. Professor Zhou Mingquan of Beijing Normal University started 3D rigid body's repair research in 1998, and made special progress on computer aided repair work of Terracotta Warriors and Horses of Qin Shihuang [21 – 24]. With fractures' information acquired by digital systems, they first performed auto-splicing by shape matching techniques, followed with a manual adjustment step to accomplish heritage's virtual repairing.

Digital museums, such as Nanjing Museum, Archeology Digital Museum of Northwest University in China, Archeology Digital Museums of Shandong University, and the International Friendship Museum in Beijing, also provide useful methods and experiences for the preservation, succession, and recreation of endangered cultural heritage using information technology.

1.5 Strategies and Requirements of Digital Preservation of Cultural Heritage

With the extension and expansion of the heritage concept, the amounts of heritages become bigger and bigger and its level become more and more abundant. But meanwhile, large amounts of heritages are damaged by wars and natural disasters. Tourists with large numbers visiting the sites also damage many cultural heritages. An important strategy of preserving cultural heritage is to use advanced computer technology with information, control, management, and decision-making, to record the precious, endangered and historic cultural heritage in a real, systematic and comprehensive way and to perform virtual representation, build permanent files and databases. The strategy could be represented by the following points:

Digital information acquisition and processing technology

Digital information acquisition and processing technology is a new technology to information architecture of cultural heritage. This technology can ensure the preservation of cultural heritage in the most comprehensive and verifiable way. Digital information acquisition and processing technology can preserve archival data such as photos and images in digital format, which makes it easy to store. It can also arrange, collect and record the information of cultural heritage with achieving high fidelity quality and displayable features which the traditional ways of preservation cannot achieve. This allows the conservation of cultural heritage in a safer and more permanent state.

Information databases and digital exhibition platform

Cultural heritage includes huge amounts of information, so there are higher requirements needed about the specific operations in preservation and representation. Simple ways of compiling the data can not work effectively. We must work under the foundation of comprehensive investigation, excavation, process, arrange, and sort codes according to the demands of digitalize and multimedia formats, then classify and edit the information systematically and load it into a database. For example, Digital Museum is a digital display platform that is suited for the transmission of cultural heritage. It differs from a traditional museum in many aspects. More than just a display of the static collection, digital museum can conduct digital programming for thousands of cultural and artistic process. These processes contain the historical development of folk crafts, existing states of crafts, files of folk artisans, classifications of folk crafts, transmissions of folk crafts, the craftsmanship, raw materials of folk crafts and the folk life style. After programming, the information will be deposited in the database networks. The digital museum can display all kinds of specific contents and essences of cultural heritage in the way of living culture.

Virtual representation technology to restore cultural heritage

Virtual representation of cultural heritage means using technologies, such as digital photography, 3D information acquisition, multimedia, and virtual reality, to create a virtual situation that can allow experience to a cultural heritage, which can provide the protection and spread of the cultural heritage. For material cultural heritage, such as relics, groups of buildings and ruins, we can use virtual representation technology to restore the appearance of cultural heritage by the models in real life and display it comprehensively. For intangible cultural heritage, we look to find the best way based on its features to reconstruct and integrate forms of visual or experience by making intangible into tangible. In addition, we can combine material cultural heritage with intangible cultural heritage and make the preservation and transmission of cultural heritage more three-dimensional and deeper.

1.6 Research Contents of Digital Preservation in Reference to Cultural Heritage

Cultural heritage can be divided into material cultural heritage and intangible cultural heritage. The contents of digital preservation of cultural heritage include digital acquisition, digital record, digital preservation, and digital reconstruction.

1.6.1 Digital Acquisition, Record and Preservation

Material cultural heritage

Archaeological excavation sometimes brings damages to ancient tombs, for example, quick decomposing of silk fabrics due to oxidation, lift and peeling of murals caused by leaking water, shrink and decay of wooden cultural relics. However, digital methods can keep in step with the archaeological sites, and record the grave's original aspect in the fastest and most comprehensive way. By means of digital photography and 3D scanning, we can make up for the destruction of cultural heritage which is caused by the elements.

Intangible culture heritage

Traditional technologies, such as written text, audio recording, video and photography, have been essential in preserving large amounts of precious intangible culture heritage. But many reasons, such as molding of books, aging of videos, color changing of videos and decay of tapes, all lead to the infidelity of information in different degrees, which affects its long-term preservation and use. However, by means of digital technology, we can preserve the intangible culture heritage with detailed information and build many kinds of information database mapping related information that is provided by the media.

1.6.2 Digital Reconstruction and Appearance

Material cultural heritage

For many cultural heritages that have already damaged or disappeared, we can reconstruct them by means of virtual technology and simulate their evolution in virtual world.

Many cultural heritages are an overall by themselves. The traditional way of preservation displays of cultural heritage is displayed in the museum. So the integrity of cultural heritage is damaged when it is removed from its original circumstance, which will cause the separation from the whole concept. Museums or related protection agencies can use digital devices and technologies such as multimedia and virtual reality to reconstruct the museum experience. which allows audiences to roam in the virtual cultural heritage space by the remote sensor, and understand the whole results of the cultural heritage, thus we can reconstruct and provide a comprehensive, complete and meaningful space.

Intangible culture heritage

Using digital virtual reality technologies such as multimedia virtual scene modeling and virtual scene coordination display, we can realistically reproduce intangible culture heritage especially for traditional handicrafts in the way of production, utilization, consumption, circulation, transmission and inheritance. Therefore, we can build a multimedia digital museum which contains text, recording, image, video, and a virtual reality.

Digital display and spread

Digital museum which is based on a digital media unified platform can integrate many kinds of intangible culture heritages with the help of technologies such as multimedia integration, digital photography, and virtual reality. It makes the display, spread and use of intangible culture heritage extremely convenient and sufficient by means of the network environment under the condition of not using the intangible culture heritage.

Digital display with the help of networks breaks the limit of time and space, and the limits of traditional museum's conditions such as building, display and visiting time. Anybody at anytime, in anywhere can get needed information from the internet conveniently. This allows huge amounts of culture resources to be displayed, and satisfies masses of consumers conveniently, quickly and efficiently. Therefore digital museum becomes a new application platform suitable for mass communication with modern technology.

References

[1] http:/www.unesco.org/. Accessed 20 May 2011

[2] http://whc.unesco.org/en/list. Accessed 20 May 2011

[3] http://en.wikipedia.org/wiki/World_Heritage_Site. Accessed 20 May 2011

[4] Richard K (2004) Safeguarding Intangible Cultural Heritage in the 2003 UNESCO Convention: A Critical Appraisal. Museum International, 56(1/2): 66 – 77

[5] Cosmas J, Itegaki T, Green D, et al (2001) 3D MURALE: A Multimedia System for Archaeology. In: Proceedings of the 2001 Conference on Virtual reality, Archeology, and Cultural Heritage, pp 297 – 306, Glyfada, Greece, 28 – 30 November 2001

[6] Grabczewski E, Cosmas J, Itegaki T, et al (2001) 3D MURALE: Multimedia Database System Architecture. In: Proceedings of the 2001 Conference on Virtual Reality, Archeology, and Cultural Heritage, pp 315 – 322, Glyfada, Greece, 28 – 30 Nov 2001

[7] Ware C (1999) Information Visualization: Perception for Design. Morgan Kaufman, San Francisco

[8] Ryder G, Flack P, Day A (2004) Adaptive Crowd Behaviour to Aid Real-Time Rendering of a Cultural Heritage Environment. In: Proceedings of the 5th International Symposium on Virtual Reality, Archaeology and Intelligent Cultural Heritage, pp 29 – 36, Oudenaarde, Belgium, 7 – 10 December 2004

[9] Gaitatzes A, Dimitrios C, Georgios P (2004) The Ancient Olympic Games: Being Part of the Experience. In: Proceedings of the 5th International Symposium on Virtual Reality, Archaeology and Intelligent Cultural Heritage, pp 19 – 28, Oudenaarde, Belgium, 7 – 10 December 2004

[10] http://www.indiana.edu/~libarchm/links.html. Accessed 10 July 2011

[11] http://cdrh.unl.edu/. Accessed 10 July 2011

[12] http://www.learn.columbia.edu/. Accessed 10 July 2011

[13] Levoy M, Pulli K, Curless B, et al (2000) The Digital Michelangelo Project: 3D Scanning of Large Statues. In: Proceedings of the 27th Annual Conference on Computer Graphics and Interactive Techniques, New Orleans, USA, 23 – 28 July 2000

[14] http://ir.lib.uwo.ca/anthropub/5/. Accessed 20 July 2011

[15] Koller D, Levoy M (2006) Computer-aided Reconstruction and New Matches in the Forma Urbis Romae. In: Proceedings of the Bullettino Della Commissione Archeologica Comunale di Roma, pp 103 – 125

[16] Bernard F (2003) Mission and Recent Projects of the UCLA Cultural Virtual Reality Laboratory. In: Proceedings of the Conference Virtual Retrospect 2003, pp 65 – 74, Biarritz, France, 6 – 7 November 2003

[17] http://www.frischerconsulting.com/frischer/FrischerWorkshopPaperIllustratedWeb_test.html. Accessed 20 May 2011

[18] Abouaf J (1999) The Florentine Pietà: Can Visualization Solve the 450-Year-Old Mystery. IEEE Computer Graphics and Applications, 19(1): 6–10

[19] Benedict J, Corey T, Diego N, et al (2008) A System for High-volume Acquisition and Matching of Fresco Fragments: Reassembling Theran Wall Paintings. ACM Transactions on Graphics, 27(3): 84: 1–84: 9

[20] Pan Y, Lu D (2003) Digital Protection and Restoration of Dunhuang Mural. Journal of System Simulation, 15(3): 310–314

[21] Lv K, Geng G, Zhou M (2003) Matching of 3D Curve Based on the Hash Method. Acta Electronica Sinica, 31(2): 294–296

[22] Fan S (2005) Research on Fractured Objects Complementary Shape Matching and Aligning. Dissertation, Northwest University

[23] Li C, Zhou M, Cheng X, Cheng R (2006) Virtual Restoration of Axisymmetric Relic Fragments. Journal of Computer-Aided Design & Computer Graphics, 18(5): 620–624

[24] Zhou M, Geng G, Wu Z (2009) A Virtual Restoration System of broken Pottery Relics. In: Proceedings of the Computer Applications and Quantitative Methods in Archeology, pp 391–396, Williamsburg, USA

2 Fundamentals of Digital Preservation of Cultural Heritage

Digital Preservation of Cultural Heritage is a new technology to preserve cultural artifacts and relics effectively through modern information technology. This is related to the variants of information technology including computer graphics, image processing, and other related subfields. Digital Preservation mainly includes the following four areas: modeling of cultural relics and ancient ruins, rendering techniques, simulation techniques, and retrieval techniques.

2.1 Representations of Cultural Relics and Ancient Ruins

In Digital Preservation of Cultural Heritage, various geometry representations are used. The five main types of representations will be introduced as point cloud, polygol mesh/triangle mesh, volume graphics, surface models and procedural models.

2.1.1 Polygon Mesh and Triangle Mesh

Polygon mesh and Triangle mesh are the most popular model to represent free-form objects. It represents a 3D free-form object through a group of polygons or triangles (see Fig. 2.1).

A polygon mesh/triangle mesh representation has two types of representation methods. One is applied as a storing model to a hard disk. The other is for storing data in memory for computing or operations. The data structure for the first one uses an array to store a group of 3D points and triangles through using a point index. Sometimes, it also stores a group of the normals, or texture coordinates of responding 3D points. The other method is applied when many operations are done on the model. Usually a half-edge structure is used, which can speed up searching of the neighborhood relationships. The half-edge structure is one of the edge-based data structures that represents the relationship among vertices, edges and faces (see Fig. 2.2).

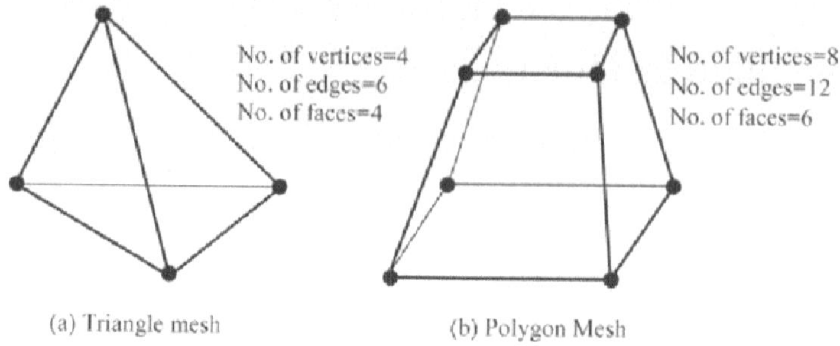

Fig. 2.1 Polygon mesh and triangle mesh.

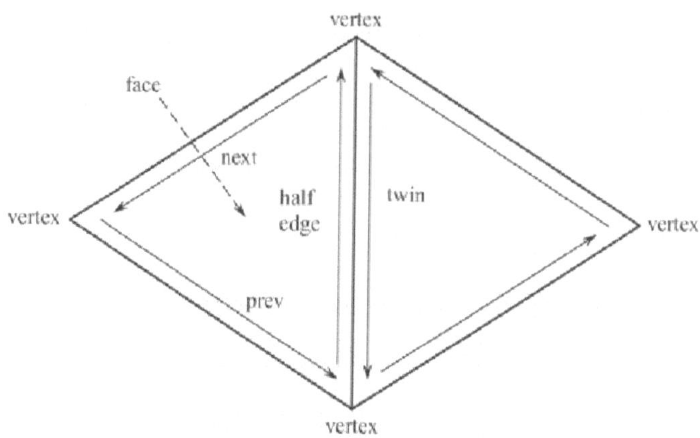

Fig. 2.2 Half-edge structure.

The advantages of polygon mesh/triangle mesh are:

(1) Rendering is fast.

(2) Boolean Operations are simpler.

(3) It is easy to obtain the model.

The disadvantages are:

(1) Data set is larger.

(2) Topological information is weak.

(3) It is difficult in computing accurate fundamental attributes like normal and curvature.

(4) It is difficult in operation and deformation activities.

(5) It is difficult in editing interactively.

2.1.2 Point Cloud

The 3D photography and 3D scanning techniques are developing and being applied rapidly. The point cloud is becoming a main representation model in many fields. It has been applied widely into the geometric representations for cultural relics and ancient ruins.

The point cloud model represents 3D objects by a group of scattered points. The point is the primary element. Therefore, the techniques of point based representation, processing, rendering, and modeling are called point based graphics.

In a point cloud model, a group of 3D points (x, y, z) or with the corresponding normal vectors (n_x, n_y, n_z) are used to represent 3D free-form objects implicitly. This data is usually from 3D data capturing instruments, like a 3D scanner. So the model is built easily.

The advantages of a point cloud are:

(1) It is easy to obtain the model.

(2) It can be used to describe internal information of objects.

(3) Boolean operations are simpler.

The disadvantages of a point cloud are:

(1) Data set is huge.

(2) There is almost no topological information.

(3) It is difficult in computing accurate fundamental attributes like normal and curvature.

(4) It is difficult in operations and deformation.

(5) It is difficult in editing interactively.

Comparing the popular representation of the polygon mesh with the point cloud, the point cloud has following advantages:

(1) There is no need to maintain a global topology. In polygon mesh, most algorithms need to maintain the topology of the physical faces. For example, when simplifying a polygon mesh, the local topological structure is changed and must be maintained. On the contrary, this topology maintenance is not needed for point cloud. Therefore, it is more flexible.

(2) Point cloud is convenient in implementing multiresolution resampling. It is more effective for implementing real time rendering or fast rendering by taking advantage of the hierarchical structure.

(3) Point cloud tends to be computed in parallel.

The original 3D point cloud data captured by 3D acquisition technologies typically brings along with noise points, floating points, dislocation of the mapping, holes, over sampling, insufficient sampling problems, and other issues. So a preprocessing step is very necessary. Preprocessing is the process of constructing a continuous and available point cloud model. Postprocessing is the process of adapting further operations on the models to meet the users' requirements. Some postprocessing steps are: resampling, polishing, simplification in multiresolution, editing, deformation, and Boolean operations. Digital geometry processing focuses on the postprocessing stage in order to implement and broaden the fundamental signal processing concepts on manifold neighborhood in the point cloud models.

We can regard polygon mesh/triangle mesh and point cloud as discrete representations. The operations based on these representations are called digital geometry processing. Digital geometry processing will be introduced in Section 2.2.

2.1.3 Surface Representation

Representing objects through mathematical functions has been a main method in the computer graphics community. In digital preservation of cultural heritage, these types of representations are often used for describing cultural relics and ancient ruins. As the representation has robust mathematical equations, computing of variant geometric properties is accurate. The dataset for the representation is small and suitable for transmission on internet. Surface representations are divided into parametric and implicit. Parametric model is more popular. In parametric surface model, Non-Uniform Rational B-Spline (NURBS) is the most widely used model.

NURBS surface

An NURBS surface is defined by rigid mathematical equation to describe 3D objects. It is flexible in geometry modeling and seen as an industry standard.

The NURBS curve is the fundamental of NURBS surface. It is a one-parameter equation. An NURBS curve is defined by a knot vector, a degree, a control point number, control points, and respective weights. The equation is as follows:

$$C(t) = \frac{\sum\limits_{i=0}^{n} N_{i,p}(t) w_i P_i}{\sum\limits_{i=0}^{n} N_{i,p}(t) w_i}, \tag{2.1}$$

where p is the order (degree+1), the control point number is $n + 1$, $N_{i,p}$ is the B-spline basis, P_i is the control points, w_i is the weight on P_i. Figure 2.3 displays an NURBS curve.

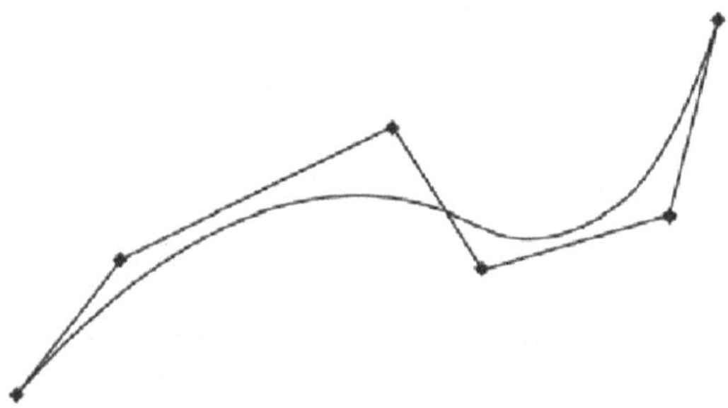

Fig. 2.3 An NURBS curve.

The NURBS surface is a two-parameter mathematical equation with two parameter directions, u and v. The NURBS surface is defined by their knot vector, degree, control point number, control points, and individual weights, respectively. The equation is as follows:

$$S(u,v)=\frac{\sum\limits_{i=0}^{m}\sum\limits_{j=0}^{n}N_{i,p}(u)N_{j,q}(v)w_{i,j}P_{i,J}}{\sum\limits_{i=0}^{m}\sum\limits_{j=0}^{n}N_{i,p}(u)N_{j,q}(v)w_{i,j}}, \tag{2.2}$$

where $N_{i,p}$ and $N_{j,q}$ are the B-Spline basis in u and v parameter direction respectively, the values of $m+1$ and $n+1$ are the control point numbers in u and v parameter direction respectively, the values of p and q are the orders in u and v parameter direction respectively, $P_{i,j}$ is the control point, $w_{i,j}$ is the weight on $P_{i,j}$. Figure 2.4 displays an NURBS surface.

Fig. 2.4 An NURBS surface.

The advantage of parameter surface are:

(1) dataset is small, even when representing a complex free-form surface.

(2) It is suitable for local or progressive transmission.

(3) It is accurate for computing geometry properties, such as normal and curvature.

(4) It is easy for operating and deforming.

(5) It is easy for interactively editing.

The disadvantages of parameter surface are:

(1) It is not easy to build the model.

(2) Boolean operations are difficult.

(3) Rendering is slow.

Implicit surface

Implicit surface technique is attracting more people in the computer graphics community as its classification of inner points and out points, computing geometry properties like normal and its efficiency in intersection and Boolean operations, and it has been used in digital preservation of cultural heritage. It is defined by an implicit equation in mathematics to constrain 3D points in a 3D space. The concrete definition is as follows:

$$S = \{P = (x, y, z) \in R^3, F(x, y, z) = C\},$$

where S is the implicit surface; F is the mapping and usually the implicit function F is algebraic $R^3 \to R$ is called implicit equation; C is a constant, usually the value is 0.

Blobby model

Blobby model is the earliest used implicit representation. It defines objects through a group of sphere base functions and an electronic density field. The density field function is defined as

$$D(r) = a\mathrm{e}^{-br^2}$$

where r is the distance from the atomic center to current point, a is the height of the center, b is the offset of the surface.

$$S = \sum_{i=1}^{N} D(r_i) \begin{cases} \text{inside}, & S \geqslant T \\ \text{outside}, & S < T \end{cases}$$

where N is the total number of atoms, T is the constant. To define iso-surface, S can be regard as an implicit surface constructed by a group of skeletal points, which accumulate N skeletons to form a scalar field. When the isovalue is T, the implicit surface S is generated.

The advantages of implicit model are:

(1) It is easy to test if a point is on surface.

(2) It is easy to compute the intersection.

(3) It is easy to control the topology.

(4) It provides direct blending, deforming, and contact detecting.

The disadvantages of implicit model are:

(1) It provides an indirectly define surface.

(2) It is difficult to describe sharp features of the surface.

(3) It is difficult in computing points on the surface.

(4) It is slow in rendering.

Implicit surface is suitable for representing dynamic objects such as fluid and soft objects.

2.1.4 Constructive Solid Geometry Representation

Constructive solid geometry (CSG) representation is one way to describe objects by primitives include cuboids, cube, cylinder, cone, pyramid, prism, torus, sphere, etc. as shown in Fig. 2.5. and a set of operations including geometric transformation and regularized intersection, union and difference.

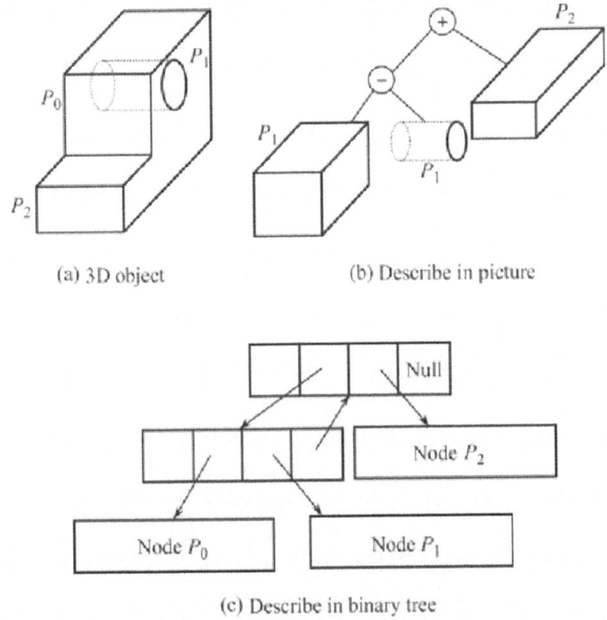

Fig. 2.5 CSG Representation.

CSG representation is simple, but its representation domain depends on primitives. In digital preservation of cultural heritage, generally it is applied to describe architecture and large ancient ruins.

2.1.5 Volume Graphics

Volume graphics is one of the main branches of computer graphics. It represents 3D objects by a group of voxels (which is counterpart in 3D of a pixel). The volume graphics model can describe the surface information of a 3D object as well as its internal information. It is widely used in 3D model analysis and medical image processing, scientific computing and visualization, and other fields.

A voxel is a cubic in 3D space. It has three kinds of relationships with its neighbor voxels:

(1) 6-connectivity: two voxels have the same face.
(2) 18-connectivity: two voxels have the same face or edge.
(3) 26-connectivity: two voxels have the same face, edge, or vertex.
Figure 2.6 shows a representation.

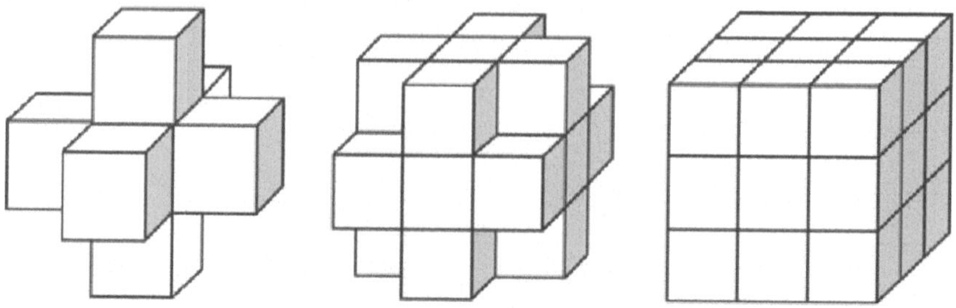

(a) 6-connectivity (b) 18-connectivity (c) 26-connectivity

Fig. 2.6 Neighborhoods in volume graphics.

2.1.6 Procedural Modeling

Physical phenomena in nature, such as cloud, smoke, and water, have no stable shape. To model such kind of phenomena a method called procedural modeling is used to calculate them instead of a mathematical formula. Usually, procedural modeling depends on not data but preset rules. It's widely used on generating complex natural phenomena and objects such as plants, mountains, cloud, fog, and fire. It is also used on modeling artificial objects such as buildings and cities. Procedural modeling includes fractals, L-systems, and particle systems.

Fractal

Fractal is a branch of mathematics. For object it is too irregular to be easily described in traditional Euclidean geometric language, it is self-similar, which means its whole part is similar with its local part. The dimension of fractal objects is not a integer but a fraction. Many natural phenomena, such as mountains, coast lins, plants, and thunder, are described well by fractals.

The fractal is implanted by an iterated function system which generates values iteratively from the initial status through a generating function or iterating geometrical construction. The Koch curve in Fig. 2.7 shows how the method works.

The shape generated by fractals has the property of self-similarity, meaning the whole has the same shape as one or more of its parts. In digital preservation of cultural heritage, it is mainly used for simulating mountains, leaves, clouds, and other non-bound objects.

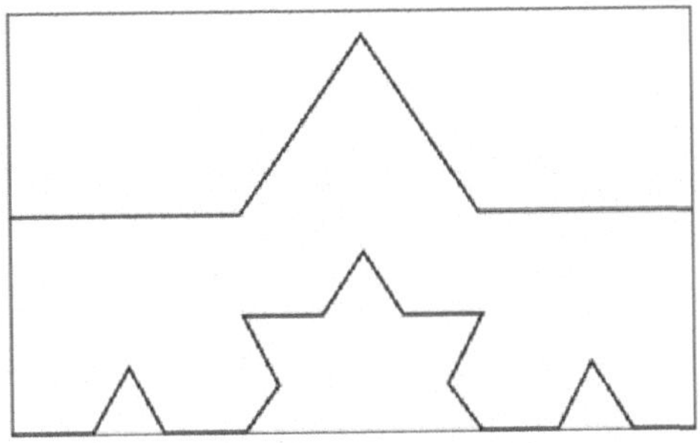

Fig. 2.7 Koch curve.

L-system

L-system is a kind of fractal methods called grammar based models. It was proposed by a Hungarian biologist named Aristid Lindenmayer in 1968 as a theoretical framework for studying the development of simple multi-cellular organisms. It has been applied to investigating higher plants and plant organisms. L-system provides a series of symbolic sets and generating rules. Simulation of plants generated by L-system is essentially a procedure rewriting symbols with rules. The replacement procedure starts from an initial structure, and then the generating rules are applied to replacing current structure during the generation operation.

Basic L-system: deterministic and context-free L-system (DOL-system)

A DOL-system is the simplest class of L-systems which are deterministic and context-free.

The formal description of DOL-systems is as follows:

Suppose V denotes an alphabet, V^* denotes the set of all words over V, and $V+$ denotes the set of all nonempty words over V. A string DOL-system is an ordered triplet $G = \langle V, \omega, P \rangle$ where V is the alphabet of the system, $\omega \in V+$ is a nonempty word called the axiom, and $P \subset V \times V^*$ is a finite set of productions.

A production $(\alpha, \chi) \in P$ is written as $\alpha \to \chi$. The letter a and the word χ are called the predecessor and the successor of this production respectively.

It is assumed that for any letter $\alpha \in V$, there is at least one word $x \in V^*$ such that $\alpha \to \chi$. If no production is explicitly specified for a given predecessor $\alpha \in V$, the identity production $\alpha \to \alpha$ is assumed to belong to the set of productions P. A DOL-system is deterministic if and only if for each $\alpha \in V$ there is exactly one $\chi \in V^*$ such that $\alpha \to \chi$.

Let $\mu = \alpha_1 \ldots \alpha_m$ be an arbitrary word over V. The word $\upsilon = \chi_1 \cdots \chi_m \in V^*$ is directly derived from or generated by μ, if not $\mu => \upsilon$, if and only if $\alpha_i \to \chi_i$ for all $i = 1, \ldots, m$. A word υ is generated by G in a derivation of length n if there exists a developmental sequence of words $\mu_0, \mu_1, ..., \mu_n$ such that $\mu_0 = \omega$, $\mu_n = \upsilon$ and $\mu_0 => \mu_1 => ... => \mu_n$. The rewriting procedure is a substitution predecessor in the father-module with successor in the child-module.

Figure 2.8 illustrates this procedure.

Fig. 2.8 Growing of a fractal leaf.

This procedure by the DOL-system is presented in the following. The symbol A will be interpreted to a light line, while the symbol I to a hard line. A and I both have unit length.

n=5

ω: A

p_1: A $\rightarrow$ I [A] [A] I A

p_2: I $\rightarrow$ I I (replacing one unit line with two unit lines)

4. Turtle interpretation

L-systems' geometric interpretation is called a turtle interpretation. It is based on a LOGO-style turtle. The state of the turtle is defined as a triplet : (x, y, α), where the Cartesian coordinates (x, y) represent the turtle's position. The angle, called the heading, is interpreted as the direction in which the turtle is facing. Given the step size of d and the angle increment δ, the turtle can respond to commands represented by the following symbols (see Table 2.1).

Table 2.1 The symbols' definition in turtle interpretation

Symbols	Respond commands
F	Move forward a step of length d. The state of the turtle changes to (x', y', α),where $x' = x + d\cos\alpha$ and $y' = y + d\sin\alpha$. A line segment between points (x, y) and (x', y') is drawn
f	Move forward a step of length d without drawing a line

(to be continued)

(Table 2.1)

Symbols	Respond commands
+	Turn left by angle δ. The next state of the turtle is $(x, y, \alpha + \delta)$. The positive orientation of angles is counterclockwise
−	Turn right by angle δ. The next state of the turtle is $(x, y, \alpha - \delta)$

Turtle interpretation of L-systems can be extended to 3D. The key concept is to represent the current orientation of the turtle in space by three vectors H, L, U, which indicate indicating the turtle's heading, the direction to the left, and the direction to top. These vectors, are perpendicular to each other with unit length, and satisfy the equation $H \times L = U$. Rotations of the turtle are then expressed by the equation $[H'L'U'] = [HLU]R$, where R is a 3× 3 rotation matrix. Specifically, rotations by angle α about vectors H, L, U are represented by the matrices:

$$R_U(\alpha) = \begin{pmatrix} \cos\alpha & \sin\alpha & 0 \\ -\sin\alpha & \cos\alpha & 0 \\ 0 & 0 & 1 \end{pmatrix},$$

$$R_L(\alpha) = \begin{pmatrix} \cos\alpha & 0 & -\sin\alpha \\ 0 & 1 & 0 \\ \sin\alpha & 0 & \cos\alpha \end{pmatrix},$$

$$R_H(\alpha) = \begin{pmatrix} 1 & 0 & 0 \\ 0 & \cos\alpha & -\sin\alpha \\ 0 & \sin\alpha & \cos\alpha \end{pmatrix}.$$

Figure 2.9 illustrates the relationship of H, L, U in the coordinate system.

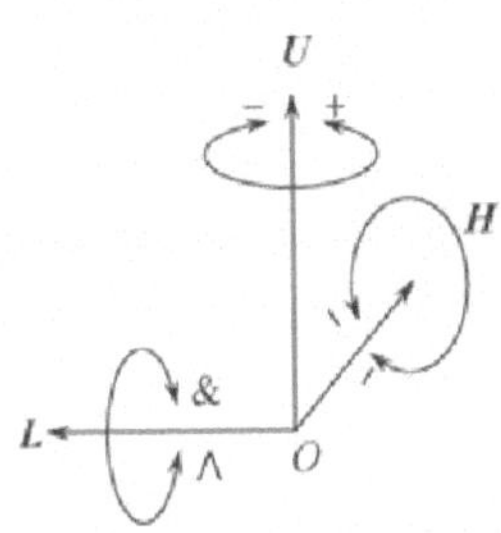

Fig. 2.9 Turtle's direction in 3D space.

Symbols in Table 2.2 control the direction of turtle in 3D space.

Table 2.2 Extended symbols of 3D turtle interpretation

Symbols	Control direction
+	Turn left by angle δ, using rotation matrix $R_U(\delta)$
−	Turn right by angle δ, using rotation matrix $R_U(-\delta)$
&	Pitch down by angle δ, using rotation matrix $R_L(\delta)$
∧	Pitch up by angle δ, using rotation matrix $R_L(-\delta)$
\	Roll left by angle δ, using rotation matrix $R_H(\delta)$
/	Roll right by angle δ, using rotation matrix $R_H(-\delta)$
|	Turn around, using rotation matrix $R_U(180°)$

Particle system

Modeling fuzzy objects, such as rain, clouds, smoke, water, and fire, has been proven difficult with the existing techniques of computer image synthesis. These "fuzzy" objects do not have smooth, well-defined and shiny surfaces; instead their surfaces are irregular, complex and ill defined. We are interested in their dynamic and fluid changes in shape and appearance.

They are not rigid objects and their motions can not be described by simple affine transformations that are common in computer graphics eigher. The method introduced by William T. Reeves in 1983 that simulates this class of objects is called particle systems [1].

Compared to the traditional surface-oriented modeling methods, particle systems modeling have the following three advantages:

(1) An object is represented not by a set of primitive surface elements, such as polygons or patches, that define its boundary, but as clouds of primitive particles that define its volume.

(2) A particle system is not a static entity. Its particles can change form and move as time passes. New particles are "born" and old particles "die".

(3) An object represented by a particle system is not deterministic, since its shape is not completely specified. Instead, stochastic processes are used to create and change an object's shape and appearance.

Particle system principle

A particle has the following seven significant properties:

(1) initial position;
(2) initial velocity;
(3) initial scale;
(4) initial color;
(5) initial transparency;
(6) shape;
(7) lifetime.

Displacement at time t_1 is calculated by the following formula:

$$S(t_1) = S(t_0) + \int_{t_0}^{t_1} v(t)\mathrm{d}t, \tag{2.3}$$

where $S(t_0)$ is displacement earlier than t_1, while t_0 is the time under status $S(t_0)$, and $v(t)$ is the velocity at time t. If the acceleration is known, $v(t)$ can be derived from the following formula:

$$v(t_1) = v(t_0) + \int_{t_0}^{t_1} a(t)\mathrm{d}t, \tag{2.4}$$

where $a(t)$ means the acceleration at time t. The two formulas are basic in the simulation of an objects motion. After finishing calculating resultant force F using Newton second law: F=$m \times a$, a (acceleration) can be got with a known m (mass), then the velocity and displacement can be easily calculated. If $\Delta t = t_1 - t_0$ is tiny enough, Eqs. (2.3) and (2.4) can be written as following

$$S(t_1) = S(t_0) + v(t_0) \cdot \Delta t, \tag{2.5}$$

$$v(t_1) = v(t_0) + a(t_0) \cdot \Delta t. \tag{2.6}$$

These two formulas can be easily implemented in a computer.

The particle system is applied to simulating natural phenomena, like smoke, dust, fog, fire, snow, rain, fountains, etc. In digital preservation of cultural heritage, it is used to simulate and recreate history scenarios realistically.

2.2 Three-dimensional Geometry Processing

Three-dimensional geometry processing is the core technique of the computer graphic and computer geometry, which covers the fields of geometric processing on triangle mesh, geometric processing on point cloud, processing in volume graphics, parametric surface, implicit surface, and other technologies.

2.2.1 Geometric Processing on Triangle Mesh

With the help of 3D scanners, 3D digital models of great details can be captured, containing large scale data, and high complexity; therefore, efficient and robust geometry processing techniques are highly required.

Denoising and smoothing

A noniterative mesh smoothing algorithm can preserve global characteristics. The algorithm is described as follows:

(1) To fit the outliers, we must distinguish spatial location and signal, and then use the predicted value to obtain a smoothed surface. That is, the predicted surface for a triangular patch q is its tangent plane Π_q, shown in Fig. 2.10.

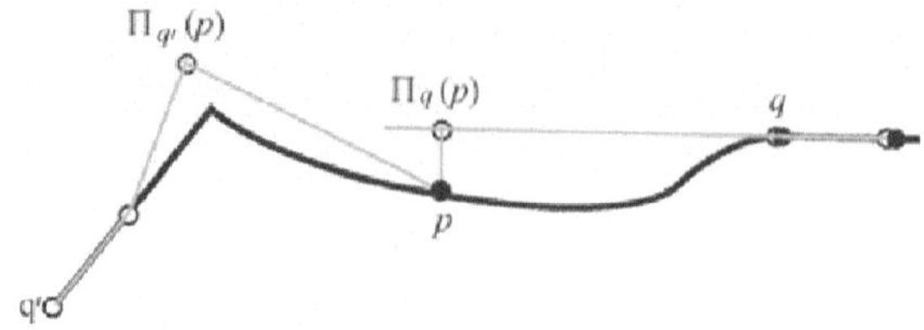

Fig. 2.10 Predicted value of surface.

(2) After smoothing, the predicted position of p is as follows:

$$p' = \frac{1}{k(p)} \sum_{q \in S} \prod_q (p) a_q f(\|c_q - p\|) g \left(\left\| \prod_q (p) - p \right\| \right), \tag{2.7}$$

where k is the normalized factor:

$$k(p) = \sum_{q \in S} a_q f(\|c_q - p|) g \left(\left\| \prod_q (p) - p \right\| \right). \tag{2.8}$$

The space weighting function f and the impact weighting function g both use the Gaussian function. The impact weighting function determines the size of the preserved features. By moving vertices to the predicted positions for each triangle a smooth mesh is achieved without other topology information by Eq. (2.7).

This predicted scheme is based on the direction of the tangent plane, that is the normal of the tangent plane; thus, by applying mollification algorithm to smooth the tangent plane normal, the predicted positions can be smoothed.

Segmentation

Fuzzy clustering segmentation algorithm has been widely used in mesh segmentation algorithms, which adopts a coarse to fine methodology. Each node of a multi-level tree represents a surface patch of a specific component of the model, with the input model as the root node. In each node, k suitable components are found, and also k decomposition methods of the node are needed.

The key idea of the algorithm is to maintain the boundary between the fuzzy components as well as to find meaningful components, and then focus on small fuzzy regions to find the precise boundary between the components. The algorithm has four steps:

(1) Based on geodesic and angular distance, the distance between every two facets is determined.

(2) By using the above distance between patches to calculate the initial decomposition, the probability of each triangular facet belonging to a component is determined.

(3) Through refining the probability of a solution, the decomposition of a fuzzy component based on an iterative clustering strategy is obtained.

(4) By using the minimum segmentation algorithm, the exact boundary of components is established. The fuzzy components become the final result.

Simplification and compression

Vertex clustering based on the simplification method is widely used for 3D model simplification. It has the advantages of low computational cost and high efficiency. It is especially appropriate for interactive applications. In a synthetic scene, when the model is far from the camera or viewer, some points of the model will be mapped to the same pixel of the displayed image. One solution is to find those points, and use only one new point to replace these points for rendering. Vertex clustering is based on this idea.

The clustering process is used to find similar points of the model, and then use one new point to represent these similar points. To measure the similarity between the points is to measure the similarity between the mesh patches. Defining different cluster sizes, different similarity thresholds are obtained. A simplified model of a different level of details (LOD) can be achieved. The detailed procedure is described as follows:

(1) Vertex weight computation: the weight of each vertex is calculated according to each vertex pair.

(2) Triangulating: the mesh is divided into individual triangles.

(3) Clustering: according to the geometric proximity, all the vertices are divided into various categories.

(4) Synthesis: with a new point to represent all the points in each cluster, some of the triangles are reduced to a number of vertices and edges.

(5) Redundancy elimination: eliminate redundant triangles, vertices, and edges.

(6) Normal adjustment: recalculate the normal for the simplified model.

The entire process is shown in Fig. 2.11.

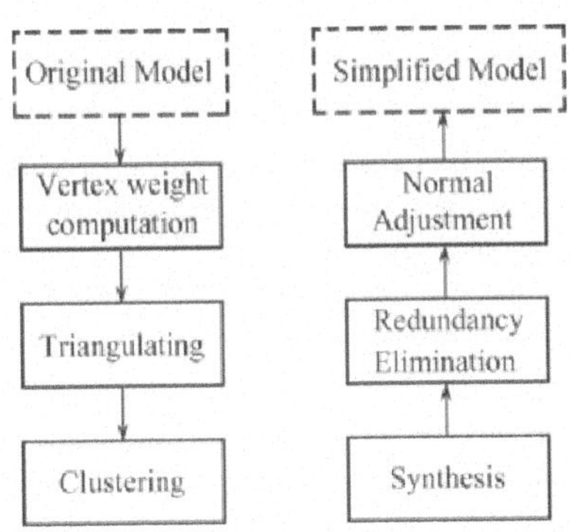

Fig. 2.11 Model simplification process.

Surface subdivision

Loop subdivision is a commonly used subdivision method for triangular models. For a regular mesh without extraordinary points, it can achieve a C^2 continuous surface. An extraordinary point is the point without six adjacent points. The mesh which has three adjacent points along the boundary is also a regular mesh. For the boundary, apply the special rules that can produce a cubic spline curve along the boundary, and the curve only depends on the points along the boundary. The entire cyclic strategy is as follows:

(1) Calculate β with the following formula, and then obtain a new point for each point on the triangle mesh. Here, k is the number of vertices adjacent points, and proper weights for the adjacent points are chosen. The following formula applies:

$$\beta = \frac{1}{k}\left(\frac{5}{8} - \left(\frac{3}{8} + \frac{1}{4}\cos\frac{2\pi}{k}\right)^2\right). \tag{2.9}$$

For extraordinary points, β is C^1 continuous. And for the regular points, the even points in Fig. 2.12 (b) replace k with 6 to calculate the weight of the points.

(2) For each edge on the mesh, calculate a new point through Fig. 2.12.

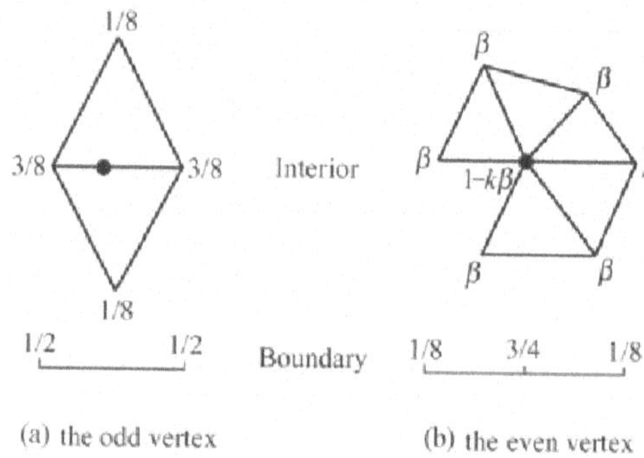

Fig. 2.12 Generating new vertex strategy.

(3) Each mesh triangle has six vertices, three of which are produced from the original three vertices, and three from the original three sides. These six points produce four new triangles.

Editing

Three-dimensional shape editing is an important research topic in the field of geometric modeling and computer graphics. The main method of modeling is parametric surface design, and this method can be extended to nonsingular subdomain parameterizations with subdivision technology. Surface editing is the core technique in geometric design and processing, which aims to provide users with intuitive and efficient editing tools for complex geometry modeling. It includes local shape adjustment, surface cut, paste, geometric texture migration, surface fusion, and large deformation. Here interactive mesh deformation and the local editing of mesh are discussed. Surface deformation and editing methods can be divided into four categories: Barr deformation method, free form deformation method based on uniform mesh (FFD), subdivision surface deformation method, and constrained deformation method. The concept of global and local deformation was first proposed in the Barr deformation method [2]. In traditional modeling methods, the object is usually represented by the CSG (constructive solid geometry) tree. Through basic object transformations (rotation, translation and scaling) and Boolean operations (union, intersection and difference), the CSG modeling method can generate very complex objects. Barr extended the traditional operations and proposed the global and local deformation as the new operators.

Free-form deformation (FFD) [3] is a deformation method that has nothing to do with the object representation. Researchers proposed many improved methods based on FFD, with the same basic idea that use Bezier, B-spline or NURBS for shape deformation. FFD method provides a general framework of spatial deformation methods. First the object is embedded in an intermediate space, and then the deformation of the space is passed to the embedded object.

Subdivision based editing method, unlike traditional surface editing methods which directly manipulate the model vertices, changes the local surface differential geometric properties, and uses optimization techniques to reconstruct new shapes. Based on this approach, users only need to use a few editing operations, and the geometric details are well preserved during deformation process. Other common subdivision methods are Loop subdivision method [4], Catmull-Clark method [5], Doo. Sabin [6], and Modified Butterfly method [7].

In 1992, Hsu [8] proposed a deformed object according to the offset point of the reverse mesh vertices to achieve the direct manipulation of free form deformation (DMFFD). This method is in fact a part of the deformation constraints. It usually requires solving a large generalized inverse matrix. The computational complexity and inconvenience interaction are disadvantages. Borrel and Rappoport [9] proposed a simple constraint deformation method using a similar deformation control method, which uses constraints spots as well as user-defined radius of influence.

Basic steps of local deformation of mesh editing are as follows:

(1) Generate a local deformation region. A closed rectangular region of deformation is determined by user interactions that can precisely control the deformation region and the deformed shape.

(2) Generate the deformation mesh. There are two ways to generate the deformation mesh: One is to parameterize the editing area onto a rectangle and uniformly sample the rectangular region. Next, take the sampling points as the control points of a generated control mesh. The control mesh is often obtained by parametric surfaces (such as B-spline surface) or the constructed control mesh with a defining mesh template, and is mapped to the deformation region. Another way is first to select control points in the deformation region and second by fitting the control points under constraints (such as

radial basis function) the surface can be deformed directly. In such a direct method, the impact range of control points can be defined and generally smooth deformed surface can be obtained.

(3) Control the deformation. If the deformation mesh is generated by the first method of step (2) is used, the manipulation of the control points is mapped to the points of the deformation region; if the second method is used, the manipulation of control points can directly impact the deformation of surrounding points, in which the impact range can be defined.

(4) Simple mesh operations include scaling, rotation, and dragging.

(5) Re-editing the boundaries of the deformation. Aliasing artifacts may occur on the boundaries of deformation because of local deformation, and it can be solved by methods like the triangle mesh editing method based on the mean value of vertices.

Parameterization

Surface parameterization was first introduced to computer graphics as a method for texture mapping. It is an important issue in digital geometry processing with various applications.

Triangle mesh is a typical representation of polygon mesh. Here parameterization of triangle mesh is introduced. Parameterization of a 3D mesh is to map the vertices of the mesh to a parameter domain under the condition of minimal geometric deformation measurements. Given a triangle mesh $S = \{T_i\}$ and a parameter domain Φ, we have to find a one-to-one mapping f from a triangle mesh to the parameter domain. The mapping keeps the topology of the mesh on the parameter domain, which is isomorphic with the original mesh, and minimizes the deformation according to certain deformation measurement. At present, most of the parameterization techniques are used to solve the minimization problem under intrinsic geometric measure. This is often related to differential geometry, equiareal mapping, harmonic mapping, and conformal mapping theory.

The plane parameterization method is a spatial 3D triangle mesh that is expanded to a triangle mesh on a plane. This ensures the effectiveness and minimization of deformation. For the plane parameterization, it is very difficult to make the length of each edge of triangle mesh unchanged. However, an angle can be locally preserved by conformal mapping. Conformal mapping theory becomes a hotspot in parameterization research. Gu et al. [10] proved that harmonic mapping and conformal mapping is equivalent for genus zero closed surfaces. Lévy et al. [11] proposed the least squares conformal mapping method based on the Cauchy-Riemann equation. By adding constraints, the conformal mapping problem can be converted to a linear optimization problem. Conformal mapping parameterization method is described in the following.

Triangle mesh model can be viewed as a set of triangular patches $G = \{V_G, F_G, P_G\}$, where $V_G = \{V_i, 1 \leqslant i \leqslant n\}$ (represents the number of vertices), F_G represents the relationship of the topological connections among all points, and P_G is the vector of all the properties on vertices.

For each triangle, a local normal basis $(x_1, y_1), (x_2, y_2), (x_3, y_3)$ is built. Consider the mapping U on the discrete triangle mesh $S : U : S \to (u, v)$. If U satisfies the condition:

$$\frac{\partial U}{\partial x} + \mathrm{i}\frac{\partial U}{\partial y} = 0, \tag{2.10}$$

U is called a conformal mapping shown in Fig. 2.13. The mapping between the two-dimensional parameter domain (u, v) and the three-dimensional mesh model preserving the angle. The conditions in the entire triangle mesh are strictly valid.

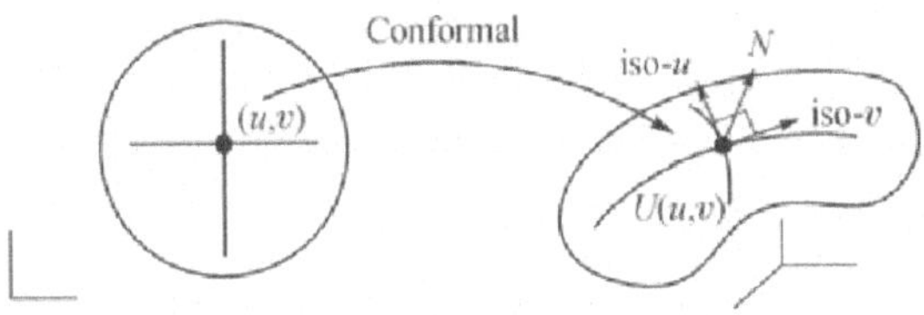

Fig. 2.13 Conformal mapping.

In order to facilitate the realization of the algorithm, assuming that the mapping in each triangular patch remains linear, U can be optimized shown as follows:

$$\operatorname*{Min}_{U} C(S) = \sum_{d \in S} \left| \frac{\partial U}{\partial x} + \mathrm{i}\frac{\partial U}{\partial y} \right|^2 A(d), \tag{2.11}$$

where d is the triangle mesh and $A(d)$ is the area of the triangle.

For each triangular patch, a local two-dimensional coordinate system is established. Each point on the triangular patches has a local coordinate (x, y) and a two-dimensional parameter domain (u, v). Set $\beta_j = x_j + \mathrm{i}y_j, \alpha_j = u_j + \mathrm{i}v_j$, then $\alpha_j = U(\beta_j)$. The vector α can be written as $\alpha = (\alpha_f, \alpha_p)$. Therefore,

$$C(S) = \|M_f\alpha_f + M_p\alpha_p\|^2, \tag{2.12}$$

where $M = (M_f, M_p)$ is a $m \times n$ sparse complex matrix (m is the number of triangular patches, n is the number of vertices). Finally, by solving the least squares optimization problem α_f is obtained. Therefore, the three-dimensional data can be mapped to a two-dimensional parameter domain.

The parameterization of conformal mapping method has good conformal characteristics after it is mapped from the original mesh to a two-dimensional parameterization domain, and it can handle these triangle meshes with a complex boundary.

Deformation

In recent years, many deformation algorithms have been developed, and one of the most commonly used is based on sketch, which can provide good user interactive experience. The procedure of sketch based on deformation is described as follows:

(1) Establish a reference curve. The user first sketches a reference curve, and then smooth it.After performing mapping of the two-dimensional curve to the three-dimensional mesh, the observation point can be caculated by reference to the first line of the intersection point with the ray. This will provide the intersection of the surface normal direction along the observation which defines the three-dimensional space and image space parallel to the plane. The projection of a plane reference curve will allow us to even out this three-dimensional reference curve.

(2) Identify regions of interest. After the reference curve has been mapped to three-dimensional space, fuzzy segmentation algorithm (fuzzy decomposition) is used to divide the model into three parts: (a) a static part, which does not change during the deformation process; (b) a part of interest, which is covered by the reference curve coverage and to be implemented in the deformation algorithm; (c) a rigid part, which is to be rigidly moved and kept in connection with the part of interest.

(3) Calculate the angle of rotation. By rotating each vertex v relative to the reference vertex v^r to the deformation of the mesh, the axis of rotation will outline the area of law. The angle of rotation $\theta(v)$, is the intersection angle v^r and v^t. To calculate the rotation angle, first define reference curves of the split line $[s_i, s_{i+1}]$, next ϕ_i as the angle with sign of rotation on the node i:

$$\Phi_i = \sum_{j=0}^{i-1} \phi_j + \frac{\phi_i}{2}. \tag{2.13}$$

For each point in $[S_i, S_{i+1}]$, interpolate the rotation angle:

$$\Phi(s) = \Phi_i + \frac{\phi_i}{2} b(2\alpha) + \frac{\phi_{i+1}}{2} b(2\alpha - 1),$$

where

$$\alpha = \frac{s - s_i}{s_{i+1} - s_i}, \quad b(x) = \begin{cases} 1, & x > 1 \\ x, & 0 \leqslant x \leqslant 1 \\ 0, & others \end{cases}.$$

Nodal rotation is

$$\theta(v) = \Phi^r(s(v)) - \Phi^t(s(v)) + \theta_g. \tag{2.14}$$

Once target position and rotation angle are calculated, the transformed vertex becomes:

$$v' = T(v^t)R(\theta(v))T(-v^r)v, \tag{2.15}$$

where T and R respectively outlines the movement and rotation functions of normal plane.

2.2.2 Geometric Processing on Point Cloud

Denoising and smoothing

A Point-based model is usually captured by 3D scanners or multiple view reconstruction methods. Due to physical measurement errors, the captured data inevitably contains a certain amount of noise. A good denoising algorithm needs to preserve the features of the model in the process of denoising. Some algorithms used in mesh denoising could be used in point cloud model, such as Laplacian, anisotropic diffusion algorithm, the vector field diffusion algorithm, bilateral filtering and local adaptive Wiener filtering method. The transplantation of the mesh model denoising methods to the point cloud denoising is the process to change the neighborhood generated from the mesh into the k-nearest neighbor in the point cloud.

Some surface reconstruction algorithms can implicitly smooth a point cloud [12–15]. They use fitting methods to generate smoothing surface, thus simultaneously achieve denoising effect. The moving least squares algorithm (MLS) proposed by Levin [16, 17] is an effective method that directly smoothes the point cloud model [12, 18]. The basic idea of the algorithm is that, given point set P is the sampling set from a smoothing surface S, MLS algorithm generates a smoothing surface M to approximate the surface S from the point set P.

Registration

Usually 3D scanning devices can only capture part of an object at a time. To get the whole data of an object, multiple scans are needed. As the multiview data are captured from different coordinate systems, they must be registered to be transformed into one coordinate system. Iterative closest point algorithm (ICP) is popular in solving the problem of three-dimensional registration, which is a high-level free-form surface based registration method proposed by Besl and Mckay [19]. It first uses the Newton iterative algorithm or search algorithm to find the nearest point-pairs between two datasets. Next it uses Euclidean distance as the objective function to iterate until the objective function of the sum of squared residual remains constant. With over ten years of development the ICP algorithm has been continuously improved. Yang and Medioni [20] and Bergevin et al. [21] proposed a point-to-plane search method for the exact nearest point-pairs. Rusinkiewicz and Levoy [22] proposed a point-to-projection method for quick search of the nearest point-pairs. Park and Subbarao [23] proposed a contractive-projection-point search method. In addition, Andrew and Sing [24] proposed a registration method based on color texture information of the data points, which utilized the color and texture information in the ICP algorithm. Natasha et al. [25] did an analysis about the quality of registrations in the ICP algorithm.

Resampling

With the improvement in accuracy of the 3D data acquisition devices, the data captured is often large and complex. For the purpose of effective storage, transmission, geometry processing and rendering of the large scale model, the model must be simplified for different requirements. In addition, due to the difficulty in controlling the scanning speed, multiple scans, and uneven sampling, the captured data is unevenly distributed and contains a lot of redundancy and some noise. Usually downsampling techniques are used to reduce of the number of sampling points in order to get the appropriate sampling density (usually evenly distributed).

Alexa [12] used greedy iterative strategy to move the positions of sampling points in the original model, and finally got the sampling points distributed evenly throughout the surface of the model. Based on the fast marching strategy, Moenning [26] proposed a uniform simplification method that is sensitive to surface features and the sampling density that could be controlled. Pauly [27] applied mesh simplification methods to point cloud models, such as vertices clustering and progressive vertices removal algorithm which demonstrates good results, based on squared errors and remeshing method. However, unlike simplification of mesh models, these simplification methods on point cloud models cannot be controlled by a predefined global error threshold. Furthermore, these methods take the points data as purely geometric. Wu [28] proposed a simplification method based on splatting. Splatting considers each point data as a point with a certain size of area (surfels). According to this method, the linear geometric properties of surfels are considered, the form of surfels and simplification procedure could be controlled by a global error, and finally a high quality of surfels distribution can be achieved. On the other hand, upsampling is necessary when the number of sampling points is not sufficient. For example, during editing or large deformation of a point cloud model, some parts of the model are extremely stretched or deformed. The model should be upsampled to satisfy the requirement of sampling density. Pauly [29] proposed a dynamic upsampling algorithm, in which those largely distorted surface splats are split to add new sampling points. In addition, repulsion-based particles simulation can also achieve uniform and dense sampling results.

Segmentation

Segmentation of point cloud data is to divide the point cloud into smaller, coherent and connected subsets, each of which contains a set of points with similar attributes. These segmented subsets should be "meaningful" parts of the original object which are to be processed according to users' interests. A complex three-dimensional model can be broken down into several parts. The decomposition of the model plays an important role in many aspects of digital geometry processing, such as shape recognition, surface reconstruction, surface parameterization, and the editing model.

The segmentation methods can be divided into two categories according to different purposes: patch-type segmentation and part-type segmentation. Patch-type segmentation refers to dividing the model into several patches. Each patch is isomorphic with a disc in topology, and the resultant patches are suitable for surface reconstruction, surface parameterization, texture mapping, and re-meshing. Part-type segmentation decomposes the model based on some significant features of the model. Usually the decomposition is along the feature sensitive areas or the areas of high curvature. The effect is that the whole model is divided into several meaningful parts, and the results are suitable for shape retrieval and editing.

Parameterization

Point cloud parameterization is the process of projecting the discrete points to a two-dimensional plane or a sphere surface. Point cloud parameterization is used in texture mapping and most of digital geometric processing procedures, such as filtering, distortion, orbital shrinkage, sculpture, etc.

Like polygon mesh parameterization, point cloud parameterization is used to construct a one to one mapping from a discrete point cloud to a parameter domain while minimizing the distortions (such as distance distortion) by some measurement. However, as the point cloud model does not provide any topology information, measurements like angle and area are difficult to calculate. Therefore, the point cloud parameterization is more difficult than polygon mesh model.

In the parameterization of point cloud model, the problem is how to minimize distance distortion. The minimization means to minimize the distance variance between sampling points before and after the parameterization. Floater [30] presented a mesh free parameterization method by solving a sparse system of linear equations, which is used in surface reconstruction. Zwicker et al. [31] proposed an interactive parameterization method in a Pointshop3D system in order to achieve minimum distortion and aliasing-free results, in which a linear least squares problem of hierarchical sampling clusters is solved.

Editing

With the wide use of point cloud models, an effective interactive editing method that directly edits on points is becoming an urgent requirement. However, due to the huge datasets and lack of topology information, the editing operation of point cloud models becomes a challenging problem. A typical work is Zwicker's PointShop3D system [31], where they extended traditional two-dimensional pixel-based editing operations to three-dimensional point cloud. By taking advantage of effective parameterization and dynamically adaptive resampling techniques, they designed an interactive mesh-free editing platform. This allows some operations like erasing, texture mapping, sculpture, filtering and resampling on point cloud to be provided.

Deformation

As the point cloud model does not provide an analytical equation about its surface or any parameterization information, the deformation of a point cloud model is a challenging problem. However, deformation on a point cloud model has its advantages in comparison with polygon mesh model:

(1) The point cloud model data structure is simple, easy to build and store. But the data structure in polygon mesh model is more complex, and its storage and maintenance during deformation is not an easy task.

(2) During deformation of a polygonal mesh, problems, such as normal direction flipping and patch distortion, often occur, while they would not happen for point cloud models.

(3) The Flowing phenomenon of particles could be seen in the deformation of large scale point data, which is more vivid than in polygon mesh deformation.

Similar to the algorithms in polygon mesh deformation, there are two steps in the deformation of a point cloud model. The first is to establish a correspondence between the source model and the target model. The second is interpolating the correspondent points. Establishing correspondence is the key and difficult issue, and the interpolation can use linear interpolation or Hermite interpolation scheme.

Unlike the polygon mesh model, large deformation operations of point cloud model can inevitably cause cracks. Thus, dynamic resampling (upsampling) during the deformation process is necessary. For example, moving least squares method could be used to implement dynamically resampling in order to fill the cracks.

In general, the deformation techniques first establish a displacement function, $d : R^3 \to R^3$, and then each surface sample point p_i is moved according to the function $p_i \to d(p_i)$, in order to achieve deforming effects.

Triangulation

The process of converting a point cloud model into a triangle mesh model is called triangulation. Another name for the process is called mesh reconstruction. Hoppe [32] proposed a method that could get a triangulated iso-surface of point cloud data. The first step is to calculate the normals by the local information of each sampling point, and then use a tangent plane that approximates the local surface to establish the distance field functions. Finally, through using the marching cubes algorithm to get the iso-surface of a triangle mesh. Amenta [33] proposed a 3D reconstruction algorithm based on the Voronoi diagram. In the method, a three-dimensional Voronoi diagram is constructed and Delaunay triangulation is applied to get a triangle mesh which precisely passes the sampling points. Floater [30] also used the Delaunay triangulation scheme, while, instead of constructing a 3D Voronoi diagram, he proposed to project the sampling points to a 2D plane and used the simple 2D Delaunay triangulation to get a triangle mesh of the projected points. Finally, the information of connections between the projected points was mapped back to the original 3D model.

2.2.3 Processing in Volume Graphics

Voxelization

Voxelization is to convert the geometric description form of an object from mathematical equations to its closest voxel representation. There are many voxelization methods. Here a simple one is introduced. Assumed that the resolution of the volume model is $N \times N \times N$, the voxelization consists of two main parts:

(1) Voxelization of surface model

At first AABB bounding box of the model is calculated. Next the bounding box is divided according to the spatial resolution of the volume model. The voxel list of each space unit $(X \div N) \times (Y \div N) \times (Z \div N)$ is achieved. Then the triangle or polygon list of the 3D model is traversed to get the bounding box of them. Then through intersection operation on the AABB and the bounding box, these voxels possibly affected by the triangle or polygons are determined. Furthermore, in order to accurately determine these voxels, intersection between the triangles with the AABB's bounding box is calculated to determine the final voxels that belong to the voxelization model. The voxelization operation of surface model is then finished.

(2) Voxelization of 3D solid objects

With completing the voxelization operation of the surface model, "surface shell" of 3D objects can be represented in a voxel model. The next operation is to voxelize the internals of the solid object. A corresponding spatial octree of the 3D model is built for usage of the intersection of triangles or polygons and rays. Second, two rays are emitted from the center of each empty voxel of the AABB of the model. Both aligned with axis in the directions but opposite to each other. For the two rays, the intersection points, normals and the distances from the voxel to the intersection point can be obtained by using the spatial octree. According to the relationship between the normal vectors of the two points, the current voxel is in the internal or external side to the 3D model that can be determined. Voxelization within the model can be completed just by applying this operation to each empty voxel.

However, applying this operation on each empty voxel is too slow to work. Hence, the approach of scan line is used to speed up this process. When determining a voxel inside the model, according to the direction of the ray and the distance of the two rays to the intersection points of the model, the adjacent voxels of the current voxel on the scan line can be marked as the status with no more judgment. Therefore, the voxelization algorithm is accelerated.

Denoising

In order to effectively use the voxel model, the noise of voxel model must be removed. There are many algorithms to implement denoising. For example, 3D data can be regarded as a series of 2D images along one of the coordinate axes. The process would be to denoise each of the 2Ds using 2D image denoising algorithms. However, because the algorithm does not consider the spatial relationship between these 2D images, it is generally difficult to obtain the expected denoising effect.

Many two-dimensional denoising algorithms can be extended to three-dimensional voxel models, such as median filtering and mean filtering. Zaroubi used wavelet transform to remove complex three-dimensional volume data noise [34]. Bao proposed an adaptive multi-scale method to reduce the noise in MRI data [35]. Non-local means is a relatively new denoising method and was first proposed by Buades in 2005. In the method, noises are removed by using natural redundancy of information in the data [36]. According to non-local mean theory, the gray value of each voxel is the weighted average of all other voxels surrounding it. In order to narrow the search only a few voxel neighborhoods around the voxel are considered. However, this algorithm is usually very time-consuming. Coupe presented a fast non-local means algorithm, and good results were obtained in MRI image data [37]. Thacker interpret the non-local means method in statistics theory [38].

Surface reconstruction

Surface reconstruction from a voxel model is to find out the t interest surface in voxel model data. In surface reconstruction each voxel not only is represented by a small cube in space, but also has a gray-scale value for the small cube. Common methods are Cuberille algorithm and Marching Cubes algorithm.

Cuberille algorithm

Cuberille algorithm is a simple and fast method, in which the cube surfaces of a voxel are used to approximate the iso-surface. Therefore such surface reconstruction is of low precision. If the data on hand is of high density, the result is improved. It is suitable for iso-surface reconstruction in medical imaging. For each voxel of the voxel model, it is regarded as a cube with same value. The six boundary surfaces of each cube are used to fit iso-surfaces, and the overlap surfaces are removed. The connected nonoverlapping boundaries of the voxels with same value approximate the iso-surface. The Cuberille algorithm is simple and easy to parallel process because the processing of each voxel is independent. The main problem is severe aliasing and the block-like nature of the resultant mesh. Therefore, it is not good for objects with rich details.

Marching Cubes algorithm

Marching Cubes (MC) algorithm is the most popular iso-surfacing algorithm from the voxel model. Each voxel is regarded as a cube whose eight vertices have different values. According to these values, the iso-surface inside each cube has 15 cases. By processing each cube one by one and connecting the patches from all cubes an iso-surface is achieved. However, there are connections on the MC algorithm of ambiguity. In order to solve the ambiguity problem, there has been proposed many effective methods [39]. Furthermore, MC algorithm is extended to a 3D solid object, i.e., Marching Tetrahedra algorithm which is developed based on the MC algorithm.

2.2.4 Parametric Surface

In a parameter surface, B-spline surface is common. Here B-spline surface is investigated.

B-spline curve interpolation

Given n data point $Q_i (i = 0, 1, \ldots, n)$, knot vector is determined through its accumulated chord length as follow,

$$\begin{cases} t_0 = 0 \\ t_i = t_{i-1} + |Q_i - Q_{i-1}|, \quad i = 1, 2, \ldots, n \end{cases}. \tag{2.16}$$

And Knot vector is,

$$T = [t_0, t_0, t_0, t_0, t_1, t_2, \ldots, t_{n-1}, t_n, t_n, t_n, t_n].$$

A B-spline curve is,

$$C(t) = \sum_{i=0}^{n+2} N_{i,3}(t) P_i. \tag{2.17}$$

Then we can get

$$\sum_{i=0}^{n+2} N_{i,3}(t_j) \mathrm{P}_i = Q_j, \quad j = 0, 1, 2, \ldots, n. \tag{2.18}$$

Plus the end constraint condition, like the tangents in the ends, or free-form end conditions, a linear equation group is created. Through solving the linear equation group, control points $P_i (i = 0, 1, \ldots, n+2)$ are obtained. Therefore the B-spline curve is determined.

Now simply discuss the end constraint conditions.

(1) Given the two tangents R_0, R_n in the start and end point, we have

$$[C(t_0)]' = 3\left(\frac{P_1 - P_0}{t_1 - t_0}\right) = R_0, \tag{2.19}$$

$$[C(t_n)]' = 3\left(\frac{P_n - P_{n-1}}{t_n - t_{n-1}}\right) = R_n. \tag{2.20}$$

(2) Free-form end conditions. It means the 2-order derivatives in the start and end point are zero, i.e.,

$$[C(t_0)]'' = 6\left(\frac{P_2 - P_1}{(t_1 - t_0)^2} - \frac{P_1 - P_0}{(t_1 - t_0)(t_2 - t_0)}\right) = 0,$$

$$[C(t_n)]'' = 6\left(\frac{P_{n+2} - P_{n+1}}{(t_n - t_{n-1})^2} - \frac{P_{n+1} - P_n}{(t_n - t_{n-1})(t_n - t_{n-2})}\right) = 0.$$

Therefore, a $n+3$ linear equation group for $n+3$ control points P_i are created. By solving the linear equation group, a B-spline curve interpolating these data points is generated. Here B-spline curve of degree 3 is used, so the linear equation group is tridiagonal equations, which can be solved by the chase method. And the solution is stable.

B-spline surface interpolation

Given data points $Q_{ij}(i = 0, 1, \ldots, m; j = 0, 1, \ldots, n)$ in a 3D space, a Bi-cubic B-spline surface is used to interpolate these data points. Here knot vectors in two parameter directions are computed by the mean accumulated chord length. Similar to B-spline curve interpolation, the following equation is obtained:

$$\sum_{i=0}^{m+2}\sum_{j=0}^{n+2} N_{i,3}(u_r)N_{j,3}(v_s)\mathrm{P}_{ij} = Q_{rs}, \quad r = 0, 1, \ldots, m; s = 0, 1, \ldots, n. \tag{2.21}$$

Plus $2(m+1) + 2(n+1)$, the end constrained condition, $(m+3) \times (n+3)$ linear equations about $(m+3) \times (n+3)$ variable vectors P_{ij}, are obtained. By solving the linear equations, a B-spline surface interpolating these data points is generated. The above method can be divided into two times B-spline curve interpolation.

Tessellation

For rendering or Finite Element method, parameter surfaces usually are tessellated into a triangle mesh model. By computing a group points of parameters $(u_i, v_j)(i = 0, 1, \ldots, m; j = 0, 1, \ldots, n)$, a group of points on the surface $P_{ij}(i = 0, 1, \ldots, m;\ j = 0, 1, \ldots, n)$ is obtained. Linking $P_{ij}, P_{i+1,j}, P_{i,j+1}$ and $P_{i+1j}, P_{i+1,j+1}, P_{i,j+1}$, two triangles are generated. Iterating the operations for all $i = 0, 1, \ldots, n;\ j = 0, 1, \ldots, n$, a triangle mesh model is generated.

Here the main work is how to compute the points P_{ij} on the surface. Usually the equidistant parameters, $u_i = i \times h$ and $v_j = j \times h$, are used. Here h is the equidistant step. Therefore, a fast computing algorithm can be used.

2.2.5 Implicit Surface

Blending can smoothly link primitives together. It can either be linear blending, hyperboloid blending, or ellipsoid blending.

Linear blending

$$B(F_1(x,y,z), F_2(x,y,z), \ldots, F_n(x,y,z)) = \sum_{1}^{n} F_i(x,y,z) - 1. \tag{2.22}$$

Hyperboloid blending

$$B(F_1(x,y,z), F_2(x,y,z), \ldots F_n(x,y,z)) = \prod_{1}^{n} F_i(x,y,z) - 1. \tag{2.23}$$

Ellipsoid blending

$$\begin{aligned} &B(F_1(x,y,z), F_2(x,y,z), \ldots F_n(x,y,z)) \\ &= 1 - \left\{ \sum_{1}^{n} [\max(1 - \alpha_i F_i(x,y,z), 0)]^{\beta} \right\}^{\frac{1}{\beta}}. \end{aligned} \tag{2.24}$$

Here parameters $\alpha_1, \alpha_2, \ldots \alpha_n, \beta$ are used for controlling the blending shapes.

Deformation

With an implicit surface function $F(x,y,z)$ and the deforming function $D(x, y, z)$, the deformed implicit surface function is $F(x,y,z) + D(x,y,z)$, thus the deformed implicit surface is $F(x,y,z) + D(x,y,z) = 0$.

Polygonization

An implicit surface is often converted into polygon or triangle mesh for rendering. The algorithm is similar to the Marching cubes algorithm which is for extracting iso-surface in volume graphics. The detail is as follows:

(1) Dividing the 3D space so the implicit surface occupies into uniform cubes.

(2) Computing these implicit function values on the cubic vertices.

(3) Obtaining edges through the computing function solution or linear interpolation.

(4) For the above edges of each cubic, link together to generate triangles or a polygon, then the polygon or triangle mesh is generated.

2.3 Rendering Technology

Rendering technology is used in the display of virtual three-dimensional models and scenes. This can have the projection of three-dimensional objects in the two-dimensional scene and produces the realistic images.

2.3.1 Methods of Rendering

Different presentation models need different rendering methods. Now, we talk about three main methods of rendering: surface rendering, point rendering and volume rendering. Among them, surface rendering is the traditional method which is well supported by graphics hardware.

Surface Rendering

Rendering is used to get the projection of the objects and then create naturally lighting effects on the visual surface to realize the realistic display. Therefore, rendering can not be performed without a lighting model. The lighting model is mainly used in calculating the light intensity of one point on the surface. Surface modeling uses the light intensity calculated by the lighting model to determine the intensities of all the projection pixels. The specific implementation processes are related to the coloring methods.

Lighting model

Lighting model contains many factors, such as the material quality transparency, diffuse reflectance, specular reflectance, and surface texture. There are also attributes of the light source such as shape and color. Another factor is the object's relative position to the light source. There is high computational complexity to accurately measure the light intensities. Just like the radiation degree algorithm, it calculates the light intensity by considering the transfer of the radiation energy between the light source and the object, which has a low computing efficiency. As a result, we employ the simplified lighting calculation and experiential model in most instances. Among these models, the light intensity usually contains four parts: emitted light, ambient light, diffused light, and specular reflection light. The four parts are calculated separately and then added up. Emitted light comes from the object and it will not be affected by the light source. Ambient light is also called bias light (flood light) since it diffuses in various directions and it is the benchmark for brightness. Diffused light is the lights that are diffused from the surface of the object. It diffuses in various directions in the same light intensity which has nothing to do with the direction of observation. Specular reflection light is the light specularly reflected from the surface of the object. It is concerned with the light incident direction and the observation direction.

Coloring method

Coloring method is used to determine the intensities and colors of all the pixels by calculating the light intensity. There are two ways used in surface rendering:

(1) Apply the lighting model to every point in each visual surface (Ray Tracing algorithm).

(2) After a small amount of calculations of the lighting model, do brightness interpolation in the surface patch (Scan Line algorithm).

Basic ray tracing algorithm builds a coordinate which the projective plane is an xy plane first. We describe the scene in this coordinate. Then, from the projective center we determine the path of light rays that pass through every screen pixel centre in xy plane. The next step is to aggregate the intensity of the illumination along this beam of light and endow the final value to the pixel. Although ray tracing technology can generate graphs of high realism, it has a strikingly huge calculation.

Common scan line algorithm also has three methods: Flat, Gouraud, and Phong shading method. The Flat method draws every polygon by a single light intensity, which means that we use one color to fill the triangle. This method has a high efficiency but it exhibits the problem of color mutants called Mach Band Effect.

Gouraud method calculates the illumination of a triangle's every vertex firstly. Then it uses the color of vertex to do interpolation in order to calculate the illumination of every point inside the triangle. This method eliminates the Mach Band Effect caused by a color mutant, but it can not truly reflect the highlights phenomenon inside the triangle.

The Phong shading method uses the normal vector in each vertex of the triangle to do interpolation and then calculates the normal vector of each pixel. Lighting effects will be determined by the normal vector of each pixel. The Phong method solves the problem of the highlights phenomenon, but its computation increases greatly.

Point-based rendering

In order to hold the results that are caused by managing the sampling point's geometrical model, better adjust, and control the process, we need to do rapid and effective rendering of the sampling point's geometrical model. We call this kind of rendering method point based rendering. Researchers propose many points based rendering technologies and methods with the classifications below.

The data flow direction in rendering can be divided into the positive draw method and reverse draw method. The positive draw method uses the projection of sampling points from the scenery space to the image space, such as the Z-Buffer algorithm. The reverse draw method begins from the display unit of the screen image space and then finds the relevant units in scenery unit by using methods such as the Ray Tracing algorithm. This method computes the intersection between the surface of point cloud model in scenery space and every sight that comes from the viewpoint, passes the pixel in the screen and then displays it in the screen.

The way of dealing with surface elements can be divided into two ways. The first way is to explain every sampling point as a directionless disk (or a square) that has a certain size directly in the image space. In this way, we usually use the positive draw method. Another way is to transform the presentation of pure geometry sampling point to the presentation of surface elements and then draw these surface elements on the screen. We can use either the positive draw method or reverse draw method.

Volume Rendering

Volume Rendering is a technology that generates a two-dimensional image directly from a three-dimensional data field. In real world, there are many scenes that can not be shown by simple faces, such as smoke, fire, cloud, and mist. In this situation volume rendering is preferable. Compared with the surface rendering, volume rendering's biggest advantage is that it can display the inner structure of the objects, which is also one of the most important reasons for it to be widely used.

In the early days of research, the algorithms of the volume rendering were divided into the Image-order volume rendering algorithm and Object-order volume rendering algorithm. Their representative algorithms are the Ray Casting algorithm and Splatting algorithm respectively. With the development of the volume rendering, people propose a mixed volume rendering algorithm based on the former two algorithms and the most representative algorithm is the Shear-Warp algorithm. In recent years, with the advances in development of hardware technology people have again proposed the volume rendering algorithm based on graphics hardware and its representative algorithm, the texture mapping algorithm. With the perfection in the theory of volume rendering, people have proposed the non-space domain volume rendering algorithm once again, whose representative algorithms are on the basis of frequency domain and wavelet domain. The structured grid algorithm agrees with the irregular grid algorithm and becomes very mature in its application. Its representative algorithm is the cell projection algorithm.

Below we will introduce the principles and processes of these mainstream algorithms.

Ray Casting

Ray Casting algorithm was first proposed by M. Levoy [40] in 1988. It is still the hot spot in many research areas and is the most classical image-order volume rendering algorithm. Ray casting algorithm simulates a process: natural lights are casted on the object, and after the effect of partial absorption and dodging when passing through the translucent object the images are formed on the other side of the illuminated object (see Fig. 2.14). When the lights are transmitted to the inside of the object the effect given by the object is sequential, but the effect cannot be achieved in the algorithm. In practice, we will resample the sequential lights as many points, do blending from front to back or from back to front, and similarly simulate the process of the light penetrating the object.

Ray casting algorithm is one volume rendering algorithm with the highest

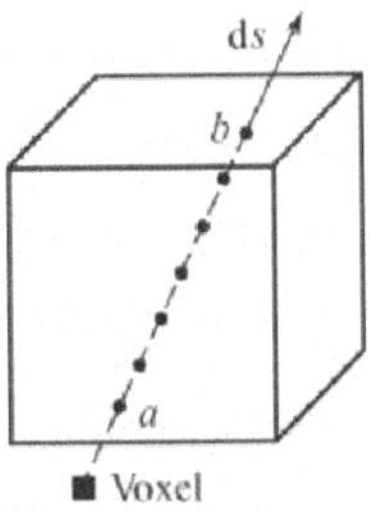

Fig. 2.14 Voxel.

drawing quality. It simulates the natural phenomenoned and has almost no aliasing when its sampling rate is high enough and the transfer function is set reasonably.

Splatting

Splatting algorithm is a kind of object-order volume rendering algorithm. It changes the traditional concept that starts from the image and turns to start from the data of rendering. This avoids the time-consuming interpolation operation and improves the speed of the drawing. The Splatting algorithm traverses every voxel in the volume data, calculates the voxel's effect to the resulting image, and mixes all the effects of the voxel. By the value of voxel and two-dimensional reconstructed kernel, we can calculate the effects to the resulting images.

The Splatting algorithm needs to traverse every voxel, and it is very time-consuming when the volume data has a very high resolution.

Shear-Warp

Shear-Warp algorithm is the fastest volume rendering algorithm so far. It is an algorithm that combines the object-order algorithm and the image-order algorithm. Shear-Warp algorithm builds a coordinate that is always perpendicular to the volume data's primary axis which divides the process into two parts. First it does vertical projections for the volume data after a shear of the middle coordinate. Next it transforms the resulting image in the middle coordinate to the projection plane. The algorithm avoids large amounts of related calculations when the projection plane is not perpendicular to the volume data's primary axis. Therefore, it simplifies three-dimensional computations to two-dimensional computations, and significantly improves the drawing speed. It also allows us to draw large scale volume data with a near real-time speed by a PC without obvious picture quality deficiency. A drawback is that it lacks 3D information and has a deformation aliasing error. This drawback makes the draw performance's reliability is hard to ensure.

Texture Mapping

Texture Mapping algorithm is a method to accelerate the volume rendering algorithm by using the graphics card in the hardware computation channel specially for image processing design. In the initial stage of volume rendering development, since general graphic cards are designed especially for model patches in traditional graphics volume rendering based on the matrix can not give full play to the advantages of the graphic card. It is also very hard for most archeological research units to be equipped with technical graphic drawing hardware because of its relatively high price. But volume rendering and general graphic drawing all belong to the same graphics field and they have many similarities. It is obvious to see the graphic accelerator's auxiliary function. Therefore, the texture mapping algorithm which is based on the graphic acceleration card and uses the texture as the basic data structure was first proposed on a graphic workstation as an individual volume rendering algorithm.

With the progress of society and the PC, people have more needs for computer vision. This usage of vision promotes the flourishing of image display hardware in general computers. Nowadays, even the most ordinary display card supports 3D texture mapping. Some high-end graphics cards also provide the function of managing the process of drawings. The development and spread of graphic display cards makes the texture mapping algorithm lose its original place and becomes an auxiliary acceleration means.

The simple texture mapping algorithm can be viewed as the splatting algorithm with only one element in its reconstructed kernel.

Non-space domain volume rendering

These algorithms discussed above all belong to space domain volume rendering. There are some other algorithms that act in non-space domain, such as the frequency domain volume rendering algorithm and the wavelet domain volume rendering algorithm.

The frequency domain volume rendering algorithm is based on the Fourier section theorem. The theorem tells us that if we extract an interface along the given sight direction in the 3D data field's corresponding frequency domain, and then do an inverse Fourier transform for this section, we could get the projection needed in the space domain's image plane. The complexity of frequency domain volume rendering algorithm is lower than space domain volume rendering algorithm. It is less than $O(N\cdot\ 2\log\ N)$. However, the shortage of 3D data information leads to low quality of the draw performance.

Wavelet is a hot research area. It is one expansion of Fourier transformation. Since wavelets have the property of multiresolution lossless compression, it has the advantages in large scale volume rendering data compression, remoting transmission and the process of perfecting the drawing performance. In applications, the data after wavelet compression is used for storage and transfering. In rendering, we still use the uncompressed space domain data, which wastes large amounts of processing time. This makes it meaningful in research on the wavelet domain rendering algorithm.

Cell projection

Cell projection algorithm was proposed by Wilhelms et al. [41] in 1991. It is an object-order algorithm, similar to the splatting algorithm, and mainly used in irregular grid data. It is different from the splatting algorithm in which the cell projection algorithm's basic cell is not voxel but a polyhedron created by the decomposition of volume data. These polyhedrons are mapped to the image plane in front to back order or back to front order and then mixed to get the resulting image.

Cell projection algorithm is not quite a point based rendering since it contains more than three-dimensional information. It is time consuming in computation. We usually use it in larger scale irregular grid data field or visualization applications that have a better space consistency.

2.3.2 Rendering Acceleration

High resolution three-dimensional models, especially large scale three-dimensional scenes, often contain tens of millions or even billions of polygons and multiple high resolution texture data. In order to achieve real-time frame rates when rendering, acceleration methods are needed.

The methods usually for rendering acceleration include: 3D scene optimizing, level of detail (LOD) technique, image-based rendering (IBR) technique, visibility culling technique and hardware supported, (i.e., GPU supported technique).

Scene optimizing

In order to effectively display a large scale complex virtual scene using the optimal data structure to arrange, the scene's data becomes very important. The common structures for scene data are Octree (Quadtree in two-dimensional case), Binary Space Partitioning (BSP) trees and scene graph.

To construct an Octree for a scene (see Fig. 2.15), we first obtain the bounding box of the scene, and then subdivide the box along the X, Y, Z axes into eight children nodes (commonly represented by the digits 0 to 7). Such subdivision is continued in the children nodes and their children nodes

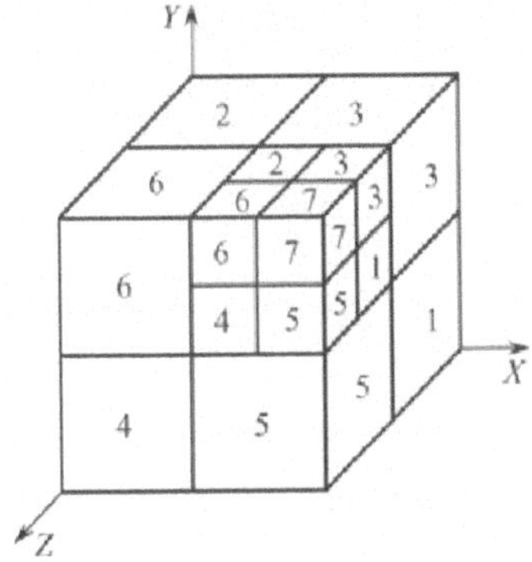

Fig. 2.15 Octree data structure.

until the end requirement is met. As a result, the three-dimensional space of the scene is subdivided into cube voxels with different sizes, which are arranged by a hierarchical structure.

Binary Space Partitioning trees are also called two-dimensional space partition tree. The basic idea of the BSP tree is that any plane can be divided into two half-spaces. The things located in the two sides of the plane belong to the two half-spaces respectively. The space partitioning is repeatedly implemented. Then you can obtain the description for the virtual scene and the various objects in the scene (see Fig. 2.16).

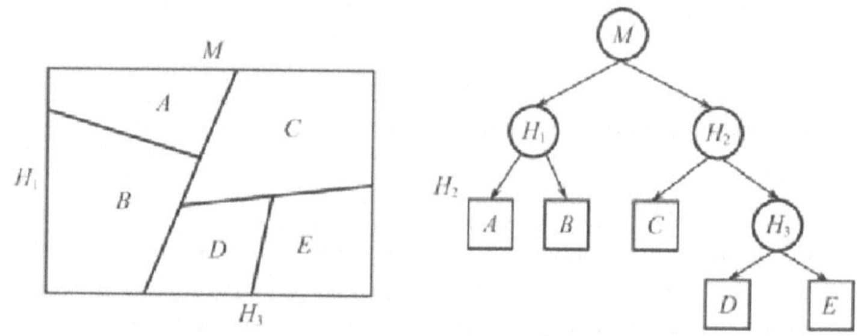

Fig. 2.16 Binary Space Partitioning tree.

In contrast with the tree structure, scene graph (see Fig. 2.17) uses the bounding volume (boundary box) to surround the objects in the scene. The scene graph is a directed and simple connection diagram. The leaf nodes of the scene graph contain geometric data of the object models of the scene. The other nodes of the scene graph contain the information of models clustering and geometric transformation.

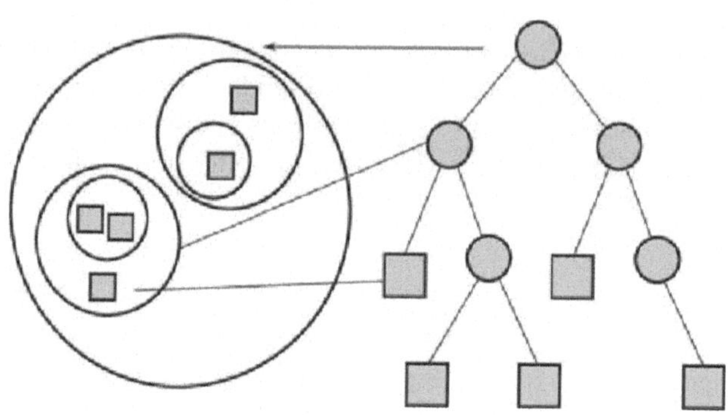

Fig. 2.17 Scene graph.

Level of details technique

LOD-based real-time rendering technique is an important research field in virtual reality. The LOD technique first constructs multiresolution models for objects of a scene during the preprocessing stage. It then chooses the appropriate level of detail models for the objects to display in the rendering stage according to the distances between the objects and the camera. If the object is far away from the camera the pixel area projected by the object on the screen space will be smaller. We can draw the object with a rough model (low resolution model). If the object is close to the camera, the high resolution model of the object will be used for drawing, as shown in Fig. 2.18.

LOD technique is closely related to simplification algorithms because it requires a simplification algorithm in the preprocessing stage to gradually simplify the model of each object of the scene from their full resolution to roughness, so as to build a model with multiresolution description. The classical simplification algorithms include: the Vertex Remove algorithm [42], the Edge Collapse algorithm [43], the Vertex Pair Contraction algorithm [44], and the Vertex Clustering algorithm [45]. For more information, please refer to the excellent review paper [46].

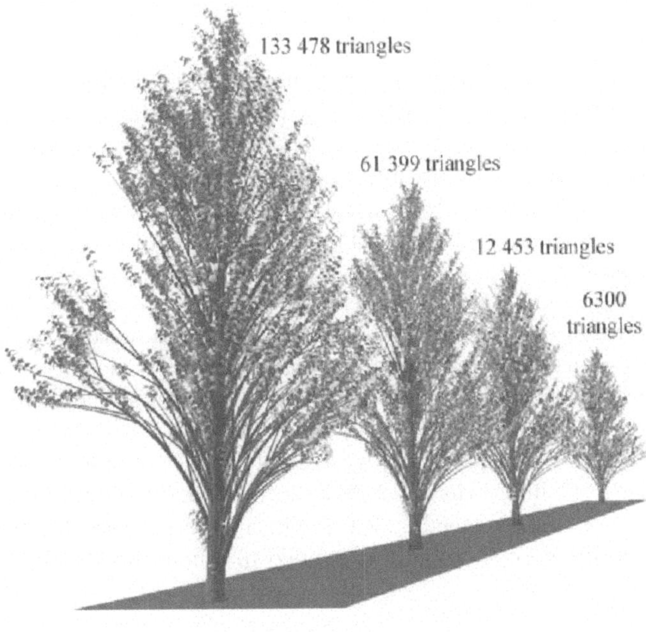

Fig. 2.18 LOD technique uses models with different resolutions for rendering.

The LOD techniques can be classified into two categories: discrete LOD models [47], and continuous LOD models [48]. The discrete LOD models use a certain simplified algorithm to obtain several models with different resolutions for each object in the preprocessing phase, and choose one suitable resolution model from them for drawing in real-time the rendering phase according to the distance from the object to the camera. This method is simple and just needs to save a few geometric models for the object. In addition, the cost of the selection of the suitable model in the rendering phase is almost negligible, thus it is very efficient. However, this method is easy to introduce noticeable popping artifacts when switching from one resolution model to another. The continuous LOD models can avoid the popping problem, but as a result it becomes more complex. It not only needs to simplify the object in the preprocessing phase but also to store the simplification process information. In the rendering phase, it requires a LOD extraction process to obtain a suitable resolution model for the object according to the distance from the object to the camera and combine it with simplification information. The time cost of the LOD extraction is usually very high, although it can ensure the continuity of simplification. The discrete LOD models are used more widely in virtual reality applications.

Image-based rendering technology

Image-based rendering (IBR) technique uses two-dimensional images to replace the complex geometric model of a static scene or an object. Compared with the traditional polygon-based rendering, the IBR technique has the following advantages:

(1) The rendering is independent of the geometric complexity of the scene or object, and it only relates with the required resolution of the images.

(2) The images for the scene or object can be either a computer synthesized, or actual photos, or the mixture of the two ways.

(3) The rendering has fewer requirements for computer resources, and can achieve real-time display for complex scenes by ordinary workstations or personal computers.

The IBR technique uses two methods to improve rendering frame rates. One is the texture mapping techniques by mapping a texture on the surface of the three-dimensional geometric model to represent the surface details of the model, the other is to use the images instead of mesh model to represent the objects.

An object can be represented by a small number of images, such as billboards, using one image that is always towards the observer, or two or three orthogonal cross images (see Fig. 2.19). This method is very efficient, but the stereo effects are poor. It usually is applied to render distant objects.

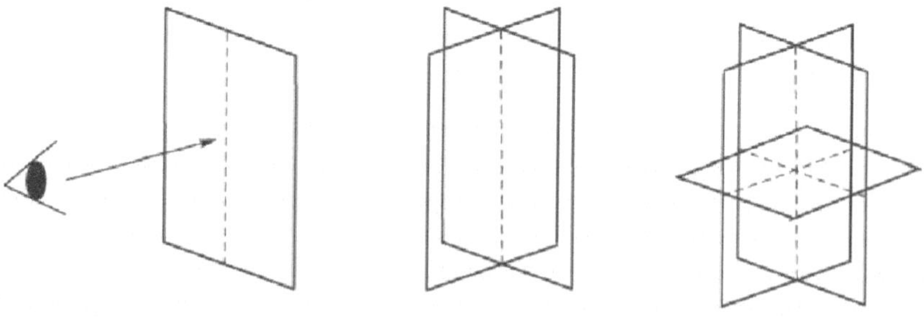

Fig. 2.19 Using billboards to represent a object.

Another way is to get a group of images of an object by taking pictures at an angle equably around the object with same focal length and lighting conditions. When rendering the object, some images can be selected based on the current viewpoint and view direction. A new image representing the object can be synthesized from the selected images by a morphing process, as shown in Fig. 2.20.

Fig. 2.20 Image based rendering.

Visibility culling technique

Visibility culling techniques aim to improve the rendering efficiency by drawing only the visible objects and ignore the other objects that locate outside of the view frustum, or the objects that locate in the view frustum which are not visible.

Visibility culling includes view frustum culling, back face culling and occlusion culling, as shown in Fig. 2.21.

View frustum culling algorithm removes the polygons outside the current view frustum, so that it can reduce the number of polygons for drawing [49]. Usually the polygons of a scene are arranged by a hierarchical data structures (such as KD tree, Octree, or BSP tree). The culling starts from the root node of the hierarchical structure. If a node is in the current view frustum, the polygons belonging to the node are considered to be visible. If a node is outside of the current view frustum, the polygons belonging to the node are considered to be invisible. If a node intersects with the current view frustum, the culling will be recursively implemented on its children nodes.

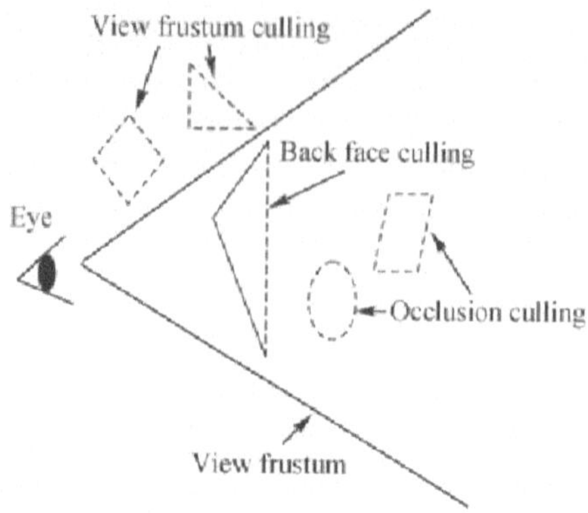

Fig. 2.21 Three kinds of visibility culling.

As a result, through the hierarchy, the culling can be done efficiently.

Back face culling removes the back polygons of an object according to the current viewpoint and view direction, and draws only the frontal polygons. In mathematics, the polygon normal vector indicates the orientation of the polygon, so the normal vector can be used to determine whether the polygon is frontal or back. We can use the dot product value of the normal vector and the view direction. If the value is negative, the polygon is back, otherwise, it is frontal.

View frustum culling can remove the polygons outside the current view frustum which are not always visible. Some polygons may be occluded or hidden by other polygons. The occlusion culling algorithm is used to remove these hidden polygons. The existing occlusion culling algorithm are Z-Buffer [50], Hierarchical Occlusion Maps (HOM) [51], and Portal Culling [52]. For details of this field please refer to articles [53].

GPU-supported rendering

The traditional graphics pipeline is completely dependent on the Central Processing Unit (CPU), but the CPU is not designed specifically for graphics operations. CPU specializes in the implementation of a serial work. However, rendering a complex three-dimensional scene often needs to deal with millions of triangle vertices and raster millions of pixels in short time. Therefore, the usage of a CPU to achieve full three-dimensional real-time rendering is very difficult. In recent years, programmable Graphics Processing Unit (GPU) developed fast with many advantages, such as powerful parallel processing techniques, multistream capabilities, broadband data transmission, increased memory capacity, and other breakthroughs. In addition, GPU itself is continuously enhancing the advanced operations for graphics, such as occlusion culling, texture mapping, transparent and translucent processing, and field depth effect processing. As a result, people began to transfer some of the graphics pipeline processing and graphics algorithms from the CPU to the GPU. This shift is especially obvious in the fields of virtual reality and computer simulation.

2.4 Computer Animation and Simulation Technology

Computer animation comes from the combination of computer graphics and art. With the development of computer hardware and graphics algorithms, it became a new highly developing technology. Computer animation offers people a new space to reveal their imaginations and artistic talents, produces colorful continuous pictures by using the knowledge of computer science, arts, mathematics, physics, and other related subjects. It has been a hot topic in the last few decades. Now it penetrates into our daily life and has formed a huge industry.

2.4.1 Physics Based Animation

Physics based animation appeared at the end of 1980s. In recent years, it has become a new animation technology with potential advantages in 3D modeling and motion simulation. Physics based animation can simulate various natural physical phenomena more realistically than traditional geometry based animation technology. However, the simulation remains computationally expensive. The real world object attributes, like quality, moment of inertia, flexibility, friction force, etc., are considered, and the behaviors of objects are calculated automatically according to physics theory. When an object is acted upon by an external force, the position, direction and shapes of the object can be calculated with Newton dynamics equation at each time step. Animators do not need to care about the details of the animation process but more about the physical properties and some constraint relations of the objects, such as quality, and external force.

In 1986, Weil introduced the elastic object based on physical model into computer animation for first time [54]. Wriggle animations of animals without legs like snakes and worms were simulated based on the mass-spring system [55]. Behavior animation was put forward by Tu in her "artificial fish" system to simulate individuals and groups movement realistically with as little as possible animator's interaction [56]. In Terzopoulos' paper [57], he prefers using continuous elastic theory to compute an object's shape and movement. By considering elastic objects' distributed physical properties, e.g., quality or elasticity, the dynamic responses to external forces can be imitated. In order to achieve a vivid sense of movement, Platt et al. proposed two kinds of constraint for elastic objects: geometry and dynamics, which made the simulation of a complex system with elastic object much easier [58]. The stochastic method is very effective for animation of natural scenery [59]. Simulation fragmentation of glasses or ceramic objects remains a complicated problem.

One possible way to obtain the fragmentation effect is using 3D particles to describe the objects [60]. Fluid dynamics could be used to simulate streams [61]. A muscle model was proposed to simulate the movement of the human mouth [62]. Albrecht gave a method to generate facial realistic animation with voice synchronized [63]. The collision detection of flexible objects on a rigid object's surface had been solved [64]. After that, Bridson achieved collision contact and friction effects on cloth [65].

Physics based animation can generate very natural, vivid animation. However, most of models and algorithms are designed for special scenes at present. The process of an object's motion is automatically controlled by the model. Users can only adjust the motion by setting abstract parameters indirectly. Since physical based simulation includes many numerical calculations, it remains computationally expensive.

2.4.2 Character Animation

3D character animation is one of the most challenge topics in the computer animation field. Character animation includes modeling characters, motion control, and rendering. In order to facilitate motion control and real-time rendering, a two-level skeleton and skin model is used to create a role's animation, which means that a role is composed by a skeleton model and a mesh skin model. A hierarchical structure of a skeleton is formed according to the characteristics of the role. Adjacent bones are linked by a joint and can do relative movement. The mesh skin is bound to its skeleton according to certain rules and each vertex of the mesh model will be influenced by some bones. The position of a vertex in the world coordinate system is computed by weighting all the influences from different bones so that the mesh skin can move the following skeleton movements. This way produces skeleton driven skin metamorphic animation, named skeleton rigging animation. The generation methods of lifelike human skeleton movement at present basically have the following categories: (1) key frame method; (2) kinematics method; (3) dynamics method; (4) procedure method; (5) motion capture method.

Key frame

The traditional key frame method relies on the animator's manual adjustment to determine the virtual role's attitude at a key frame moment. The intermediate frames can be calculated with many kinds of interpolation methods, like linear interpolation, spherical interpolation, and spline interpolation. Key frame can easily control the movements of characters. However, animators need to adjust a role's attitude manually to modify the animation, which makes animators' workload extremely heavy. Determining the exact moment of each key frame is very difficult. So the effects of the animations created by key frame method rely heavily on the animators' experiences. Another problem of key frame interpolation is that these interpolations between the nodes are relatively independent. For example, the interpolations of a shoulder node and an elbow node have no direct relationship. But the distance between the shoulder and elbow should be fixed as common sense dictates. This restriction cannot be guaranteed by using the key frame method. Kinematics method is an alternative solution for the problem.

Kinematics

Kinematics method computes the movement without considering the quality and external forces, which includes forward kinematics method and inverse kinematics method. After giving a virtual character and the rotation angles of its joints, forward kinematics can calculate the position of each bone in a global coordinate system. However, the inverse kinematics method calculates joints' angles inversely with a given aimed attitude of the role. Forward kinematics method requires each joint' angle, while inverse kinematics method only requires the aimed situation. Therefore, inverse kinematics method is more intuitive and easier to control the roles' behaviors.

Dynamics

The fidelity of key frame or kinematics is heavily dependent on the experiences of the production staff. It is difficult to verify physical fidelity of both methods. The dynamics method calculates each joint's acceleration and speed according to force and torque, and finally determines all the attitudes of a role during its movement. Compared with the former two methods, Dynamics method's physical effect is much better. Nonetheless, to obtain external forces and torques on a role is difficult and not intuitive. This problem can be settled by inverse dynamics and constraint-based method.

Procedural animation

For some cyclical movements, such as walking and running, Boulic [66] tried to obtain the motion data and set up a corresponding empirical formula to generate the movement. The procedure method determines exact movements according to role's characteristics (e.g., height, length of legs), and movement characteristics (e.g., speed). It is manageable and the effects are authentic, but the applicable scope is limited.

Motion capture

This method uses sensors to capture movements of human body in a three-dimensional space and records the data. Then it drives the virtual human into virtual environments according to the recorded data. Motion capture techniques can overcome a heavy workload and a lack of fidelity of traditional assigning displacements of bones and joint angles by animators. Motion capture method can capture the real data of human movement quickly, make the effect authentic, and generate many complicated movements. The captured data describes the skeleton structure and all the parameters at all time. The most common data format is the BVH file format, which consists of two parts:

the file header and data section. BVH files store joints' movement data. The file header section describes the connections between the joints and the offset values. The data section describes a joint's move at each sample point.

2.4.3 Group Animation

Group animation is an abbreviation of group behavior animation. It is the technology to simulate a species group's behaviors on a computer and record them as an animation. As the computer does the simulation automatically of making a group animation, the animator's workload is reduced greatly and the key work turns to designing group behavior. With proper behavior control constraints, the group will act independently and in familiar ways.

At present the main research of group animation is divided into two directions: simulation cluster and behavior control. Simulation cluster has been applied in many areas including artificial life, computer animation, games, interactive computer graphics, virtual reality, robots, aerospace, education, biology, and physics. Behavior control includes common behavior control, such as simulating pedestrians and traffic, simulating emergencies of a crowd, autonomic learning and evolution, behavior control in a game, and path planning. In fact, these two directions are inseparable: behavior control describes the basic rules and algorithms of simulation clustering.

Groups are self-organized. Complex behaviors of a group emerge from the interaction of many simple individuals. The behavior of an individual depends on its perception of its surroundings and system's behavior control rules. This makes the three key modules of group animation: virtual environment, individual perception mechanism, and behavior control mechanism. Individual perception mechanism obtains detailed data of a scene from the virtual environment model. Behavior control mechanism is a group of constraints that tells each individual to act as required. The combination of behavior mechanism and perception mechanism gives the individual independent behavior ability.

Group animation must be based on group characteristics. It is necessary to understand the knowledge of swarm intelligence when design behavior control mechanism.

Swarm intelligence has the following features

- The control mechanism is distributed, and there can be no control center. Thus it adapts to work under current network environment. It also needs strong robustness to avoid the situation that one broken individual makes the whole system collapse.
- Each individual of the group is able to change the whole environment. This is a way of indirect communication between individuals called *stigmergy*. Swarm intelligence can make information transmission and cooperation through indirect communication ways. When the number of individuals

increases, the growth of communication overhead becomes smaller. So it has good scalability.

- Individual's ability and behavior rules are very simple, thus the realization of swarm intelligence is convenient.
- The group has emergent intelligence which means its complex behaviors emerge from the interaction of many simple individuals. Groups are self-organized.

Group behavior modeling based on artificial life

The main purpose of group behavior modeling is in the pursuit of reality about behavioral expressions. The wide application of group animation has attracted many researchers to study the modeling methods of group behavior for over 10 years. Whereas group behaviors rely on the virtual environment, the group behavior modeling would be limited. Here several mature modeling techniques are introduced in the following:

Group behavior modeling based on artificial life

The artificial life method creates group behavior through the interaction between individuals and the interaction between the individual and the environment. It focuses on the self-organization process and the emergence intelligence of a group. This method is based on the theory of biology. It mainly investigates reproduction, evolution, synergy, competition, and organization of natural life systems, like boids [67]. Boids can simulate behaviors of flocks, herds and schools.

Group behavior modeling based on particle system

The Particle system method was proposed by Reeves WT in 1983 [1]. It has promoted the development of the computer graphics greatly. The system is very powerful to simulate some specific fuzzy phenomenon in the computer graphics field, such as explosion, flying flags, and meteors. Eric Bouvier investigated a crowd behavior simulation model based on particle system [68]. The model assumed that everyone was a "particle" and the crowd was a particle system. Each particle's attribute, like position, velocity, and acceleration, is calculated through Newtonian mechanics mechanism and random events simulation. It fits crowds with simple behaviors very well, but not very well for crowds that contain complex emotional factors or need advance knowledge for decision-making.

Group behavior modeling based on dynamics system

The dynamics method assumes that each individual wants to move to a specific position. This position can be obtained by calculating the group's speed and investigating the currently visible obstacles and neighbors. Drick Helbing analyzed the internal force of particle system and created a simulation model for emergency evacuation of crowds [69]. The model simulated the evacuation of a crowd under a panic state, calculated out the individual movement speed, and deduced possible casualties by combining with the speed of the crowd's passing through an export. However the method has some limitations. For example, solving dynamic equations remains a big problem.

ViCrowd Model

Daniel Thalmann's group proposed ViCrowd [70]. They divided and defined the behavior level, control level and other attributes of a human crowd. The behavior level includes crowd, group, and agent. Agents in the same level get the same path planning. Control level consists of three degree levels, including guide behavior, plan behavior and autonomy behavior. The attributes includes faith, knowledge and intention. ViCrowd abstracts crowd behaviors and gives a general method for movement modeling.

2.5 Content-Based 3D Model Retrieval Technology

In this section, 3D model retrieval systems and feature extraction technology are introduced. The algorithm of feature extraction technology includes histogram-based features, topology-based features, view-based features, transformation-based features and symmetrical feature extraction.

3D model retrieval systems

With the technology development of 3D model and the popularity of 3D model data, 3D model retrieval is becominghot topic in research institutions and industry. 3D model retrieval research currently focuses on content-based 3D model retrieval technology. Some content-based 3D model retrieval systems have been developed by research institutions and companies. The traditional way to retrieve 3D models is to use two-dimensional or three-dimensional sketches as input.

The Princeton Shape Retrieval and Analysis Group in Princeton University is one of pioneers in 3D model retrieval and has successfully developed a WEB based 3D model search engine. It offers three search methods: text keyword searching, 3D sketch and 2D sketch retrieval [71]. The group has collected more than 30,000 general 3D models to form a 3D model database in OFF format. The Communications and Multimedia Laboratory of China Taiwan University developed a 3D model retrieval system, in which the 2D projection image from 3D model is used to capture characteristics of a 3D model of the content descriptors [72] to achieve content based 3D model retrieval. The National Institute of Multimedia Education in Japan developed the Ogden VI system [73], which is used in distance learning for dealing with polygon models. By using rotation invariant shape descriptors, the content feature extraction of a 3D model is achieved. The Laboratory of Computer Graphics Image Processing of the University of Leipzig in Germany developed a VRML based online 3D model retrieval system through extracting the content characteristics to achieve three-dimensional model retrieval [74]. The Advanced Multimedia Processing (AMP) Lab at Carnegie-Mellon University developed a 3D model retrieval system [75] in which each mesh model is regarded as a solid 3D model of the binary region through the extraction rate of body surface area models and composed of moment invariants in ten information contents of a new set of model features. There are other 3D models based on the content retrieval system like the National Institute of Ephesus Canadian search engine [76] , the 3D retrieval engine at Utrecht University [74] and the 3D search system at the Informatics and Telematics Institute, Greece [77].

Feature extraction technology

For 3D shape matching, features represent geometric and topological properties of 3D models, 3D models can be discriminated by measuring and comparing their features. Feature based methods can be divided into four categories according to the type of shape features which are used: histogram-based features, topology-based features, geometry-based features, and view-based features. New features can be generated by integrating various features of a 3D model. Vranic mentioned the use of the composite features of a 3D model for searching. The composite feature vector consists of the depth of the image, projection profile, and polygon mesh expansion characteristics of the ray composition [74]. The retrieval results using the method will be better than the single feature algorithm. However, because feature extraction operation of a three-dimensional model will conduct much iteration for multifeature integration, the algorithm takes a lot of time and reduces the efficiency of retrieval.

Histogram-based features

Histogram statistical distribution-based feature extraction method is the most commonly used method to obtain three-dimensional model characteristics. In current study, the following statistical characteristics are mainly used: the additional information of the model (such as color, texture, etc); the geometric relationship between the model's vertices (such as distance, angle, normal direction, etc.); and the model vertex's curvature distribution characteristics. Paquet proposed to use normal vector histogram to describe the characteristics of a three-dimensional model. However, the characteristics are not sensitive to the bump feature so that a large number of models have same characteristics [78]. Osada [79] showed different distribution characteristics depending on the geometry relationship between the surface vertices and attempted to make the complex feature extraction problem from an arbitrary that may be a degraded three-dimensional model and maybe a relative simple shape probability distribution problem and calculate the similarity of the characteristics distribution. Zhang took some of the model's geometrical parameters (such as area, volume, and some constructed special vector) as the feature vector [80].

Paquet took the relationship between the vertices and some axis as the characteristics and proposed a method based on the connection [78]. The Zaharia method provided the object's internal shape index description according to some local geometric surface properties (such as the curvature of a point) [81]. Ankerst enfoldd the centroid of the three-dimensional model, divided the model space into a series of profiles and sectors, and then calculated the three-dimensional shape histogram according to [82].

Topology-based features

Topology based three-dimensional model feature extraction method uses a graph to describe the relationship between different parts. Topology map based method is divided into the Reeb graph and skeleton diagram.

The definition of a Reeb graph can be traced back to 1946 [83]. In recent years, the Reeb graph had been introduced as shape descriptors to analyze the three-dimensional model shape characteristics in computer graphics and the analysis results are used in a variety of applications [84]. An extended Reeb graph could be used to handle three-dimensional model grid data [85]. The choice of the real value mapping function defined in the surface of the model determines the final result of the Reeb graph extraction. Biasotti [86] compared the different three-dimensional model matching results using Reeb graph that is generated from different functions.

The skeleton of three-dimensional model is a representation of the topology structure. It is a visual description of the model's main features and is consistent with human visual characteristics. Sundar used a skeleton map as the shape descriptor to perform the geometry and topology information of the three-dimensional model. This algorithm uses the controlled parameters based thin-oriented algorithm to extract the model's skeleton. This is suited for any three-dimensional model that is described in a voxel [87]. The skeleton node in this algorithm lies the center of the partial model and the lean of the parameters controls the density of nodes. Therefore, the parameters directly affect the quality of the extraction of the skeleton. The thinning algorithm is abnormally sensitive to the noise and small perturbations will lead to the wrong skeleton extraction. Meanwhile, due to the recursive computation and comparison for every voxel distance's conversion values, this algorithm is computationally expensive. The skeleton based model feature extraction algorithm requires a good closure of the model. The need for the original model's information is very strict and the model needs to be a closed polygon grid or strict voxel description. The extraction for a model formed by a loose polygon is meaningless, and may lead to incorrect results when dealing with some degradation models. At the same time, due to different methods of skeleton extraction, the model will be very sensitive to noise. Iyer [88] used the iterative erosion strategy to thin the voxel in the model into one pixel in order to get the skeleton graph and compared two graph's isomorphism using the decision tree method. This algorithm stores all the graphs' indexes in the decision tree form in the database which leads to that the algorithm's time complexity and space complexity that increases exponentially as the graph nodes increase. Therefore, this algorithm is only suited for small models. Iyer also proposed the method of using multi-scale level of the skeleton graph. This method only stores the local shape information, such as the normalized distribution of the physical length and curvature. So the space complexity is greatly reduced. This algorithm also uses the heuristic genetic methods to find two skeleton graph's isomorphism [89].

Another graph theory based method includes the model graph based method, which is mostly used in the feature extraction of the CAD model. The most representative algorithm among them is the boundary representation (B-rep) algorithm and the learning and physical mapping algorithm (CSG). B-rep describes the model's vertices, edges, and faces [90]. CSG uses a Boolean operation set that is used for the basic geometric entities such as a cube, or a cylinder to describe the model [91]. The model graph based method can be effectively used in the CAD/CAM models, but it is very difficult to apply to ordinary models, such as human models or animal models.

View-based features

View-based method is used to extract from the point of view of human vision to compare the two 3D models similarity. If two 3D models are similar, they still are similar from different points of view [92]. Then a very intuitive 3D model of feature extraction from the visual idea from the point of view of a 3D model will be in a particular plane for projection. The use of projection of 2D contour extraction image in a three-dimensional model of the corresponding features will be expressed.

Loffler using a 2D image as a 3D model retrieval conditions for library projection shown a similar model [93]. Satoshi used a hand-painted 14 sketch as retrieval conditions on the 3D model search projection [94]. Wang [95] extracted six projected two-dimensional image characteristics from 3D model as 3D model's features. Then six groups of features from two models are calculated respectively. Lastly similarity is calculated through cross comparing the six groups of characteristics. Funkhouser also used 2D sketch as retrieval conditions, in the pre-treatment stage that will be used to describe the 3D model of the outline projection image as a model 13 descriptor, with 13 of the 2D images to represent a three-dimensional model. It can not very well react to 3D model internal local characteristics change [96]. Vranic used six projection maps of model along X, Y, Z coordinate axis to get different 2D contour information. Then Vranic calculated the FFT spectrum shape characteristic coefficient as the energy vector [97]. Ohbuchi proposed the 42 different points of the depth of the shape of the image as descriptors. Each image with a rotation invariant of the Fourier descriptor was stated, and the shape of the model by this descriptor provided 42 of characteristic vector, compares the two models by calculating the similarity of the characteristic vectors [98]. It is used for feature extraction of 3D model projection image. The more matches the better the results. Chen from the model visualization angle even had a 3D model of one hundred projections that provided calculation of the projection Zernike torque and Fourier transformation. This is extracted from the Fourier transformation coefficients as the characteristic value of model [99]. A 3D model of the plane of the outline projection can be extracted. A 3D model features have close observation of the visual perception of human body, but this feature can not reflect the spatial structure information and bumping characteristics of 3D model well, thus the feature matching accuracy is not good enough.

Transformation-based features

Using transformation coefficients as a feature of 3D models is an important method on describing the 3D model characteristics. Vranic proposed to use three-dimensional model of the spherical harmonic functions to extract three-dimensional model characteristics and then used the KL transformation method on posture correction [100]. Yu put forward another similar method. This method calculates the intersection points of all the rays from the origin and the model, and calculates these Fourier transformation coefficients on these intersection points. Then similarity between two models is determined through calculating the Euclidean distance between these coefficients. [101]. Kazhdan improved Yu's method by using a rotation independent and modeled spherical harmonic transform method, the use of the harmonic transform for feature extraction [102]. Novotni proposed using three-dimensional Zernike moment as a 3D model descriptor [103]. Zernike moments and spherical harmonic functions for retrieving the contents of the effect of three-dimensional model is not very different, however, Zernike moments are used within the model to better understand the relationship between, while this method is still computationally complex and has problems. Ricard introduces a 3D perspective transform of the radial shape descriptors. This method is from 2D image radial angle wavelet [104].

Based on the mathematical transformation of feature extraction method we can usually model to get a good retrieval effect, but this method usually is not space related. The extracted features can not provide performance of the model space relevance, so it does improve support to the space structure matching, and therefore could not give reasonable search results, feedback, and not to judge the retrieval results similarity either.

Symmetrical feature extraction process

The symmetry of a three-dimensional object is one of its important geometric features. In the world of three-dimensional objects are showed using strong symmetry. In recent years 3D model symmetry research has increased over 3D model segmentation, identification, matching, and other 3D model analysis fields. 3D models symmetry and rules structure are more and more recognized [105, 106]. These results also are based on symmetrical characteristic for the 3D model retrieval and further research provided a condition. Kazhdan (3D model proposed by the reflection of symmetrical descriptor) proposed a 3D models feature which will be used in a 3D model symmetry of feature extraction [107]. First, the 3D model of the body element is defined, then the 3D model of the plane of the reflection in different distance value are symmetrical according to the distance between reflections of the symmetric descriptor from a three-dimensional model of the characteristic expression.

References

[1] Reeves WT (1983) Particle Systems: a Technique for Modeling a Class of Fuzzy Objects. ACM Transactions on Graphics, 2(2): 91–108

[2] Barr A (1984) Global and Deformations of Solid Primitives. In: Proceedings of the 11th Annual Conference on Computer Graphics and Interactive Techniques, July 1984, 18(3):21-30, ACM Press, New York

[3] Sederberg TW, Parry SR. (1986) Free-form Deformation of Solid Geometric Models. ACM SIGGRAPH Computer Graphics, 20(4): 151–160

[4] Loop CT (1987) Smooth Subdivision Surfaces Based on Triangles. Master's thesis. Department of Mathematics, University of Utah, Utah, USA

[5] Catmull E, Clark J (1978) Recursively Generated B-spline Surfaces on Arbitrary Topological Meshes. Computer Aided Design, 10(6): 350–355

[6] Doo D, Sabin M (1998) Behaviour of Recursive Division Surfaces Near Extraordinary Points. ACM Press, New York

[7] Zorin D, Schroder P (2000) Subdivision for Modeling and Animation. Course Notes for SIGGRAPH, ACM Press, New York

[8] Hsu WM, Hughes JF, Kaufman H (1992) Direct Manipulation of Free-form Deformations. ACM Press, New York.

[9] Borrel P, Rappoport A (1994) Simple Constrained Deformations for Geometric Modeling and Interactive Design. ACM Transactions on Graphics, 13(2): 137–155

[10] Gu X, Yau S (2003) Global Conformal Surface Parameterization. In: Proceedings of ACM Symposium on Geometry, pp 127–137 Aire-la-Ville, Switzerland

[11] Lévy B, Petitjeans S, Ray N, et al (2002) Least Squares Conformal Maps for Automatic Texture Atlas Generation. In: Proceedings of the SIGGRAPH 2002, ACM Press, New York

[12] Alexa M, Behr J, Cohen-Or D, et al (2001) Point Set Surfaces. In: Proceedings of the IEEE Conference on Visualization, pp 21–28, San Diego, California, 21–26 October 2001

[13] Carr JC, et al (2001) Reconstruction and Representation of 3D Objects with Radial Basis Functions. In: Proceedings of the SIGGRAPH 2001, ACM Press, New York

[14] Ohtake Y, Belyaev A, Alexa M, et al (2003) Multi-level Partition of Unity Implicits. In: Proceedings of the SIGGRAPH 2003, ACM Press, New York

[15] Kazhdan M, Bolitho M, Hoppe H (2006) Poisson Surface Reconstruction. In: Proceedings of the SGP 2006, Aire-la-Ville, Switzerland, pp 61–70

[16] Levin D (1998) The Approximation Power of Moving Least-squares. Mathematics of Computation, 67(224): 1517–1532

[17] Levin D (2003) Mesh-independent Surface Interpolation. Geometric Modeling for Scientific Visualization, pp 37–49, Springer, Heidelberg

[18] Dey TK, Li G, Sun J (2005) Normal Estimation for Point Clouds: A Comparison Study for a Voronoi Based Method. In: Proceedings of the Eurographics/IEEE VGTC Symposium on Point-Based Graphics, pp 39–46

[19] Besl PJ, McKay HD (1992) A Method for Registration of 3-D Shapes. IEEE Transactions on Pattern Analysis and Machine Intelligence, 14(2): 239–256

[20] Yang C, Medioni G (1992) Object Modeling by Registration of Multiple Range Images. Image and Vision Computing, 10(3): 145–155

[21] Bergevin R, Soucy M, Gagnon H, et al (1996) Towards a General Multi-View Registration Technique. IEEE Transactions on Pattern Analysis and Machine Intelligence, 18(5): 540–547

[22] Rusinkiewicz S, Levoy M. (2001) Efficient Variants of the ICP Algorithm. In: Proceedings of the of the International Conference on 3-D Digital Imaging and Modeling, pp 145–152

[23] Park SY, Subbarao M (2003) An Accurate and Fast Point-to-plane Registration Technique. Pattern Recognition Letters, 24(16): 2967–2976

[24] Johnson AE, Kang SB (1999) Registration and Integration of Textured 3D Data. Image and Vision Computing, 17(2): 135–147

[25] Gelfand N, Ikemoto L, Rusinkiewicz S, et al (2003) Geometrically Stable Sampling for the ICP Algorithm. In: Proceedings of the Fourth International Conference on 3-D Digital Imaging and Modeling, pp 260–267

[26] Moenning C, Dodgson A (2003) A New Point Cloud Simplification Algorithm. In: Proceedings of the 3rd International Conference on Visualization, Imaging and Image Processing, pp 8–10

[27] Pauly M, Gross M, Kobbelt LP (2002) Efficient Simplification of Point-sampled Surfaces. In: Proceedings of IEEE Visualization, pp 163–170

[28] Wu J, Kobbelt L (2004) Optimized Sub-Sampling of Point Sets for Surface Splatting. Computer Graphics Forum, 23(3): 643–652

[29] Pauly M, Keiser R, Gross M (2003) Multi-scale Feature Extraction on Point-sampled Surfaces. In: Proceedings of Eurographics 2003, 22: 281–289, Blackwell, London

[30] Floater MS, Reimers M (2001) Meshless Parameterization and Surface Reconstruction. Computer Aided Geometric Design, 18(2): 77–92

[31] Zwicker M, Pauly M, Knoll O, et al (2002) Pointshop 3D: An Interactive System for Point-based Surface Editing. ACM Transactions on Graphics, 21(3): 322–329

[32] Hoppe H, Derose T, Duchamp T (1992). Surface Reconstruction from Unorganized Points. Computer Graphics 26(2): 71–78.

[33] Amenta N, Bern M, Kamvysselis M (2002) A New Voronoi-based Surface Reconstruction Algorithm. ACM Transactions on Graphics, 21(3): 322–329

[34] Zaroubi S, Goelman G (2002) Complex Denoising of MR Data via Wavelet Analysis: Application for Functional MRI. Magnetic Resonance Imaging, 18(1): 59–68

[35] Bao P, Zhang L (2003) Noise Reduction for Magnetic Resonance Images via Adaptive Multiscale Products Thresholding. IEEE Transactions on Medical Imaging, 22(9): 1089–1099

[36] Buades A, Coll B, Morel JM (2005) A Review of Image Denoising Algorithms, with a New One. Simul, 4: 490–530

[37] Coupe P, Yger P, Barillot C (2006) Fast Nonlocal Means Denoising for 3D MR Images. In: Proceedings of the International Conference on MICCAI, pp 33-40, Copenhagen, Denmark, 1 – 6 October 2006

[38] Manjon, NA, Manjon JV, Bromiley PA (2010) A Statistical Interpretation of Non-Local Means, 4(3), 162–172

[39] Newman T, Yi H (2006) A Survey of the Marching Cubes Algorithm. Computers & Graphics, 30(5): 854 – 879

[40] Levoy M (1988) Display of Surfaces from Volume Data. IEEE Computer Graphics and Applications, 8(3): 29–37

[41] Wilhelms J, Gelder AV (1991) A Coherent Projection Approach for Direct Volume Rendering. Computer Graphics, 25(4): 275–284

[42] Schroeder WJ, Zarge JA, Lorensen WE (1992) Decimation of Triangle Meshes. Computer Graphics, 26(2): 65–70

[43] Algorri ME, Schmitt F (1996) Mesh Simplification. Computer Graphics Forum, 15(3): 77–86

[44] Garland M, Heckbert PS (1997) Surface Simplification Using Quadric Error Metrics. In: Proceedings of the 24th Annual Conference on Computer Graphics and Interactive Techniques, pp 209–216

[45] Low K, Tan T (1997) Model Simplification Using Vertex-clustering. In: Proceedings of the Symposium on Interactive 3D Graphics, pp 75–82

[46] Cignoni P, Montani C, Scopigno R (1998) A Comparison of Mesh Simplification Algorithms. Computers & Graphics, 22(1): 37–54

[47] Gumbau J, Ripolles O, Chover M (2007) LOD Manager: A Framework for Rendering Multi-resolution Models in Real-time Applications. In: Proceedings of the 15th International Conferences in Central Europe on Computer Graphics, Visualization and Computer Vision, 29 January – 1 February 2007, Plzen, Czech Republic

[48] Ripolles O, Chover M, Gumbau J, et al (2009) Rendering Continuous Level-of-detail Meshes by Masking Strips. Graphical Models, 71(5): 184–195

[49] Slater M, Chrysanthou Y (1997) View Volume Culling Using a Probabilistic Caching Scheme. Proceedings of the ACM Symposium on Virtual Reality Software and Technology, ACM Press, New York

[50] Greene N, Kass M, Miller G (1993) Hierarchical Z-buffer Visibility. In: Proceedings of the SIGGRAPH 1993, ACM Press, New York

[51] Zhang H, Manocha D, Hudson D, et al (1997) Visibility Culling Using Hierarchical Occlusion Maps. Computer Graphics, 31: 77–88

[52] Airey JM, Rohlf JH, Brooks Jr FP (1990) Towards Image Realism with Interactive Update Rates in Complex Virtual Building Environments. Computer Graphics, 24(2): 41–50

[53] Cohen-Or D, Chrysanthou YL, Silva C, et al (2003) A Survey of Visibility for Walkthrough Applications. IEEE Transactions on Visualization and Computer Graphics, 9(3): 412–431

[54] Weil J (1986) The Synthesis of Cloth Objects. In: Proceedings of the SIGGRAPH 1986, 20(4): 49–54, ACM Press, New York.

[55] Miller GSP (1988) The Motion Dynamics of Snakes and Worms. Computer Graphics, 22(4): 169–173

[56] Tu X, Terzopoulos D (1994) Artificial Fishes: Physics, Locomotion, Perception, Behavior. In: Proceedings of the 21st Annual Conference on Computer Graphics and Interactive Techniques, pp 43–50

[57] Terzopoulos D, Platt J, Barr A, et al (1987) Elastically Deformable Models. In: Proceedings of the SIGGRAPH 1987, Computer Graphics, 21(4): 205–214

[58] Platt JC, Barr AH (1988) Constraints Methods for Flexible Models. Computer Graphics, 22(4): 279–288

[59] Shinya M, Fournier A (1992) Stochastic Motion-Motion Under the Influence of Wind. Computer Graphics Forum, 11(3): 119–128

[60] Norton A, Turk G, Bacon B, et al (1991) Animation of Fracture by Physical Modeling. Visual Computer, 7(4): 210–219

[61] Kass M, Miller G (1990) Rapid, Stable Fluid Dynamics for Computer Graphics. Computer Graphics, 24(4): 49–57

[62] Sera H, Morishima S, Terzopoulos D (1996) Physics-based Muscle Model for Mouth Shape Control. In: Proceedings of the IEEE International Workshop on Robot and Human Communication, pp 207–212, Tsukuba, Japan, 11–14 November 1996

[63] Albrecht I, Haber J, Seidel H (2002) Speech Synchronization for Physics-based Facial Animation. In: Proceedings of the WSCG 2002, pp 9–16

[64] Nadia BL, Thalmann NM, Thalmann D (1991) Cloth Animation with Self-collision Detection. In: Proceedings of the Conference on Modeling in Computer Graphics, pp 179–187, Springer, Heidelberg

[65] Bridson R, Fedkiw R, Anderson J (2002) Robust Treatment of Collisions, Contact and Friction for Cloth Animation. ACM Transactions on Graphics, 21: 594–603

[66] Boulic R, Ulicny B, Thalmann D (2004) Versatile Walk Engine. Journal of Game Development, 1(1): 29–52

[67] Reynolds CW (1987) Flocks, Herds and Schools: A Distributed Behavioral Model. Computer Graphics, 21(4): 25–34

[68] Bouvier E, Cohen E, Najman LC (1997) From Crowd Simulations to Airbag Deployment: Particle System, a New Paradigm of Simulation. Journal of eletronic Imaging, 6(1): 94–107

[69] Helbing D, Farkas I, Vicsek T (2000) Simulating Dynamical Features of Escape Panic. Nature, 407(6803): 487–490

[70] Musse SR, Thalmann D (1997) A Model of Human Crowd Behavior: Group Inter-relationship and Collision Detection Analysis. In: Proceedings of the Workshop of Computer Animation and Simulation of Eurographics, pp 39–51

[71] Lee J, Funkhouser TA (2008) Sketch-Based Search and Composition of 3D Models. In: Proceedings of the Fifth Eurographics Workshop on Sketch-based Interfaces and Modeling, Annecy, France, 11–13 June 2008

[72] Shen Y, Chen D, Tian X, et al (2003) 3D Model Search Engine Based on Lightfield Descriptors. EUROGRAPHICS Interactive Demos, Granada, Spain, 1–6 September 2003.

[73] Suzuki M (2001) A Web Based Retireval System for 3D Polygonal Models. In: Proceedings of the 20th NAFIPS International Conference, Vancouver, Canada, 25–28 July 2001

[74] Vranic DV (2005) DESIRE: A Composite 3D-shape Descriptor. In: Proceedings of the IEEE International Conference on Multimedia and Exp, pp 962–965, Amsterdam, Netherlands, 6–8 July 2005

[75] http://amp. ece. cmu. edu/projects/3DModelRetrieval/. Accessed 20 May 2011

[76] Paquet E, Murching A, Naveen T, et al (2000) Description of Shape Information for 2D and 3D Objects. Signal Processing: Image Communication, 16(1): 103–122

[77] http://3d-search. iti. gr/3DSearch. Accessed 20 May 2011

[78] Paquet E, Rioux M (1998) A Content-based Search Engine for VRML Databases. In: Proceedings of 1998 IEEE Computer Society Conference on Computer Vision and Pattern Recognition, IEEE Computer Society, pp 541–546, Santa Barbara, USA, 23–25 June 1998,

[79] Osada R, Funkhouser T, Chazelle B, et al (2002) Shape Distributions. ACM Transactions on Graphics, 21(4): 807–832

[80] Zhang C, Chen T (2001) Efficient Feature Extraction For 2D/3D Objects in Mesh Representation. In: Proceedings of the 2001 International Conference on Image Processing, pp 935–938, Thessaloniki, Greece, 7–10 October 2001

[81] Zaharia T, Preteux F (2001) 3D Shape-based Retrieval within the MPEG–7 Framework. In: Proceedings of SPIE Conference on Nonlinear Image Processing and Pattern Analysis XII, 4304: 133–145, San Jose, USA, January 2001

[82] Ankerst M, Kastenmller G, Kriegel HP, et al (1999) 3D Shape Histograms for Similarity Search and Classification in Spatial Databases. In: Proceedings of the 6th International Symposium on Advances in Spatial Databases, pp 207–226, Springer, London

[83] Reeb GC (1960) Sur les Points Singuliers d'une Forme de Pfaff compl Tement int Grable ou d'une fonction Numrique. Comptes Rendus Acad Sciences, 222: 847–849

[84] Biasotti S, Giorgi D, Spagnuolo M, Falcidieno B (2008) Reeb Graphs for Shape Analysis and Applications. Theoretical Computer Science, 392(1–3): 5–22

[85] Biasotti S, Marini S, Mortara M, et al (2003) An Overview on Properties and Efficacy of Topological Skeletons in Shape Modelling. In: Proceedings of the International Conference on Shape Modeling International, pp 245–254, IEEE Computer Society, New York

[86] Biasotti S, Marini S, Mortara M, et al (2003) 3D Shape Matching through Topological Structures. Discrete Geometry for Computer Imagery, Lecture Notes in Computer Science, 2886: 194–203

[87] Sundar H, Silver D, Gagvani N, et al (2003) Skeleton Based Shape Matching and Retrieval. Proceedings of the Shape Modeling International. In: Proceedings of the International Conference on Shape Modeling and Applications, IEEE Computer Society, pp 130–290, Seoul, Korea,12–16 May 2003,

[88] Iyer N, Janyanti S, Lou K, et al (2004) A Multi-Scale Hierarchical 3D Shape Representation for Similar Shape Retrieval. In: Proceedings of the TMCE 2004, pp1–10, Lausanne, Switzerland, 12–16 April 2004

[89] Iyer N, Jayanti S, Lou K, et al (2005) Three-dimensional Shape Searching: State-of-the-art Review and Future Trends. Computer Aided Design, 37(5): 509–530

[90] EI-Mehalawi M, Miller RA (2003) A Database System of Mechanical Components Based on Geometric and Topological Similarity. Part I: representation. Computer Aided Design, 35(1): 83–94

[91] Cicirello V, Regli WC (2001) Machining Feature-Based Comparisons of Mechanical Parts. In: Proceedings of the International Conference on Shape Modelling and Applications, IEEE Computer Society, pp 176–185, Genoa Italy, 7–11 May 2001

[92] Zarpalas D, Daras P, Axenopoulos A, et al (2007) 3D Model Search and Retrieval Using the Spherical Trace Transform. EURASIP Journal on Applied Signal Processing, pp 207–207

[93] Loffler J (2000) Content-based Retrieval of 3D Models in Distributed Web Databases by Visual Shape Information. In: Proceedings of the International Conference on Information Visualisation, IEEE Computer Society, pp 82–87, London, UK, 19–21 July 2002

[94] Kanai S (2008) Content-based 3D Mesh Model Retrieval From Hand-written Sketch. International Journal of Interact Design Manufacture, 2(2): 87–98

[95] Wang Y, Liu R, Baba T, et al (2008) An Images-based 3D Model Retrieval Approach. Lecture Notes in Computer Science, pp 90–100, Springer, Heidelberg

[96] Funkhouser T, Min P, Kazhdan M (2003) A Search Engine for 3D Models. ACM Transactions on Graphics, 22(1): 83–105

[97] Vranic DV, Saupe D, Richter J (2001) Tools for 3D-object Retrieval: Karhunen-Loeve Transform and Spherical Harmonics. In: Proceedings of the IEEE 2001 Workshop Multimedia Signal Processing, pp 293–298, Cannes, France, 3–5 October 2001

[98] Ohbuchi R, Nakazawa M, Takei T (2003) Retrieving 3D Shapes Based on their Appearance. In: Proceedings of the 5th ACM SIGMM International Workshop on Multimedia Information Retrieval, pp 39–45, ACM Press, New York

[99] Chen D, Tian XP, Shen YT (2003) On Visual Similarity Based 3D Model Retrieval. Computer Graphics Forum, 22(3): 223–232

[100] Vranic DV (2001) 3D Model Retrieval. In: Proceedings of the Spring Conference on Computer Graphics and its Applications, pp 89–93, Budmerice, Slovakia, 3–6 May 2000

[101] Yu M, Atmosukarto I, Leow WK, et al (2003) 3D Model Retrieval with Morphing-based Geometric and Topological Feature Maps. In: Proceedings of the IEEE Conference on Computer Vision and Pattern Recognition, pp 656–661

[102] Kazhdan M, Funkhouser T, Rusinkiewicz S (2003) Rotation Invariant Spherical Harmonic Representation of 3D shape Descriptors. In: Proceedings of the Symposium on Geometry Processing, pp 156–164, Aire-la-Ville, Switzerland

[103] Novotni M, Klein R (2003) 3D Zernike Descriptors for Content Based Shape Retrieval. In: Proceedings of the 8th ACM Symposium on Solid Modeling and Applications, pp 216–225, ACM Press, New York

[104] Ricard J, Coeurjolly D, Baskurt A (2005) Generalizations of Angular Radial Trans form for 2D and 3D Shape Retrieval. Pattern Recognition Letters, 26(14): 2174–2186

[105] Mitra NJ, Guibas LJ, Pauly M (2006) Partial and Approximate Symmetry Detection for 3D Geometry. ACM Transactions on Graphics, 25(3): 560–568

[106] Li M, Langbein FC, Martin RR (2008) Detecting Approximate Symmetries of Discrete Point Subsets. Computer Aided Design, 2008, 40(1): 76–93

[107] Kazhdan M, Chazelle B, Dobkin D, et al (2004) A Reflective Symmetry Descriptor for 3D Models. Algorithmica, 38(1): 201–225

3 Digitization of Cultural Heritage

With digital technology and devices rapid development, all the details and information of an artifact can be preserved forever. This chapter consists of four parts, the first part reviews information technology of devices to the heritage and cultural artifacts protection; the second and third parts introduce technology details about the procedure for artifacts reconstruction based on multi-view range images and 2D images respectively; the fourth part describes digitalization of cultural site scenes, including 3D terrain and site scenes modeling.

3.1 Digitization Technology

The archaeological research objects are the ancient artifacts and remains, which exist on the ground or have been excavated from underground. The information can be completely captured and collected by scientific archaeological surveys and excavations. Digital preservation of cultural heritage uses various means to capture archaeological information that involves multiple levels. From technical level, it is divided into various applications. Archaeologists' mission is to capture information, such as excavation diaries, discovered records, photographs, archaeological drawing, and video recordings of the archaeological site. These are usually used as a means in the archaeological recording of the digital capture of archaeological information needed to use in computer related hardware and application software, such as digital cameras, electronic total stations, three-dimensional laser scanners, Global Positioning Systems (GPS), Remote Sensing, Geographic Information System (GIS), and other digital acquisition hardware.

Digital Photography

Onsite photography of cultural heritage sites and objects excavated at archaeological sites in archaeological works are important and indispensable. It records in real-time the entire process of the archaeological work. Early archaeological work used traditional analog cameras and archaeological photographic data was in the form of photographs and negatives. The advancement of scanner technology is used in digitizing the early archaeological photographs to permanently preserve archaeological data and information and avoid photo negatives and color failure due to storage decay. The emergence of high resolution digital cameras has brought greater convenience to archaeological work and makes the recording of archaeological photographs even more convenient.

Because the images will have perspective prejection effects using a digital camera, the ratio will not be equal. In order to minimize image distortion, the use of a long distance telephoto lens camera can provide great results. This method usually requires a larger space and takes a lot of time. It should be understood even given the above conditions it is not possible to get complete orthographic images.

The complete orthogonal camera device (Fig. 3.1) is developed by using a radiation mirror telemetric optical system. The device can eliminate the image with the efferct of near-large and far-small and the size of the image will not change because of a change in shooting distance. The device includes an ordinary digital camera taking pictures by a computer controlled camera and confirmation of the shot can be viewed on the computer. According to different requirements of an image, the device can change photographic conditions and immediately rephotograph, which delivers improved efficiency. The device has a deep depth of field and allows the vertical parts of an object to be clearly demonstrated. If the relic size is bigger than the imaging range, we can capture overlap photographs, and then use image processing software to achieve image mosaic on the computer.

Fig. 3.1 Complete orthogonal camera device.

Digital Camera Technology

Digital camera technology used for true recording of archaeological excavation sites in archaeological work is more convenient than using traditional analog cameras. Digital video gives clearer and more vivid images. Traditional video cameras used video tape to record and analog media to save the image which causes tape wear and tear in the video editing, and caused signal attenuation. Tape will become invalid exceeding working life. Tape is not conducive to the preservation of image data. In order to edit image data people must use computer related equipment to transform analog signals into digital signals for digital information preservation which increases complexity. Digital cameras record images using a digital signal. This is beneficial for nonlinear editing of video/data and repeated use will not cause image signal attenuation.

The use of video technology to record and assist the archaeological excavation process is of increased importance to deliver archaeological information. The nonlinear editing system including computer, digital cameras, analog cameras, CD burners, and other storage devices can complete an archaeological information enterprise system. With nonlinear editing software, the archaeological data is captured and digitalized by computer video capture and compression. Another method is to capture archaeological data that is shot by a digital video camera and directly stored it into the computer as materials. Through a nonlinear editing system, color photographs, audio introduction, background music, subtitle editing allows the synthesization of archaeological feature films. It also allows organization of the camera's data, which can be burned to CD, DVD, or transcribed to videotape. Figure 3.2 is a photographic laboratory in Xiamen University. Figure 3.3 shows electronic total station.

Fig. 3.2 Photographic laboratory in Xiamen University.

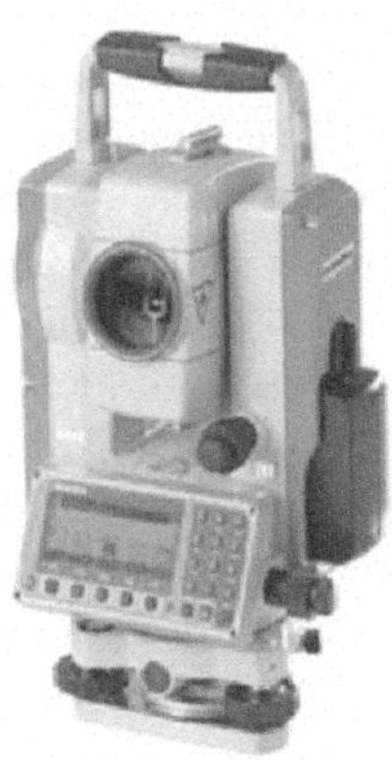

Fig. 3.3 Electronic total station.

Total station

Total Station is referred to as the station's electronic speed measuring device (Fig. 3.3). It mainly is composed by the electronic distance meter (EDM), electronic theodolite and microprocessors measuring the slope distance, vertical angle, and horizontal angle. It can automatically record, calculate and can show the horizontal distance, slope distance, height, elevation, coordinates, and other relevant data. It is called a total station because the station can finish all the survey work at one station. Total Station is a common measurement tool used in construction, water conservancy, environmental protection and other sectors, but the application to the archaeological industry has only just begun. Only a few universities and cultural institutions use it. The broad prospects of total station in the field of archaeologic have yet to be fully developed and applied to archaeology work.

The main workflow of total station measurements is firstly reconnaissance allowing one to choose the station, set up the equipment and run the complete field work shooting. A secondary workflow is its ability to download mapping data and editing it into a map. Live mapping can be done in the room or can be done on site. Total station is mainly used in profile mapping, topographic mapping, pit flat map, single cutaway diagramming, caves sites mapping, and other site mapping in archaeological collection.

High precision, high efficiency, low intensity, and conventional operations take days to complete the work, in contrast the total station take a few hours to complete. The results of total station can be modified to any ratio output. Vector formatting can deliver a variety of data and calculation such as the formation area, volume, the distance between sites, and poor direction. Quantitative information reflects important field information and provides important reference for the archaeological research.

Three-dimensional laser scan technology

The emergence of three-dimensional laser scanning technology makes three dimensional data more accurate, fast, and convenient. The designs of the laser scanning systems are very different basis for the application, including contact and non-contact. So far, two-dimensional non-contact scanner is used more. According to the principle of three-dimensional scanning system is divided into three types, phase interference scan, radial scan and triangle method scan. Because of different principle of different types of scanning systems, so here is a big different in the scan range. In the above three types of scanning systems, triangular scan and phase interference scan method is applied to the small scan range (short distance) and data acquisition (generally less than 50m), however, relative to a wider scan range (far distance), radial scanning system is a good choice. Now, the major manufacturers of the three-dimensional laser scanner to obtain data for a wide range at home and abroad: Switzerland's Leica, Canada's Optech, Austria's Riegl and I-SiTE Pty, shown in Fig. 3.4.

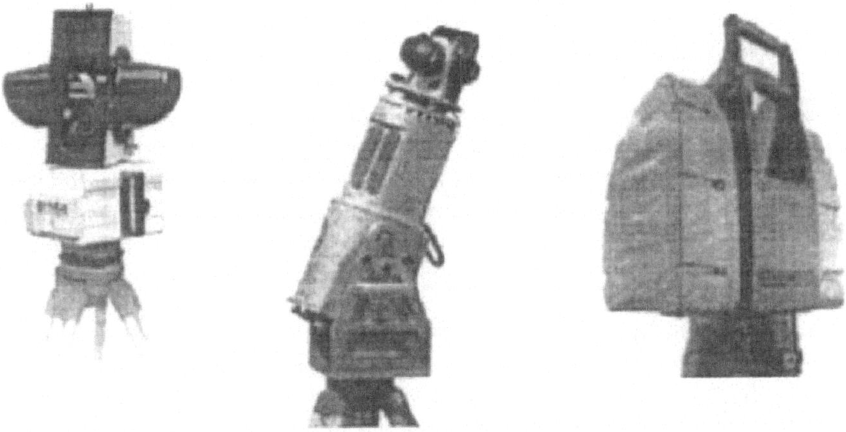

(a) I–SiTE system (b) Riegl LMS system (c) HCS3000 system

Fig. 3.4 Long-range three-dimensional scanners.

For the shorter distance scanning, there are a number of corresponding three-dimensional scanning-systems. For three-dimensional data acquisition of large scenes and long distance scanning is not enough. For small unearthed cultural relics and long range scanning systems have not been suitable because of quality problems and errors. Three-dimensional hand-held scanning systems (such as HANDY 3D SCAN) aim to solve this problem. The scanning system not only gives a real-time 3D mesh model of the object, but also delivers the access texture data, real-time rendering, and output in various data formats. The most important feature of hand-held scanners is its high precision reaching to 0.2 to 0.3 mm, as shown in Fig. 3.5.

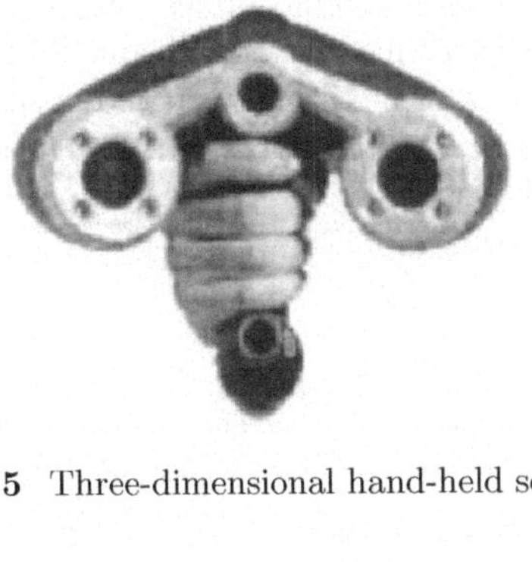

Fig. 3.5 Three-dimensional hand-held scanner.

A three-dimensional laser scanning system is composed of hardware and software systems. Hardware is the most important part of the system, while the software is also essential. To make the scanned data more realistic, texture data access is particularly important. This cannot be done without the aid of digital cameras. Three-dimensional laser scanning technology is becoming more accepted as a default device without match. In mapping study the use close-range photography and photos to reconstruct two-dimensional ancient ruins is cumbersome, inefficient and rebuilding models for realism is difficult. For the mapping community the birth of three-dimensional laser scanning technology opens up new avenues for data acquisition and site protection.

3S Technology

3S technology includes GPS, Remote Sensing (RS), and GIS. These constitute a highly automated, real-time, and intelligent geographic information system. It is a powerful tool for analysis of spatial information timely capture, processing, updating and dynamic geographical process and for providing decision support information. In recent years, 3S technology plays an increasingly important role in the conservation monitoring, archaeological surveys, and cultural heritage protection research [1].

GPS technology

GPS is a measurement-based system that is able to achieve with range of millimeter many advantages in the archaeological field such as high-precision three-dimensional positioning, design, and distribution that are convenient and flexible, and geographical conditions and operating conditions that are low and highly efficient.

Remote sensing technology

Remote sensing of archaeological research is a new archaeological method. It uses information technology with remote sensing to measure a target. Installed various remote-sensing features of a satellite can sense the earth from outer space with detail of mountains, rivers, plants, and trees. It can provide insight into buried underground mines, display underground geological situations and forecast earthquakes and volcanic activity.

Because of its features of flexibility, speed, depth of vision, information-richness, and ability of quick detection, remote sensing technology has been used widely by the archaeological community. Remote archaeological research has to become a new discipline.

GIS technology

GIS is a geographical technology rapidly developed in the 1960s as a result of interdisciplinary studies. Based on the geographical space database and geographical coordinates (latitude and longitude), GIS provides a variety of space and dynamic geographic information. It has the ability to handle a variety of geographic data and provides services for geography research and geographic decision-making. GIS acts as a computer hardware and software system; but internally it is a geospatial information model consisting of computer programs and geographical data.

With the emergence of "Digital Earth", GIS is developing from a 2D system into a multidimensional dynamic system or network system, to meet the urgent needs from theoretical development and many other fields such as resources management, environment monitoring, and city planning. One of these technical developments is based on a client/server architecture to ensure that the data and procedures on the server are accessible to its end-user. Another is based on the Internet, Internet GIS, or WEB-GIS to access various geospatial data remotely, including graphics and images, and to carry out various kinds of geospatial analysis. This "Cloud Computing model" further develops the connection of GIS to the information highway through modern telecommunication technologies.

3.2 Three-Dimension Based on Range Image Reconstruction

With the rapid development of three-dimensional digital acquisition devices, three-dimensional laser scanners, structured light scanners, and other non-contact devices have been widely used in digital modeling. The basic principle is that the laser or visible light is projected onto the surface, and then CCD cameras of the equipment are used to capture the reflected light to calculate the surface range. Range can be calculated in two ways. The first is by calculating flight time to gain information of the range between laser's return and shooting. The second method is based on optical triangulation method. Two CCD cameras and the laser projection point on the artifact surface constitute of the vertex of the triangle and then the depth information can be calculated [2]. This method is suitable for small object modeling. Devices based on the above principle can capture the range of image and texture information at the same time (such as Vivid910, VIUScan, and other equipments).

Because of the limitation of the sight scope of scanning equipment in capturing data, the complete reconstruction of a model cannot be achieved in only one time scan. Therefore, the following three methods are used in data capturing:

(1) Multiple scanners from different perspectives to capture three-dimensional data.

(2) The artifact is placed at a fix position and the complete information is captured by moving the scanner to different perspectives.

(3) The scanner is placed at a fix position and the complete information is captured by moving the artifact around axis.

The two-dimension point clouds are captured by laser scanner, and the value of each point is the depth image which can generate three-dimension point of artifact, called range image. All the range images from different views are called multiview range images. Due to each range image is located at the different local coordinate system, we should register multiview range image to a common coordinate system to construct the artifact model under the constraint with making the distance of overlapping region of neighbor range images minimum. The complete procedure is called registration. The accuracy of registration is directly determining the quality of the model reconstruction. Poor registration will make the details of integration result fuzzy and even more the wrong registration will make the reconstruction fail directly. Therefore the registration method is the core technique of range image modeling.

Artifact's data captured by a laser scanner has the following three advantages:

(1) the modeling accuracy of this method is usually higher than based image data modeling;

(2) the texture information can be obtained to enhance the realism of heritages;

(3) the device is easy to carry, and more suitable for modeling of archaeological excavation sites of cultural relics.

Through these digital devices, the texture information of the heritage can be captured to make a more realistic model, but due to the need for range image registration, the algorithm complexity is very high.

The key of multiview range image registration is in the calculation of the transformation matrix on the basis of the feature correspondence of the overlapping regions between the range images. Searching for the feature correspondence and calculating the transformation matrix are the two difficulties in multiview range image registration. Correspondence is to identify the overlapping region and the transformation matrix is to make the corresponding distance minimum. If there is a correspondence, a transformation matrix can be calculated. If the transformation matrix has been obtained, the nearest point between the two range images can be considered as the corresponding points.

At present, the research of multiview data registration includes two aspects. The first is the registration between two range images. It is the foundation of multiview data registration and ensures the accuracy of registration. The second is the registration between multiple range images, i.e., the multiview registration. On the basis of pairwise registration, it is important to make sure that the registration errors are evenly distributed to all the data so as to eliminate accumulated error.

Assuming the initial position is concerned or not, registration between adjacent range image is divided into rough registration and accurate registration. Rough registration is used to calculate the transformation matrix of the position of the range image based on the feature invariant. The common features include statistical invariants, geometric partial differential invariants, geometric features, and spin image or texture features [3]. Rough registration can also be achieved by means of manual interactive markings, and the position tracker along with other hardware devices [4].

Accurate registration is based on rough registration. It means to accurately estimate the rotation and translation matrices between the range image. Through continuous iterations it can accurately estimate the rotation and translation transformation matrix to make the distance of the overlapping region between two images minimum. ICP (Iterative Closest Point) and its improved algorithm are now widely used in the accurate registration method. The following three aspects must be considered. First, define the effective accelerated ways in order to search for the nearest point. Second, define the method of measuring the minimum distance. Third, define the transformation matrix method considering iterative. Equipment calibration errors, lens errors, moving objects, and different sensors may make the acquired range image distorted or deformed. Rigid registration methods cannot solve these problems. A nonrigid registration algorithm is used to eliminate most of these errors and improve the details of the model.

In the multiview data registration process, if the range image is registor with the next scanned range image for pairwise alignment, only n times of the accurate registration algorithm can achieve accurate registrations of n data. This method will produce accumulate errors, such as the error in the previous registration will accumulate in the next registration, resulting in obvious gaps between the first and the final range image. This makes the registration results not completely closed [5], as shown in Fig. 3.6.

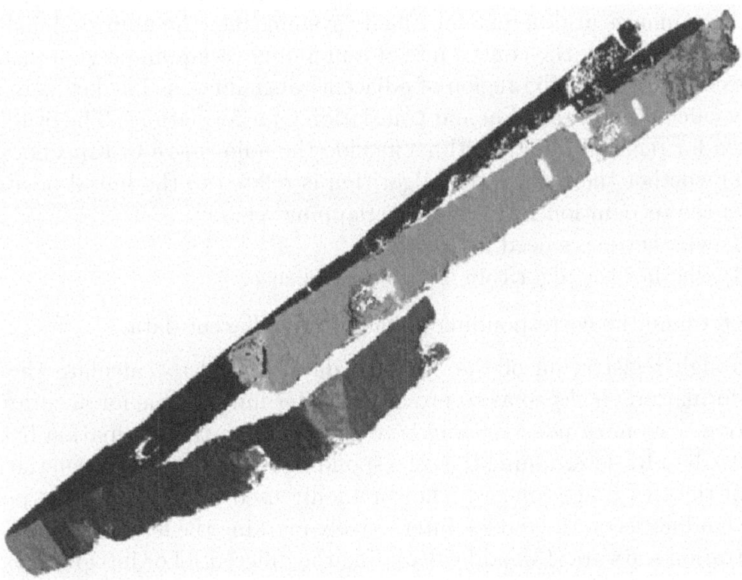

Fig. 3.6 Error accumulates with each scan (with permission from Brown) [6].

It is necessary to study the multiview registration method to be able to make the registration errors evenly distribution among all the range images.

Currently, the graph theory based multiview registration algorithm is the widly used. The range image is taken as the node of graph, the image's adjacent edges form a graph, the data registration errors are shown as weights and the minimum spanning tree is used to distance multiview registration strategies [7]. Another measure can be directly constructed a multifunction of the overlapping region. This makes the measurement function in the principle a minimum value. This method can directly estimate the rigid transformation matrix for each range image under the constraint with the value of the defined distance multi function minimum [8].

Brown et al. [9] placed the model on the turntable whose rotation angle can be controlled to achieve data acquisition and rough registration. He proposed a multi way ICP algorithm to achieve the registration of multiple data at the same time, improving the registration speed and accuracy. Kari [10] proposed the graph-based global registration algorithm, effectively eliminating the accumulated errors in the process of the adjacent data registration. Bernardini et al. [11] proposed the constrained global registration method based on the results of the paiwise registration, making the errors evenly distributed. Fleishman et al. [12] designed the digital acquisition program, in which he achieved the semi-automatic registration of data by manual calibration and introduced the image-based registration method to improve the accuracy of the ICP algorithm.

The rigid registration between the two data sets essentially to transforms the range images at different coordinate systems into the unified global coordinate system with the constraints of minimum overlapping region distances between the overlapping region of adjacent range images. The key is to accurately calculate the rotation and translation transformations. The evaluation criteria for registration algorithms include the following four aspects:

(1) whether the registration algorithm is related to the initial position;
(2) the recognition rate of the overlapping region;
(3) whether users need interaction;
(4) whether the algorithm is fast convergence.

To determine the corresponding points of the adjacent data

The rough registration of the adjacent data is used to calculate the rigid transformation (R, T) so as to provide a better initial value for accurate registration. The most effective way is to calculate the transformation between the two data by determining the corresponding relationship between the point sets of the two range images. The commonly used methods include posting some landmarks on the model, interactively marking the feature points in the registration software [13], and calculating the differential or integral invariant to find features [14].

Different types of three-dimensional information acquisition devices may obtain different information of the cultural models. For example, some devices can obtain both the texture image and range image of the model at the same time, while some can only get the range image of the model. Therefore, the data from different devices and the automatic registration of the adjacent data will employ different methods. If there is only range image, Wei [15] proposed a new pairwise range image registration algorithm. The first step is to map the data of the range image into a two-dimension image according to the pixel information and the curvature value of the vertices. The second step is to use the scale-invariant feature transform (SIFT) algorithm to determine correspondence point of the two-dimension image and range images. Next, obtain the correspondence points of the two range images according to the mapping relationship between the range image and the two-dimension image. The third step is to use the voting and pre-registration methods to remove the mismatches, achieving the registration of the adjacent image ranges. Yang [16] proposed an automatic registration method for the range image with texture image and non texture, which is suitable for both pairwise registration and multiview registration. When registering two range images, the first choice is to extract the texture image from the scanned data. If the scanned data does not contain the texture image, you would generate the texture image directly based on the geometric invariant of the range image. Next, use the SIFT algorithm to identify the candidate set of the matching pixels and use Random Sample Consensus (RANSAC) algorithm. The three-dimensional geometric information are used to matching pixel and their corresponding matching vertex set. Based on the final matching point set is the transformation matrix of the range calculated image Random Sample Consensus to achieve the rough registration of the two range images. Finally, the modified ICP algorithm is used to achieve the accurate alignment of the model.

In order to improve the accuracy of determining the corresponding features in the image, scale space is introduced in search of the image features. This aims to simulate the multi-scale features of images. SIFT feature matching algorithm is the most effective way in the field of matching feature points. With the features of scale, rotation, perspective changes, illumination, and invariance of accurate transformation, can be effectively achieved feature matching [17] between two images. Koenderink [18] proves that the Gaussian convolution kernel is the only kernel to achieve scale transformations. Lindeberg et al. [19] further prove that the Gaussian kernel is the only linear function.

Two-dimensional Gaussian function is shown as follows:

$$G(x, y, \delta) = \frac{1}{2\pi\delta^2} \mathrm{e}^{-(x^2+y^2)/2\delta^2}, \tag{3.1}$$

where δ represents the variance of the Gaussian normal distribution.

The two-dimensional images at different scales can be expressed as the convolution of the images and the Gaussian kernel:

$$L(x, y, \delta) = G(x, y, \delta) \cdot I(x, y), \tag{3.2}$$

where (x, y) represents the positions of the pixels, δ is the scale space value, and L is the scale space of the image.

Lowe [20] proposed to use the scale space extreme of the Gaussian differential function to detect the key points in the scale space. The function is generated by the Gaussian differential kernel of the two adjacent scales and the image convolution:

$$\begin{aligned} D(x,y,\delta) &= (G(x,y,k\delta) - G(x,y,k\delta)) \cdot I(x,y) \\ &= L(x,y,k\delta) - L(x,y,\delta). \end{aligned} \tag{3.3}$$

The Gaussian differential function value of each pixel is calculated at different scales, then the function values is connected to constitute the characteristic scale track. The local extreme point is considered to be the feature of the scale.

The generating algorithm of the SIFT eigenvector includes the following steps. First, the scale space extremum is detected When detecting, compare the 8 pixels of the adjacent surrounding regions and the same scale with the 18 pixels of the corresponding positions of the adjacent scale. Second, determine the location and scale of feature points of the image and then remove the low-contrast feature points and the instable edge points. Third, specify the direction parameter for each key point based on the distribution of the gradient direction of the neighboring pixels of the feature points. Each key point includes location, scale and direction. Fourth, generate the SIFT eigenvector. After the generation, we use the Euclidean distance of the feature points to measure the similarity of the feature points in the two images. When the distance is less than the threshold, the feature points in two images are regarded as the corresponding points.

Rough registration of the adjacent data

Based on determining the registration point set of the range image, singular value decomposition method can be used to achieve rough alignment between the adjacent data.

Decompose the range image as $scan = \{scan_i | i = 1, 2, \ldots, n\}, P = \{p_i\}, i = 1, \ldots, n$ is the set of registration points of $scan_i$ and $Q = \{q_i\}, i = 1, \ldots, n$ is the set of registration points of $scan_j$, then, the specific process of the rough registration algorithm is as follows:

Step 1: Calculate the k-nearest neighbor of each registration point in sets P and Q. Next, put these points in sets P and Q.

Step 2: Calculate the covariance matrix of sets P and Q denoted by $covq$, $covq$ separately;

Step 3: Calculate the rotation transformation $R = U_1 U_2^{-1}$, in which U_1, U_2 are the eigenvectors of covariance matrix cov$p$ and cov$q$;

Step 4: Calculate the translation transformation $T = \overline{p} - \overline{q} \times R$, in which $\overline{p}, \overline{q}$ are respectively the center of the registration point sets P and Q.

However, in the calculation process of this algorithm, if the corresponding relationship between the registration point sets is unknown, which the correspondence of p_i and q_j is not clear. The direction of two data sets after alignment maybe 180 degrees. This is because the main directions based on the above calculation have positive and negative directions. Rotating the model can achieve the data registration. Therefore, the normal vector constraints should be introduced, that the normal direction after registration should be consistent, otherwise, reverse the range image.

The accurate registration between adjacent data sets

The registration between adjacent range images is defined as

$$F(\alpha_1, \ldots, \alpha_N) = \sum_{i,j=1}^{N} \gamma_{ij} d^2(\alpha_i(scan_i), \alpha_j(scan_j)), \tag{3.4}$$

where $\gamma_{ij} \in [0, 1]$ is the representation and overlap of S^i and S^j, d^2 is distance metric of overlap zone, α_i is rigid transformation that makes the distance metric function of overlapping region minimal. Usually a fragment is selected as a fixed position, so α_1 is the identity matrix. Currently, the iterative closest point algorithm is the most accurate registration algorithm.

Definition $P = \{p_i\}, i = 1, \ldots, n$ and $Q = \{q_i\}$, P and Q are the two-dimensional point sets. p_i and q_i are the points of the P and Q, and p_i and q_i are correspondence. Calculate the rotation and translation transformations through the iterative method, making the measurement function minimal. The measure ment function is defined as the distance from point to plane:

$$E = \min \sum_{i=0}^{n} ((R \cdot p_i + T - q_i) \cdot n_i)^2, \quad T = [t_x, t_y, t_z, 1]^{\mathrm{T}}. \tag{3.5}$$

According to the results registration can be estimated by overlapping regions of two depth of the image $scan_0$ and $scan_1$. In overlapping regions the depth of the image selected point set $H = \{h_i\}$ that H covers the entire overlap region. The depth of the image search corresponding set of points satisfies the following two principles:

(1) Have the same differential properties of the nearest point

Define the nearest point of the measurement function:

$$neighbor = \|h_i - k_i\| + \lambda \|curH_i - curK_i\|, \tag{3.6}$$

where $curH_i$ and $curK_i$ represent the Gaussian curvature.

The measurement function consists of two parts: the first part meets the minimal distance between corresponding points. The second part meets the Gaussian curvature approximately the same. While the neighbor ascending order, just choose $p\%$ point pairs which the value of neighbor are minimal, thereby enhancing the correct rate of the correspondence between the registration point sets.

(2) High stability of the set of points

$$E = \min \sum_{i=0}^{n} ((p_i - q_i) \cdot n_i + r(p_i \times n_i) + t \cdot n_i)^2, \tag{3.7}$$

where $r = [\alpha, \beta, \gamma]^{\mathrm{T}}, T = [t_x, t_y, t_z]^{\mathrm{T}}$.

Therefore, the following linear equations can be solved for the rotation and translation matrix:

$$AX = b, \tag{3.8}$$

where

$$A = \begin{pmatrix} p_1 \times n_1 & \dots & n_1 \\ \vdots & & \vdots \\ p_k \times n_k & \dots & n_k \end{pmatrix},$$

$$X = \{\alpha \;\; \beta \;\; \gamma \;\; t_x \;\; t_y \;\; t_z\}^{\mathrm{T}},$$

$$b = \{-(p_1 - q_1) \cdot n_1 \dots - (p_k - q_k) \cdot n_k\}^{\mathrm{T}},$$

$$A^{\mathrm{T}}AX = A^{\mathrm{T}}b, \tag{3.9}$$

$$C = A^{\mathrm{T}}A = \begin{pmatrix} (p_1 \times n_1)^{\mathrm{T}} & n_1^{\mathrm{T}} \\ \vdots & \vdots \\ (p_k \times n_k)^{\mathrm{T}} & n_k^{\mathrm{T}} \end{pmatrix} \begin{pmatrix} p_1 \times n_1 & \dots & p_k \times n_k \\ n_1 & \dots & n_k \end{pmatrix}. \tag{3.10}$$

Relationship between the rigid transformation and metric function in the registration process:

$$\Delta E = (\Delta r^{\mathrm{T}} \;\; \Delta t^{\mathrm{T}}) C \begin{pmatrix} \Delta r \\ \Delta t \end{pmatrix}. \tag{3.11}$$

It can be seen whether the registration is stable relating related with the covariance matrix. If the value is larger, the registration is more stable. The characteristic value of the covariance matrix corresponds to rigid transformations translation, rotation and other six degrees of freedom. When the characteristic value is small, then the current point is shifted or is not stable. Therefore, choose k-nearest neighbor of p_i point, and then calculate the eigenvalue and eigenvectors of the covariance matrix C according to the neighborhood adjacent vertices. If the eigenvalue is large, then p_i is the stable point.

As you view the complexity of range image, looking for correspondence among the registration point sets may introduce error correspondence between points. To remove these error matches, set the following three conditions to verify.

Condition 1: Constraints of differential properties, if the points set is corresponding, then use the normal direction, the Gaussian curvature should be approximately the same.

Condition 2: Remove border points, because it is the boundary point of the first data set is likely not a boundary point in another data set.

Condition 3: Distance threshold, if the distance between corresponding points is greater than the threshold θ, then it is a wrong match, where the threshold can be set according to scanning resolution. Scanning resolution is

$$e = \frac{1}{n} \sum_{i=1, p_i, q_i \in edge_k}^{n} \|p_i - q_i\|. \tag{3.12}$$

In order to verify whether correspondence of a registration point set is correct after the above method, a metric function is defined as follows:

$$DRMS^2(P, Q) = \frac{1}{n} \sum_{i=1}^{n} \sum_{j=1}^{n} (\|p_i - p_j\| - \|q_i - q_j\|)^2.$$

3.3 3D Reconstruction Technology Based on 2D Images

Traditional methods to obtain three-dimensional scene information use a laser scanner. Three-dimensional laser scanners are expensive. They require a lot of manpower and resources, do not capture data quickly, and with some special artifacts. It can deliver vary degrees of damage. With the popularity of digital cameras, the cost of three-dimensional reconstruction based on two-dimensional images is getting lower, and delivering higher efficiency. Three-dimensional reconstruction based on two-dimensional images can be divided into several types: geometric model reconstruction based on a single image, geometric model reconstruction using a stereo vision method, geometric model reconstruction based on the silhouette contour, and geometric model reconstruction based on depth of the image and geometry of scene recovery from uncalibrated images with camera movement. This chapter describes some key technologies of three-dimensional reconstruction based on two-dimensional images. Some examples are camera calibration,

Fig. 3.7 Instance image of 3D reconstruction based on 2D images.

stereo matching, and three-dimensional reconstruction. Archaeologists discovered an ancient Medusa head statue in a Roman bath archaeological site of Sagalassos, Fig. 3.7 shows 3D reconstruction of an ancient Medusa head based on two-dimensional images.

3.3.1 Stereo matching

Three-dimensional reconstruction based on 2D images requires that the extracted feature points in the object structure could reflect the objects structure and at the same time achieve high matching accuracy. This requires that the reconstructed objects surface could correctly express the geometry structure, or geometric appearance of an object maybe distorted. Stereo matching requests the extracted characteristics with not only reflecting physical characteristics but also matching high precision. Feature extraction is a critical step in stereo matching.

Feature extraction

Feature-based stereo matching describing the difference of the selected features can be divided into point features matching, line features matching and surface features matching. They all have their own advantages, so it is difficult to precisely say which method is superior than others. Point feature is widely used. We introduce several classic point feature extraction methods.

Harris corner detection algorithm

The idea of Harris feature extraction algorithm is to design a part detection window in the image. When the window makes a small move in all directions, the average energy of the study window is changed. When changes to the value of the energy exceed a threshold set, it will be to extract the center pixel point of the window for the corner pixels.

SIFT Feature Point detection algorithm

In SIFT feature point detection method you firstly examine the extreme scale space testing in the scale place and identify key points location and scale. Next, you identify the subpixel for feature points by fitting the three-dimensional quadratic function to determine the location and scale of key points function to accurately, while removing low contrast of the key points and unstable edges correspondence in order to enhance the match stability and improve noise immunity.

Feature matching

Stereo matching of three-dimensional reconstruction is a key issue. When feature points matching in different images is established, many important visual applications, such as 3D reconstruction and motion analysis can be solved successfully. Whether one can achieve the right match is critical, therefore the matching process uses a variety of constraints.

The Stereo matching algorithms generally can be divided into two categories: area-based matching and feature-based matching.

Area-based matching method

The area-based matching method was the earliest to be investigated. It is the simplest and easiest for hardware to implement. The method makes use of the pixel gray value and applies certain constraints to find the pixels corresponding relationship of stereo images in the matching algorithm. The basic idea is to assume that corresponding points in the small neighborhood of two images have a similar gray distribution. View the image with a statistical point of view as a one-dimensional signal and apply the related methods, uses image local relevance to determine matches of the two corresponding points.

Feature-based matching method

Feature-based matching method does not directly use the image gray values, but prior to detect the corner, edge of the stereo image, then it matches the features. Therefore, it can overcome the issues of area-based matching method. It is relatively stable in contrast and apparent light changes. At the same time, feature-based matching can be achieved by a simple comparison of features and attributes. Therefore, it is much faster than the area based matching method. This method has the advantages of less matching and small computation, however, feature-based matching usually only gets the sparse disparity map, and sometimes it needs interpolation. SIFT feature matching is commonly used for feature-based matching method.

3.3.2 Camera calibration

Camera calibration is a process which is used to seek parameters of the camera. It is used to determine the mapping process between the actual camera coordinate system and objects in three-dimensional space coordinate system. Camera calibration precision is a key factor in determining whether three-dimensional reconstruction is successful. The camera calibration method is divided into two types: the traditional camera calibration and camera self-calibration. The traditional camera calibration needs specific experimental conditions that have a calibration reference. The traditional camera calibration method has relatively high accuracy. Here we introduce some classic traditional camera calibration methods and the self-calibration method.

Traditional camera calibration methods

Abdel-Aziz and Karara firstly proposed Direct Linear Transformation (DLT) method in 1971. The DLT method gets the camera model parameters by solving linear equations. This method does not consider distortion factors. The DLT method improved afterwards. It considered some nonlinear factors and solved problems by some nonlinear methods. In 1986, Tsai pointed out the two step method for the first time. This method first solves the camera parameters by using the perspective transformation matrix. The parameters were regarded as the initial value of nonlinear optimization, and put in some distortion factors. To further improved the precision, it also uses the optimization algorithm to solve other parameters. Zhang's plane template calibration method is a classic plane template calibration method. It considered some camera parameters including the radial distortion and tangential distortion. This method demands that the camera gets at least three or more template image which are shot from different angles. Through the homography of the template point and point's corresponding points in the image, this method determines the camera intrinsic parameters. We can then determine the camera's external parameter. At present, Zhang's plane template calibration method is widely used. We can use this method to estimate the intrinsic parameters and movement parameters of the camera. The experimental results are shown in Fig. 3.8.

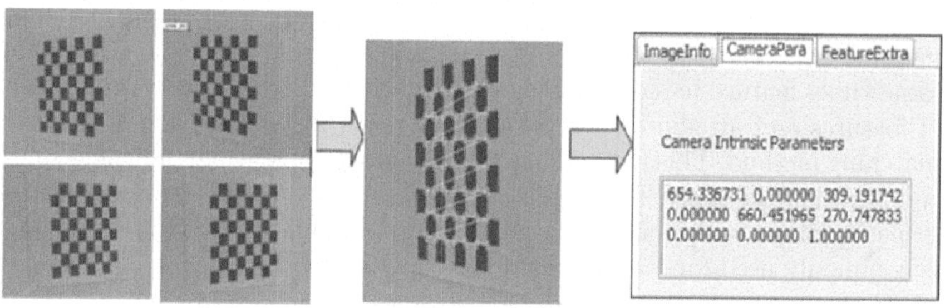

Fig. 3.8 Calibration results.

Camera self-calibration method

In the middle and late period of the 1990s, the camera self-calibration method rose in the computer vision research field. Faugeras and Maybank put forward the concept of self-calibration [21]. The camera self-calibration was more flexible and did not need a calibration board. It can calibrate the camera parameters by using only the corresponding relations between many images. By using the theory of projective geometry, Faugeras proved that the two images' quadratic nonlinear constraint, where there are two Kruppa equations existing between these two images [22]. By solving the Kruppa nonlinear equations, we can get the camera parameters. But the calibration method which is based on the Kruppa equation is not stable. The calibration precision is poor. Lei gave the reasons why the Kruppa equation is not stable [23].

3.3.3 Three-dimension reconstruction based on images

Most images which are received from an image acquisition device are based on a 2D plane, although it can contain a 3D object's space information. Therefore, to know the real objects from the image, we need to recover 3D spatial information from the 2D images. This is the task that 3D reconstruction completes.

Stereo vision is able to restore the 3D point's coordinates in the space using two or more cameras. The method of structure from motion is to restore the structure of the object or scene from the single camera's images

$$M' = RM + T, \tag{3.13}$$

where M is the point's coordinate in the camera coordinate system, M' is the point's coordinate in the world coordinate system,

$$R = \begin{pmatrix} r_{11} & r_{12} & r_{13} \\ r_{21} & r_{22} & r_{23} \\ r_{31} & r_{32} & r_{33} \end{pmatrix}, \quad T = \begin{pmatrix} t_x \\ t_y \\ t_z \end{pmatrix}.$$

Through the previous section of the camera calibration, we have already known the camera's intrinsic parameters. This problem is similar to the stereo vision problem, but the difference is that in the stereo vision problem we know the relative position between the two cameras. In the Structure from motion method we use R and T to describe the camera's movement parameters.

We can use the structure from motion principle to get the camera's movement parameters R and T, and then achieve the three-dimensional reconstruction. The specific methods are: first, according to the fundamental matrix of matching solve to find the essential matrix, and then use Singular Value Decomposition to essential matrix and produce the candidate value R and T, and then judge if R and T meet the formula, determine a unique set of solutions, and finally calculate the spatial three-dimensional points that are corresponding to the feature points, realizing three-dimension reconstruction.

Essential matrix of acquisition

In the case of an ordinary digital camera that will take pictures of objects or scenes in two different positions where they are relatively close, propose that the two positions are position A and position B. Regard the position A's camera coordinate system as the world coordinate system, then $[I|0]$ is the camera external parameter matrix at position $A, P_A = K[I|0]$ is the camera projection matrix at position A. The camera's projection matrix at position B is $P_B = K[R|T]$, where I is the unit matrix of three lines and three columns. K is the camera intrinsic parameters matrix. R and t respectively is rotation matrix and translation vector of the camera which is in position B relative to the world coordinate system. Because K has been obtanued, P_A is known, we only need to solve out R and T, then P_B will be able to be discovered. According to the Triangle Principle, the 3D coordinate of the spatial point would be calculated.

For any pair of points which match each other, For example we get m, m', $m \in I_1, m' \in I_2$, the homogeneous coordinates are $m = (x_1, y_1, 1)^{\mathrm{T}}, m' = (x_2, y_2, 1)^{\mathrm{T}}$, then we get

$$\begin{cases} s_1 m = K[I|0]M \\ s_2 m' = K[R|T]M \end{cases}, \tag{3.14}$$

where s_1 and s_2 is the constant factor, M is homogeneous coordinates which is correspondence between the feature point and the 3D object point. F is the fundamental matrix of the front. We calculate, then $(m')Fm = 0$, find $F = K^{-\mathrm{T}}[T]_X RK^{-1}$. The vector $[T]_X$ is the vector $T = (T_x, T_y, T_z)^{\mathrm{T}}$ of the anti-symmetric matrix.

The camera movement parameters R and T determine the essential matrix and has nothing to do with the intrinsic parameter $E = [T]_x R$. The essential matrix of singular value decomposition is also singular value decomposition (SVD) decomposition. It can calculate the camera movement parameters R and T in the case of a difference of a constant factor.

Camera movement parameters of acquisition and symbols judgment

Based on the essential matrix of SVD can be calculated the camera movement parameters R, T

$$E = UAV^{\mathrm{T}}, \tag{3.15}$$

where $A = diag(r, s, t)$, if match point correctly. In theory essential matrix E meets $r = s, t = 0$. However, in practice, due to the existence of noise, so $r > s > t$. Therefore, it is necessary to amend the formula, we command $k = (r + s)/2$, to get the modified diagonal matrix $A = diag(k, k, 0)$, with A' instead of A', obtained by a modified essential matrix E', and then the E' to a singular value decomposition:

$$E' = UDV^{\mathrm{T}}.$$

Through the decomposition you get two of the three-order unitary matrix, a third-order diagonal matrix s, set

$$w = \begin{pmatrix} 0 & -1 & 0 \\ 1 & 0 & 0 \\ 0 & 0 & 1 \end{pmatrix}, \tag{3.16}$$

we can say $R = UWV^{\mathrm{T}}$ or $R = UW^{\mathrm{T}}V^{\mathrm{T}}$, $t = u_3$ or $t = -u_3$, with u_3 is the last column of U. So P_B will have four kinds of cases. Which group is the right value? According to whether the depth of field is positive value to judge which one set of values satisfies the matching point to the corresponding 3D coordinates. Find out the correct R and T. So two images corresponding projection matrix is as follows:

$$\begin{cases} P_A = K[I \quad 0] \\ P_B = K[R \quad T] \end{cases}. \tag{3.17}$$

Set P_{A1}, P_{A2}, P_{A3} are the projection matrix P_A corresponding row vectors, set s is constant factor, $(u_i, v_i, 1)^{\mathrm{T}}$ is homogeneous coordinates of the spatial point corresponding to the i match point in the position A of the pictures, X_i is the homogeneous coordinates of the i match point with the corresponding spatial point. So

$$s\begin{pmatrix} u_i \\ v_i \\ 1 \end{pmatrix} = \begin{pmatrix} P_{A1} \\ P_{A2} \\ P_{A3} \end{pmatrix} X_i$$

eliminates the constant factor. From the above equation can get

$$\begin{pmatrix} P_{A3}u_i & -P_{A1} \\ P_{A3}v_i & -P_{A1} \\ P_{B3}u_i' & -P_{B1} \\ P_{A3}v_i' & -P_{B2} \end{pmatrix} X_i = 0. \quad \text{Suppose } A = \begin{pmatrix} P_{A3}u_i & -P_{A1} \\ P_{A3}vu_i & -P_{A2} \\ P_{B3}u_i' & -P_{B1} \\ P_{A3}v_i' & -P_{B2} \end{pmatrix}, \tag{3.18}$$

Eq. (3.17) has three unknown variables, then $AX_i = 0$. Because X_i is defined in several factors, increase constraints bring $\|X_i\| = 1$. This solution of the problem equals to solving the corresponding to $A^{\mathrm{T}}A$ minimum eigenvalue of the eigenvectors. Put A on SVD decomposition:

$$E = USV^{\mathrm{T}}.$$

So X_i is the last column of the last unitary matrix V, M is homogeneous coordinates. 3D ordinary coordinates need each element of the coordinate vector divided by the fourth component to account.

Triangulating space points

The 3D space points calculated above is discrete points. It can be displayed with OpenGL. But the reconstructed points for some simple models is poor visualization. It is necessary to triangulate these discrete points. Through the triangulation algorithm, it can triangulate the 2D feature points mapping the division 2D point to 3D space. Then it would achieve space point triangulations.

Texture mapping

When triangulated, 2D image is map into the three-dimensional space. In dealing with this process the image has been divided into some triangulation of texture. This already corresponds to a mapping with the three-dimensional point. We take these triangle textures mapping into space in a grid. This allows us to get the texture with the 3D models or scene.

Suppose $(x_1, y_1, z_1), (x_2, y_2, z_2)$, and (x_3, y_3, z_3), respectively corresponding to three points in the space. The three points are just a triangle. Within a triangulation set (u_1, v_1) and (u_1', v_1') the pixel coordinates and texture coordinates of the corner corresponding of point (x_1, y_1, z_1), because image coordinate system provides the upper left corner is the origin of the coordinates. In the texture coordinate, the bottom left corner is the origin of the coordinate system, so

$$u_1' = \frac{u_1}{width}, \quad v_1' = \frac{height - v_1}{height},$$

where *width* and *height* are image width and height respectively. Similarly the texture coordinates of $(x_2, y_2, z_2), (x_3, y_3, z_3)$ can also be obtained. OpenGL can achieve the texture mapping.

Figure 3.9 is a corner photo of stairs from two different angles of Western Han Tomb. We reconstruct the 3D model as shown in Fig. 3.10.

Fig. 3.9 Original Stair Corner images of Western Han Tomb.

Fig. 3.10 Reconstructed results.

3.4 Digitalization of Cultural Site Scenes

The objects in the scene of a cultural site can be roughly divided into three categories: terrain, the main body of the sites, and other objects including cultural relics. The terrain is the carrier of other objects. This provides the base for geometric position. The main body of the site usually includes buildings, bridges, tombs and accessory pit, with cultural relics that are the variety of objects unearthed at the sites. Because the three kinds of objects have different sizes, and have different precision requirements in the digital protection, appropriate data is needed to be captured for each kind of object according to its characteristics. Then a three-dimensional model can be reconstructed based on the data. As shown in Fig. 3.11, terrain modeling usually requires to capture satellite RS, GIS data, and geological radar data or paper maps with contour lines. The main site modeling often needs to capture point cloud and texture data usaung three-dimensional scanners, photos, video, surveying and mapping data, and historical information and data. Cultural relics modeling often needs to capture point cloud and texture data using three-dimensional scanner and camera. After reconstructing the three-dimensional models for all the objects in the scene, an integration of these models will be implemented. The format and coordinates of each object will be uniform and a complete scene can be finally built.

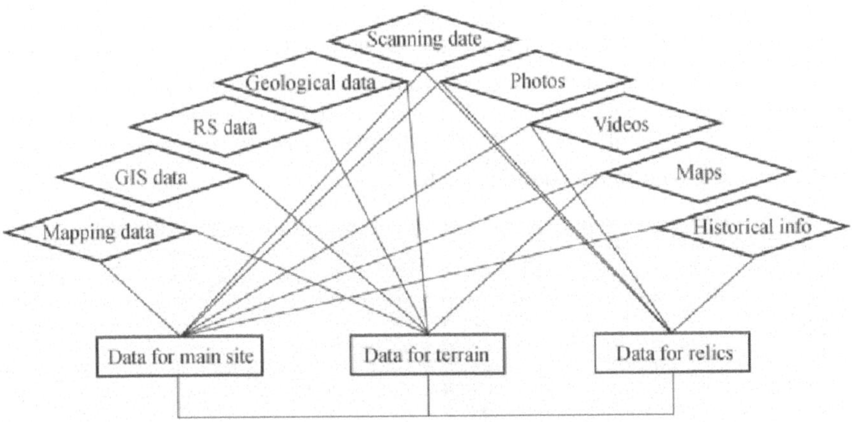

Fig. 3.11 Data capture for the reconstruction of cultural sites.

3.4.1 Generation of 3D Terrain

In a virtual ancient site environment, the terrain model plays a very important role. It is the basic tool of space continuation and the carrier of other features and the basis of the geometric positioning.

Terrain generation technology can be divided into two kinds: based on the algorithm of the terrain generation and based on real terrain of the generation. The algorithm Based on the terrain generation method uses the parameters' surface or fractal simulation algorithm to approximate reality terrain, and carries on the optimization control. Using the surface of the 3D terrain is a traditional terrain generation method. It usually uses some parameter surfaet such as Bezier surface, Coons surface, and Nurbs surface. Through interpola, fitting a 3D terrain is achieved. Its advantage is the guarantee of the adjacent slope continuity. The disadvantage is surface is equation and the parameters are not easy to control. The other disadvantages are the generated terrain is too smooth and the realism is poor. Many base their assumptions on the fractal modeling method in current use. This can be divided into Poisson faulting, Fourier filtering, Midpoint displacement, Successive random additions, Summing band limited noises, Wavelet transform, and so on. The advantages of this method are that it works with a small amount of data. The disadvantage is that the complexity of the algorithm is high and has no real terrain and geomorphology contact. Therefore, it only applies to the virtual scene terrain modeling.

Based on the real terrain generation method mainly uses the digital elevation model (DEM) in its creation. DEM is a GIS that uses the part of the earth's surface to provide the terrain of the 3D vector limited sequence. DEM is a commonly used modeling method and it can be divided into two methods (Fig. 3.12): based on rules Grid of modeling and based on the triangle nets (triangulated irregular network, TIN) modeling. The advantages of the rules grid model data structure is that it is simple, easy to use and easy to manage. The disadvantage is that it takes large storage and has data redundancy. TIN model is used with different levels of resolution to describe the surface topography. A particular resolution can use less space and more accurate express a more complex surface.

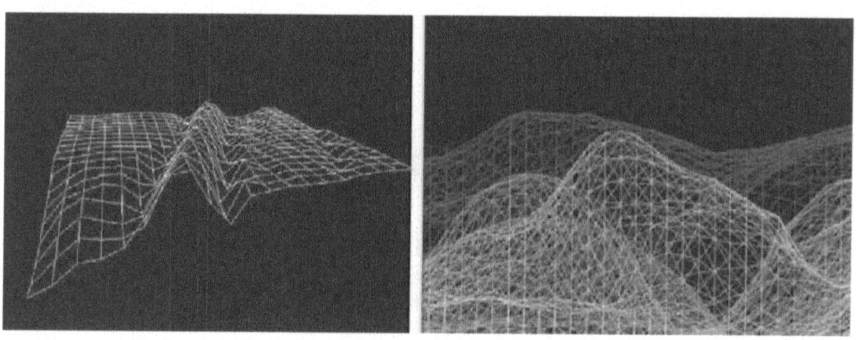

Fig. 3.12 Terrain expressed by Grid (left) and terrain expressed by TIN (right).

To provide 3D terrain, usually there is a need to be given materials and textures, this makes it more expressive and adds realism through an aviation image or satellite pictures (DOM data) to deliver real terrain texture. Using tools such as Photoshop, one can perform manual generation of terrain texture.

There are many mature 3D terrains constructing model software. Some examples are 3Ds Max, MultiGen Creator, Creator Terrain Studio, and VT Builder (as shown in Fig. 3.13). Through these software tools, we can use DEM data or the contour of the building real terrain model. This allows us to not rely on the features of the data only, but through interactive work get a similar terrain. The use of geographical virtual reality modeling language GeoVRML establishes a 3D terrain model.

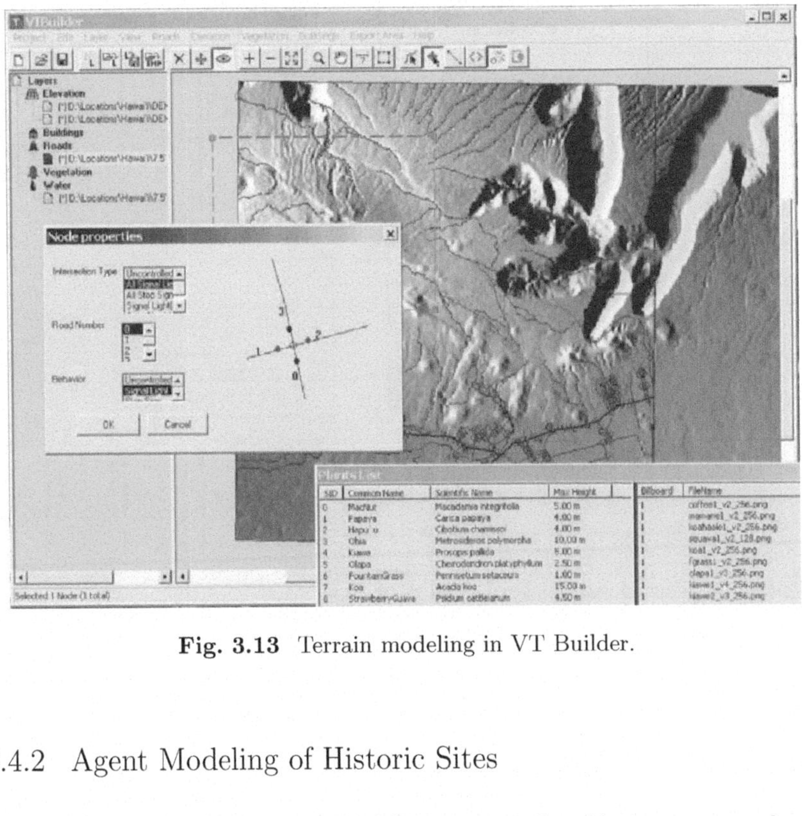

Fig. 3.13 Terrain modeling in VT Builder.

3.4.2 Agent Modeling of Historic Sites

The main body of historic sites usually consists of architecture, mausoleum, and grave sites, which is shown in the landscape. The common modeling method contains the 3D modeling method baeed on scanning. The surveying and mapping data incorporating with the third-party software modeling method, and image based modeling method.

3D modeling method based on scanning

The advantages of building huge historic sites using the 3D laser scanner lie in that it can acquire the 3D information quickly and conveniently, and has high precision.

The usual practice is to combine the 3D scanner and digital camera to scan the main body of the historic sites. The 3D scanner can get the point cloud data of the scene and the digital camera can get the texture information. Then, we generate the realistic 3D model by processing the data acquired in a later period.

Modeling usually contains three stages: data acquisition, data pre-processing, and geometric model reconstruction. The working process model is shown in Fig. 3.14.

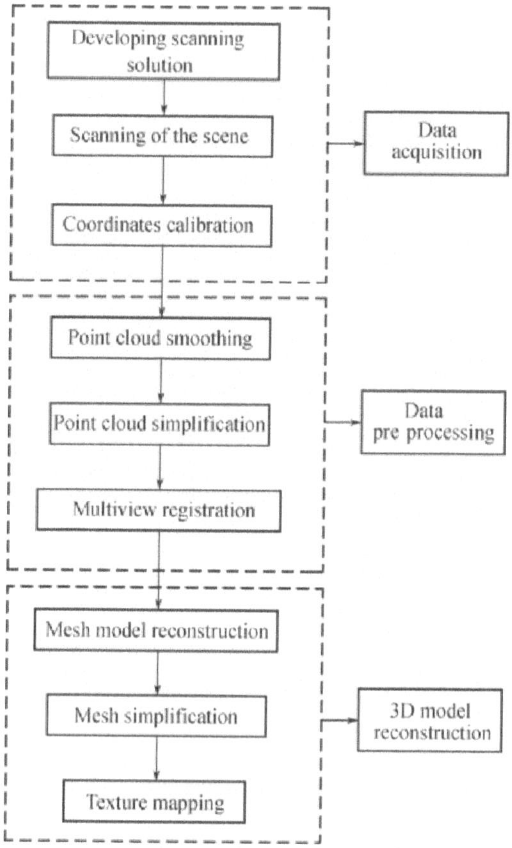

Fig. 3.14 Process of 3D laser scanner based modeling.

Data acquisition is the premise of realizing the 3D modeling of the historic relics. The main work in this stage includes:

(1) Developing scanning solutions, including determining the position of the scanner, planning the path of the scanner, setting the scanning compensation parameters and determining the scanning precision of different scanning seats.

(2) Set targets, total station and some other auxiliary equipment, use the methods of the combination of distance method and the closed loop method

to do stereo, accurate, and rapid scanning.

(3) Perform digital photography along the view of the scanner to acquire the color and texture information.

(4) Perform calibration between the scanner's own coordinate system and the camera coordinate system. Unify them to guarantee the accuracy of the texture mapping.

Data preprocessing not only provides reliable point cloud for the reconstruction of the 3D model, but also reduces the complexity of the model construction. The main work in this stage includes:

(1) Perform filtering and smooth processing for the original point cloud data in order to remove the interference data that has nothing to do with the reconstruction. Examples include the noise and fly spots.

(2) Under the premise of guaranteeing the geometric accuracy, do necessary simplification for the original point cloud data in order to reduce the complexity of point cloud data fusion and model reconstruction.

(3) Make registration and fusion processing for the data scanned from different views, and through the coordinate transformation get a complete 3D point cloud model of the site, as shown in Fig. 3.15.

Fig. 3.15 Point cloud models in three perspectives of the Small Wild Goose Pagoda.

Model reconstruction is on the basis of preprocessing and through texture mapping in order to realize the realistic reconstruction.

The main work in this stage includes:

(1) Perform triangulation for the point cloud data to reconstruct its 3D mesh model, as shown in Fig. 3.16.

(2) According to the application requirements for the 3D virtual display, the model is simplified by LOD and other methods.

(3) In order to improve the realism of the scene, the laser synchronous optical image based texture mapping method is used. The two-step method in the process of error estimation and compensation is used to improve the precision of the texture mapping.

Fig. 3.16 Reconstruct mesh and surface model of the Small Wild Goose Pagoda.

Modeling based on the surveying and mapping data and third-party software

Another widely used method of modeling is manual modeling. This is based on the surveying and mapping data, and use of third-party modeling software. There are many different types of modeling software. Some commonly used tools are MultiGen Creator and 3Ds Max. In comparison, 3Ds Max is powerful and can obtain models with more details. It is suitable for fine modeling. However, fine models usually contain a large amount of polygons, and cannot meet the requirements of real-time rendering unless acceleration methods are adopted, such as mesh simplification and the removal of redundant data. MultiGen Creator is one product of the MultiGen-Paradigm Company. It is specialized for industrial applications of visual simulation. It is designed for providing models to construct complex virtual scenes, which can be rendered in real-time. But the details of the models can not be compared with those models generated by 3Ds Max.

Three-dimensional modeling software usually uses hierarchical data structures to manage the models of a scene. In the modeling, in order to provide manual modeling methods, some softwares also provide additional functionality to support modeling using CAD data or a height map. Some commercial softwares also provide materials and rendering functions which you can easily see the final results of the modeling.

In general, the modeling method based on third-party software and mapping data has the advantage of low equipment requirements, and low technical difficulty. The drawbacks to this method are that it is heavy, and the efficiency is low. In addition, it is very difficult to model objects with complex shapes. Therefore, this method is only suitable for modeling the heritage site scenes with many simple objects that are easily measured.

Image-based 3D modeling

Image-based 3D modeling first gets two or more photos or videos of a scene that are viewed from different positions around the scene. Next, the three-dimensional information is retrieved by part of the scene using the technique of computer vision.

3.4.3 Cultural Heritage and Other Objects' Modeling

Historic Sites usually have many cultural heritages. In order to guarantee the integrity of the scene, we need to perform modeling for these cultural heritages. In addition, we need to add some models such as plants and sky, which improve the realism of the scene of historic sites.

Artifact modeling

For the digitalization of the artifact, the general method includes a three-dimensional scanner, which can capture more details of artifact, and a manual way based on photos. An introduction to these methods can be seen in Section 3.2.

Tree modeling

As common objects of the environment, trees are vital natural elements to many scenes in historic sites. Common tree models usually can be divided into two aspects: three-dimensional models and two-dimensional image models. Three-dimensional models have a high fidelity but complexity as well. No matter which approach taken, including based on three-dimensional scanner, based on image modeling, or manual modeling, it is very hard to get trees model with a high fidelity. It will also affect the rates of the scene's roaming because of the trees model's high complexity. Therefore, the trees two-dimensional image models are more widely used in virtual scenes in contrast with the three-dimensional models and it mainly contains two common ways: billboard technology and cross representation. These types of trees can be widely used in the scenes because of its low complexity but the fidelity decreases in close observation.

Sky modeling

The use of the hemisphere model to model the sky and texture mapping is used in order to improve the realism of the sky. Furthermore, we can use the texture moving technology to produce a dynamic sky. The technology's main idea is to build the hemisphere model at first; then use one layer of the sky's background as the texture of the geometrical model; last attach the second texture layer of the clouds. We can also set the moving matrix of the texture layer based on time, which can make the clouds move. Meanwhile, joining the stochastic model can also make the movement of the clouds more realistic.

3.4.4 Seamless Integration of Scene Modeling

The process of constructing the whole scene of the sites involves many models such as the terrain model, the site model and the cultural heritage model. The resource data and modeling environment of the three models may have big differences. What is more, it is relatively independent in the process of modeling, which can lead to total distinctions in the data format and the coordinate system. Therefore, in order to integrate all kinds of models into a unified environment so that we can get the holistic site scene, we need to do seamless integration to different models of different data formats and coordinate systems.

Blending different data formats

We need to determine the ultimate issue environment and the data format that the environment supports. Then, transform the data in different data formats to the object format. This conversion usually can be achieved by the software's auxiliary function. If the object format is in the user defined format, we should do independent programming in order to transform the data. The thing to notice is that we are better off in choosing common formats (such as ∗.3ds format and ∗.obj format) to store the data. These kinds of formats have already formed general standards and many software tools support them. If we use the data format that the issue environment supports originally, the workload will be reduced.

Blending different coordinate systems

The models in the scene maybe in different coordinates and the ratio scale can also have variances. We need to transform (zoom or translation) the models of the sites and the cultural heritage into the scene of the terrain model. Next, set the models in the relative position of the scene and combine the scenes using their relative position on the basis of the real position in reality.

In addition, the terrains in the scene usually employ a level of detail models. So we should be careful in the process of scene fusion, the terrain elevation may change when the terrain transitions from a level of detail to another level of detail. In this situation, the scene in the terrain should perform relevant changes.

References

[1] Liu J (2007) Theory with Practice for Number Archaeology. Relics From South, 1: 2–5

[2] McIvor A, Valkenburg R (1998) Accurate 3D Measurement Using a Structured Light System. Image and Vision Computing, 16 (2): 99–110

[3] Salvi J, Matabosch C, Fofi D, et al (2007) A Review of Recent Range Image Registration Methods with Accuracy Evaluation. Image and Vision Computing, 25(5): 578–596

[4] Zhang H, Zhang G, Li Z, et al (2004) Surface Reconstruction and Range Image Registration with Cloud Data Points. China Mechanical Engineering, 15 (18): 1626 – 1629

[5] Sharp G, Lee S, Wehe D (2004) Multiview Registration of 3D Scenes by Minimizing Error Between Coordinate Frames. IEEE Transactions on Pattern Analysis and Machine Intelligence, 26 (8): 1037 – 1050

[6] Brown B, Rusinkiewicz S (2007) Global Non-rigid Alignment of 3-D Scans. ACM Transactions on Graphics, 26 (3): 1 – 9

[7] Hou F, Qi Y, Shen X, et al (2009) Automatic Registration of Multiple Range Images Based on Cycle Space. The Visual Computer, 25 (5–7): 657–665

[8] Yang S (2010) Based on Depth Image 3-D Modeling Technology Research. Doctoral dissertation, Beijing University of Aeronautics and Astronautics

[9] Brown BJ, Toler-Frankin C, Nehab D, et al (2008) A System for High-Volume Acquisition and Matching of Fresco Fragments: Reassembling Theran Wall Paintings. ACM Transactions on Graphics, 27 (3): 1 – 9

[10] Kari P (1999) Multiview Registration for Large Data Sets. In: Proceedings of the Second International Conference on 3D Imaging and Modeling, pp 160 – 168, Ottawa, Canada, 4 – 8 October 1999

[11] Bernardini F, Rushmeier H, Martn I, et al (2002) Building a Digital Model of Michelangelo's Florentine Pieta. Computer Graphics and Applications, 22 (1): 59 – 67

[12] Fleishman S, Iddo D, Daniel C, et al (2003) Bilateral Mesh Denoising. ACM Transaction on Graphics, 22(3): 950 – 953, New York, USA, July 2003

[13] Luo X, Zhong Y, Li R (2004) Data Registration in 3-D Scanning Systems. Journal of Tsinghua University (Science and Technology), 44(8): 1104 – 1106

[14] Pottmann H, Huang Q, Yang Y, et al (2006) Geometry and Convergence Analysis of Algorithms for Registration of 3D Shapes. International Journal of Computer Vision, 67(3): 277 – 296

[15] Wei H, Zhang L, Liu S, et al (2010) An Algorithm on Registration of Multi-view Range Images Based on SIFT Feature Matching. Journal of Computer-Aided Design & Computer Graphics, 22(4): 654 – 661

[16] Yang C, Qi Y, Shen X et al (2010) Rapid and Automatic Method for 3D Scanned Data Registration. Journal of Software, 21(6): 1438 – 1450

[17] Lowe D (2004) Distinctive Image Features from Scale-invariant Keypoints. International Journal of Computer Vision, 60(2): 91 – 110

[18] Koenderink J (1984) The Structure of Images. Biological Cybernetics, 50(5): 363 – 370

[19] Lindeberg T (1988) Feature Detection with Automatic Scale Selection. International Journal of Computer Vision, 30(2): 79 – 116

[20] Lowe DG (1999) Object Recognition from Local Scale-invariant Features. In: Proceedings of the Seventh IEEE International Conference on Computer Vision, 2: 1150 – 1157, Los Alamitos, USA

[21] Stephen J, Olivier D (1992) A Theory of Self-calibration of a Moving Camera. International Journal of Computer Vision, 8(2): 123 – 151

[22] Faugeras O, Luong Q, Maybank S (1992) Camera Self-calibration: Theory and Experiments. In: Proceedings of the Second European Conference on Computer Vision, 588: 321 – 334

[23] Lei C, Wu F, Hu Z (2001) Kruppa Equations and Camera Self-calibration. Acta Automatica Sinica, 27(05): 621 – 630

4 Digital Management of Cultural Heritage Protection

Digital preservation of the extension of cultural heritages supports the applications like information query, virtual exhibition, auxiliary research and surroundings monitoring, etc. Digital management within the context of cultural heritage includes information visualization, virtual analysis, spatial geographic information system, data mining, knowledge discovery, nonimmersion virtual reality, and other technologies. These technologies aim to achieve better protection, research, and promotion of cultural heritages. In terms of protection, digital models contain an enormous rich space, texture, and semantic information, which can be used as a permanent and intact digital copies of cultural heritage. Digital models can be based on the original appearance of an ancient site. The goal is to reproduce and restore the ancient sites to their original forms. In terms of research, with the support of a spatial platform, researchers can quickly and accurately retrieve the relevant documentation information, 2D images, 3D models, and simulate the natural evolution of ancient sites through artificial intelligence and spatial visualization. In terms of promotion, the use of virtual-reality technology to draw 3D site scenes can provide virtual-realistic scenes for visitors. This allows enjoyment the ancient arts more fully. Computer-aided manufacturing systems can help make artistic works and tourist souvenirs with the characteristics of cultural heritage.

This chapter focuses on the applications of digital management of cultural heritage protection in digital auxiliary investigation, the digitalized surrounding of archaeology and the dynamic surroundings of monitoring items. The examples of Archeological Site Space Information Systems introduced in this chapter are expected to be helpful for digital information services of cultural heritage.

4.1 Digital Auxiliary Investigation

Archaeological excavation is the foundation of the cultural heritage research and an important method to protect ancient cultural heritage. The use of digital aided measurement systems can help to automatically obtain the pit profile, and the bottom graph to aid in data processing. The original 3D scene of the excavation site is built with the help of charts and other data. The ancient human surroundings are simulated and reproduced for the 3D model.

During the process of archaeological excavation, a lot of archaeological site information with the characteristics of spatial distribution is generated. For example, the location and extent of the archaeological site can be marked on space coordinates with all the remains and artifacts in the site. The ability to accurately mark a specific location, allows further research by archaeologists, as shown in Fig. 4.1. Because of its plane figure and text-based query ability, traditional methods cannot satisfy the archaeological team's needs for spatial inquiry for archaeological information and the relevant visual analysis. Traditional systems can only provide text, pictures, and video information organized in two-dimensions. A traditional system cannot provide content-based retrievals, 3D virtual presentations, and other capabilities. The archaeological team expects carrying out intelligent management and visual analysis on massive and multi-dimensional information to the excavation site. Benefits must be measured to cultural and tourist enthusiasts looking forward to the 3D visual and virtual tours of the excavation site.

Currently, there still exist the following problems in the excavation and research of field archaeology in China.

(1) To some people the archaeological excavation means destruction of the ancient sites because the excavation of any ancient cultural heritage sites will change their original surroundings. At present, data acquisitions and

Fig. 4.1 Archaeological excavation.

Fig. 4.1 Continued.

recording instruments are not perfect. Data measurements and charts drawings are still performed manually, which inevitably lead to very low efficiency. The differences of data accuracy and drawing quality can be quite large because of individual differences of skill.

(2) The vast majority of exploration projects are carried out in a closed state. The quality and progress of an excavation are quite different because of the different skill levels of team leaders and members. Therefore, a misjudgment of stratum and remains will hinder remote monitoring, expert judgment, and data sharing at the excavation site.

4.1.1 Research Contents of Digital Auxiliary Investigation

From a practical point of view, the digital auxiliary investigation should focus on the management and integration of dynamic data of the field archaeological excavation. The integration of the written records, charts, and image data allows a holistic view of the archaeological excavation data. 3D reproduction of archaeological surface features in its original surroundings allows collaborative management of the excavation project. The remote consultation provided over the unearthed surface features allows the simulation and reproduction of the ancient human surroundings, and other functions like decision-making and spatial analysis. Digital auxiliary investigation contains the following five parts:

(1) Automatically obtaining the archaeological pit profile, bottom line graph of the excavation site, and acquiring, managing and processing text information.

The work involves four steps: First, image capture, management and processing, and line graph automatic generation. Second, graphics and image database construction, image correction, image mosaic, and vector chart extraction of the profiles from data acquisition system. Third, construct a 3D surface model of the bottom plane; extract opening lines of the remains, and design and implementation of other data processing functions. Fourth, acquisition, management, and processing of text information involving data acquisition, classification, storage management, queries of statistics, and tabulation output, including design of the archaeological excavation database, and formulation of various data acquisition and processing standards.

(2) Building a 3D scene of the original excavation site. Based on the archaeological information such as charts and images, a 3D scene of the original excavation site is developed to reproduce the ancient human surroundings of certain cultural stratum. The scene involves all the cultural levels and the construction, integration, and processing of the 3D models various surface features (such as houses, tombs, pits, etc.) in the archaeological excavation.

(3) Construction of the static scene of field archaeology. Applying digital close-range photogrammetry techniques, fast and efficient data acquisition solutions to the construction of a static scene of field archaeology can be obtained. Furthermore, real-time storage, transmission, updates, and management of all the static and dynamic attribute data, image data and graphical data on the excavation site in remote areas are implemented based on the capability of the wireless network.

(4) Data mining techniques on spatial-temporal database. Investigating the original surroundings in which the archaeological surface features remained the spatial-temporal development and changes of ancient human surroundings are reproduced and simulated based on the data mining techniques of the spatial-temporal database. Meanwhile, by analyzing, synthesizing, and extracting the field archaeologists' experiences, and standardizing and formalizing the experiences, the space knowledge base of field archaeology is established based on appropriate knowledge base models to describe and express overall domain knowledge.

(5) Establishing virtual archaeological geographical surroundings based on wired and wireless networks. With integration of the research results of Web GIS, 3D GIS, and the international standards for distributed interactive technology, virtual archaeological geographical surroundings are established based on wired and wireless networks. This enables field archaeologists in different areas to have discussions about certain problems and supports experts to make judgments and decisions remotely.

In summary, the digital auxiliary investigation system is a link to the excavation site of the field archaeology together with the concerned cultural relic protection agencies, functional departments, and research institutions as an interactive whole by means of wired and wireless networks. Storage of the information remains at the excavation site and relevant expert knowledge is employed to formulate and adjust major excavation schemes and to resolve the issues on the field excavation site. Therefore, the quality and level of field excavation are improved.

4.1.2 Functions of Digital Auxiliary Investigation Platform

Achieving comprehensive, accurate, and visual geographic information and remains information on the site is prerequisite for smooth archaeological excavations. This requires the digital auxiliary investigation platform to provide not only the two-dimensional information on the excavation site (including engineering data, pictures of cultural relics, exploration video, etc.) but also the release, management, retrieval and display of the 3D information (including point cloud models, solid models, surface models, etc.) for archaeologists.

Data management

The various data elements of a major archaeological excavation site at different stages of excavation need to be acquired. These elements include the location, geometric shapes, spatial distribution, and color texture of the unearthed surface features. Some of the data forms include excavation records, engineering drawings, site scenes, and 3D point cloud models of the cultural relics and video records of the excavation process. The large and diverse forms of the data and their complex temporal and spatial associations require careful study of the relationship between the data and its reasonable classification to form a layered visualization database. The layered visualization database can provide the implementation of the multi-dimensional information management of archaeological excavation site from the perspectives of time, three-dimension space, and properties of the relics.

Nonlinear editing

Recording the archaeological excavation process through use of dynamic image technology is an important part of the digital aided measurement system. A nonlinear editing system is composed of the computer, digital video camera and DVD or other network storage devices. The nonlinear editing system can implement the input, storage, editing, and video creation of the image information of archaeological excavations. The system can compile feature films on archaeological excavation from color photographs by use of digital cameras, voice introduction, background music, subtitles, and so on. It can also organize the components together to produce image data discs of certain archaeological work.

Intelligent retrieval

Because of the amount of unearthed cultural relicsat an excavation site, text retrieval is not preferred. Query techniques based on key words, contents, multiviews and multi-dimensional profiles and the high-level semantic query techniques based on shape features and image descriptions should be applied to the information retrieval of archaeological excavation projects [1].

Archaeological drawings

Archaeological drawings are the fundamental work unit in compiling the data of cultural relics. These are used in excavation report illustrations, illustrated papers, monographs, textbook illustrations and other media. These unearthed relics and remains in archaeological excavation are needed to generate archaeological drawings. The traditional hand-drawing method is not only time-consuming, but also inconvenient for storage and use. To avoid the issues of hand-drawing defects, an automatic archaeological drawing generation method is implemented based on 3D laser scanning technology. Using the technique of extracting feature lines, curvature estimation, and detection of featured regions from the obtained 3D model captured by 3D laser scanner, automatic drawing functions such as the drawing of plane graphs, profile chart and contour maps, 3D mapping and measurement can be implemented. The method is flexible and convenient for users.

Prediction and analysis

Archaeological researchers are not only concerned about the attribute information of unearthed relics such as the cultural layers but also the about spatial information such as the distribution of the unearthed relics. In recent years, with the expanded use of simulation and virtual tours of sites, archaeologists need visual, interactive, easy to use tools to predict and analyze the cultural sites. Therefore, it is necessary to integrate the spatial information and attribute information of the unearthed relics to provide spatial queries of the cultural sites and visualization analysis. Therefore, users can obtain the relevant information of the archaeological sites through systems tools such as WebGIS and VRGIS.

Virtual touring

The virtual archaeological site scene is constructed through a combination of data captured in archaeological excavation site and historical documents. The digital auxiliary investigation platform provides an interactive touring system that allows users to see 3D images, tour freely in the virtual archaeological site scene, and interact with the relics they are interested in. Either a VRML/X3D-based virtual scene description or the XML-based scene description language can achieve a unified mark and description of the 3D virtual scene and implement virtual tours. This allows display of the excavated site scene [2].

4.1.3 Key Techniques

Multi-dimensional digital recording of relics

In the process of archaeological excavation, an intelligent digital mapping system can integrate GPS with total station instrument. An intelligent digital mapping system can acquire, input, edit, map, output, and manage the spatial data of the site terrain and can effectively improve the archaeological mapping accuracy and efficiency. The process of digital mapping data mainly includes data transmission, data preprocessing, data transformation, data computing, graphics generating, image editing, management and the application of graphical information. Data preprocessing includes the coordinate transformation, various data matching, unification of map scales, and data conversions. Data processing can generate digital map files to exchange information with the external devices. The control of map layers can compile and output various thematic maps (including plane graphs, topographic maps, maps of site distributions, etc.).

Knowledge reasoning and wireless network distribution

Based on the functions of GIS spatial analysis,the spatial statistical analysis, comparative analysis, buffer analysis and visible range analysis about relics and remains, and spatial layers models about ruins can be implemented. This allows the location features and combination of characteristics of the relics to be revealed. The spatial relationships between various cultural levels and excavated objects then can be investigated. Furthermore, through knowledge reasoning based on a spatial knowledge base of field archaeology, space distribution rules of human activities in the ancient surroundings can be inference and verified. The work includes the following:

(1) Integration and inter operability of the virtual archaeological environment system and the three-dimensional visualization technology;

(2) Construction of a field archaeological database and the spatial-temporal data exploration mechanism;

(3) Construction of an intelligent model of collective decisions and the collaborative and interactive working mechanisms [3];

(4) On this basis, the wireless network technology and Web GIS technology serve to achieve the functions of near real-time remote monitoring, expert judgment, holistic inference of the remains, comparisons of layer relationships, and error warnings during the course of field archaeological excavations.

Arrangement and management of massive data

Cultural sites are usually of large scale, and inevitably, the related spatial geometric data and terrain texture data are so massive that high-end graphics workstations cannot achieve real-time results. Therefore, it is vital to investigate 3D data models and data structures to describe various cultural layers and archaeological excavated objects. The representation models for the distribution features of ancient culture layers and attribute features of various relics and remains allow the build of a 3D multisource spatial data fusion framework model [4].

Data structure

The DEM-standard files describing terrains have different data structures such as Grid, TIN, and the mixture of Grid and TIN. A TIN represents a surface as a set of non overlapping contiguous triangular facets, of irregular size and shape [5]. These structures have different advantages. Storage space for terrain descriptions of the large scale scene and the operating complexity are the two key issues to determine the overall data structure. Grid is very suitable for large scale use and management because of its compact storage, simple structure, and ease of operation. Some features such as the regular array of square grid, the elevation of each grid's values outside the network, allow only the need to record the location of a starting-point from the coordinates and grid interconnection. A grid network with topological relationships between points in the array implies the ranks of its numbers. Therefore, this structure is more appropriate for large scale scene data storage and management due to small storage, simple structure, and ease of operation. The TIN data structure shows a better solution to overcoming problems caused by the nonstationary property of the terrain surface. Also, for some applications such as shading, cataloging, and visibility, TIN has a nice implementation.

The two primary ways to render terrains on the 3D scene are volume rendering and surface rendering. Volume rendering attempts to provide real 3D features, which leads to complex data structures and large data storage requirements. Surface rendering, whose data structure is vector data structure in nature, is suitable for object rendering of the visualization of large scale scenes for the sake of practical applications.

Data partitioning

Visualization of large scale 3D scenes requires pre-separation of spatial data. Visualization of large scale scenes is hindered by limited memory capacities, computing power, and rendering ability that are unable to process massive spatial data from external memory sources for processing at onetime. This causes data to be partitioned for processing. Different granularity settings can be applied for rendering based on different distances of the scenes from the eyes. It is advisable to adopt the level of detail (LOD) method to simplify surface details to reduce the complexity of the scene's geometry and retain the images when possible so that the effect of visual images is not affected. Thus, the efficiency of rendering algorithms is improved [6]. Visualization of 3D scenes involves data such as DEM data of terrain rendering, vector data of land form texture data, and metadata of the scene.

- DEM data partitioning

Adopting a Grid data structure makes DEM data partitioning easier. Grid data structure is a square grid array at regular intervals. Given the coordinates of the start and end points of a data partition and the size requirements after partitioning, the original DEM can be partitioned into many fragments with the same size. Using application software and hardware, QuadTree-based simplification can be adopted in the rendering stage. The grid numbers of each columns of the DEM fragment should be limited to $2N$ (N is an integer greater than 2).

- Surface features data partitioning

Surface features data partitioning is used to create an association between surface features and DEM fragments. Surface features data can also be processed by LOD. However, as experimental results are concerned, surface features of different detailed levels often produce sudden flashes while switching. Therefore, whether to use LOD or not depends on a machine's performance and application requirements [7].

- Texture data management

The method of texture mapping can significantly increase the realism of 3D scenes. At the same time, it increases the amount of internal storage and the complexity of the rendering. Without effective and optimized mechanisms, the real-time scene's rendering performance will be significantly reduced. For further optimization, image processing tools can be adopted to process image maps in detailed levels to reduce the storage space that a terrain texture occupies in the distance observation. When observation is made at long distance, a similar color can be used.

- Metadata management

Metadata (Metadata) is the data about data. It is an important base for spatial data sharing. It describes the data content, quality, condition, and other features to help people locate and understand data. In the exploration of large scale scenes, usually a relational database is used to store metadata and to indicate the identification information, quality information, data organization information, release information, and other factors. After the scene is partitioned, the sub-scenes often share all the original metadata.

Data coding

After the partition of the spatial data, the original large scale 3D scene is replaced by many subscenes with different granularities and different sizes. Although each subscene can be rendered independently, it cannot support the global perspective rendering for real-time roaming. Therefore, in order to achieve real-time scheduling of many site scenes, subscenes must be coded to set up mutual spatial relationships.

Spatial relationships between the subscenes include two main aspects. One is the level of detail, which is reflected in the "father-child" relationship between one bigger subscene and multiple smaller subscenes. The other is the location of the same level, which expresses the adjacent spatial relationship between the subscenes in the same level of detail. The scene code has a significant impact on the effects of final rendering. To define the principles of data coding should not only fully reflect the spatial relationship between the subscenes, but also ensure the coding rules being clear and easy to locate, so as to avoid a complex search process. The following encoding scheme can be used:

$$[\text{LayNum}][\text{RowCode}][\text{ColCode}]$$

Here LayNum represents the level of detail of the subscene, RowCode and ColCode are the increasing codes in the row and column of the layer, respectively, in accordance with the direction from north to south and from west to east. Suppose the scene coding of the current subscene where the view point locates is [3] [3] [5], the row and column codes plus 1 or minus 1 can determine the codes of eight adjacent sub-scenes on the same level (which are respectively [3] [2] [4], [3] [2] [5], [3] [2] [6] ...). And the "father and son" relationship between the subscenes on different levels of detail can be easily described through another Tree Index, as shown in Fig. 4.2.

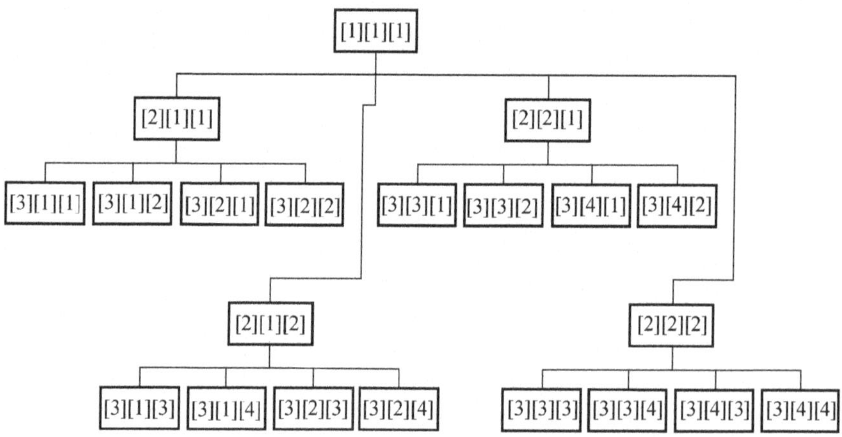

Fig. 4.2 Coding structure of the cultural sites scene.

Spatial data pyramid

According to the encoding mechanism described above, spatial data of a large scale 3D scene are eventually organized into a pyramid-type data structure consisting of a number of subscenes of different levels of detail. The pyramid-type data structure indicates that the cell sizes decreases successively from the top layer to the bottom layer. This means that the rendering of the scene has increased detail from the top layer to the bottom and the scene is progressively larger from the far to the near. Based on this method of organizing data, the spatial data structure of the whole scene is shown in Fig. 4.3.

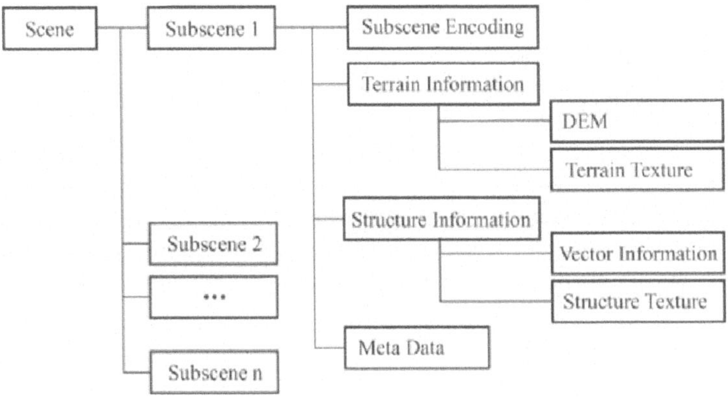

Fig. 4.3 Spatial database structure of the cultural sites.

4.2 Digital Environmental Archaeology

As a nondestructive detection system that allows for an extension to different scales of space, 3S technologies (GPS, RS, and GIS) have made great achievements in the archaeological exploration in recent years. The spatial information capture and analysis techniques combined with 3S technologies as a core can effectively extract the spatial distribution features and modes of the cultural sites. The spatial information and techniques serve to analyze the trajectory of cultural and historical heritages and the rules of the evolution of ancient environments, and provide a scientific research approach to understanding and discovering the formation and evolution processes of human cultural heritage [8]. Compared to traditional methods, application of modern information technologies such as, 3S technologies and virtual reality (VR) technology to environmental archaeology have shown their advantages.

4.2.1 Concept of Digital Environmental Archaeology

In a broad sense, the goal of digital environmental archaeology is to integrate advanced information means and tools (including remote sensing technology, satellite positioning, digital photogrammetric, spatial database, geographic information systems, and virtual reality technology) to achieve the complete digitization of cultural heritage information such as the ancient surroundings, sites and remains. Based on traditional environmental archaeology, artificial intelligence is applied into analyzing, filtering, calculating, and restructuring geographical and archaeological data to form the knowledge base of environmental archaeology, logic database, method database, and model database. Then a digital space is built to expand time and space dimensions of the ancient ruins and surroundings and ultimately achieve the overall digitization of the archaeological process. In a narrow sense, digital environmental archaeology refers to the regional environmental archaeological GIS supported by 3S and VR technologies.

Digital environmental archaeology is used to explore how to apply modern information technologies to solve practical problems in environmental archaeology. The creation of environmental archaeological GIS has the functions of capturing, processing, managing, analyzing and applying multi-source but heterogeneous information of cultural sites based on traditional environmental archaeology.

4.2.2 Process of Digital Environment Archaeology

From a technical perspective, digital environmental archaeology is the process of capturing cultural heritage information, digitalization, model analysis, information extraction, knowledge and rules discovery, and decision-making assistance. Its main technical support is the modern information technologies such as remote sensing technology, global positioning satellite, digital photogrammetry, spatial databases, geographic information systems, and virtual reality technology.

Specifically, the process of digital environment archaeology includes following five steps:

(1) Digital management, which means to store the archaeological data, geographic data, and environmental data obtained from a variety of sources into the digital environmental archaeology system though the way of texts, forms, digital images, and graphics.

(2) Information management. Useful data is extracted from massive data marts through mathematical statistical analysis, graphics identification, and dynamic conversion of time and space.

(3) Knowledge management. Spatiotemporal data, attribute data, and image data are studied to discover informative laws or patterns by using various domain-specific models.

(4) Reproduction. According to the objective laws, through virtual simulation, the natural or social process of the environmental archaeology is reconstructed, and the developmental trend is predicted. Moreover, several possible solutions to the problems in environmental changes and cultural resource protection are provided.

(5) Decision-making. Decision-making authorities could choose feasible solutions from above suggestions.

The technical structure is shown in Fig. 4.4.

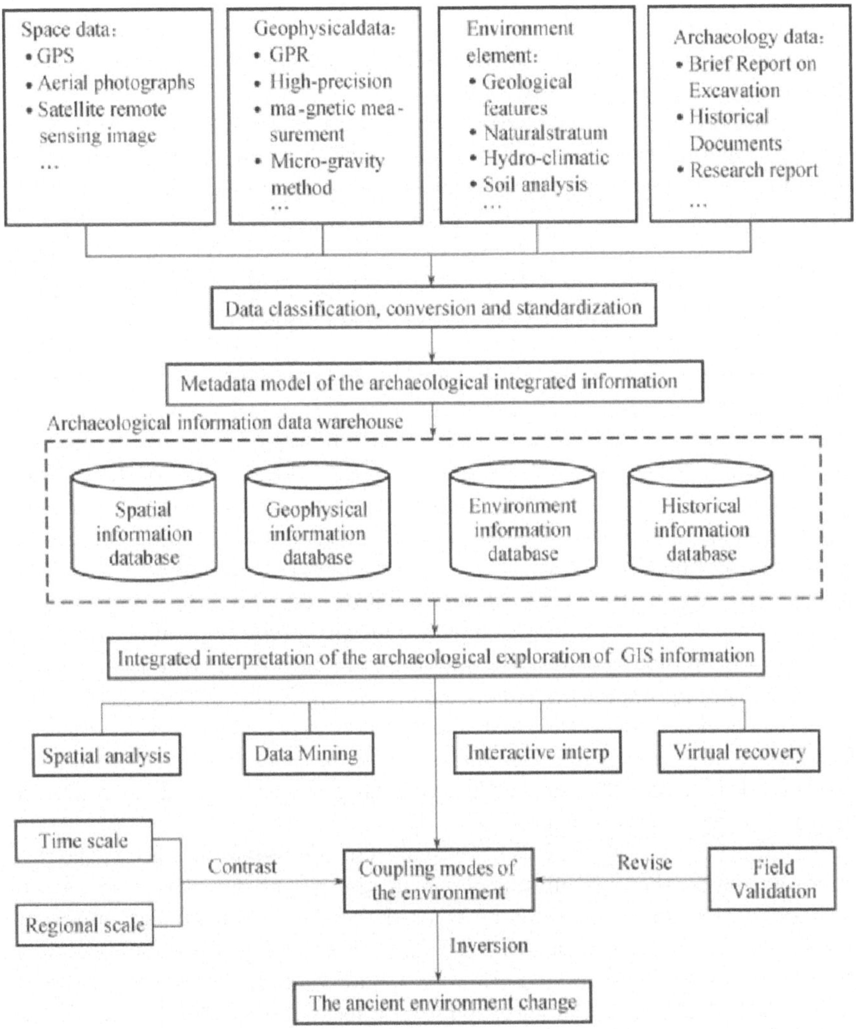

Fig. 4.4 Technical architecture of the archaeology digital environment [9].

4.2.3 Typical Application Analysis

The rapid development and mutual integration of RS, GPS, GIS, and VR technologies are becoming the forefront in environmental archaeology. In integrated applications, RS technology can be implemented effectively with the preliminary exploration of the ancient ruins in vast areas. GPS technology can provide the exact location of the site and surface information data accurately. GIS technology has strong functions of managing and analyzing the spatial data in archaeology. VR technology can visually reproduce the living surroundings of human beings and its evolution over time, create virtual surroundings of the key archaeological sites, and achieve 3D dynamic visual displays of the large scale site scenes.

In the large scale archaeological excavation of Zhougong Temple site in Qishan, Shanxi Province, GPS, GIS, and RS technologies were first applied in China to the course of archaeological excavations. On the basis of airborne remote sensing technology, the site location was determined and the field archaeological investigation database was established. With more than 30 million square meters around the site, synchronous drillings and mappings created the framework of a digital archaeology database [10], which provided foundations for further excavations.

In the research of settlement archaeology, taking advantage of DEM-based elevation changes and valley buffer analysis respectively, Xia Zhengkai [11] and Hu Jinming [12] discussed the relationship between cultural landscapes and environmental elements from the topographic background of the cultural distributions. Using analysis functions of the buffer zone in GIS, the activity scope of ancient inhabitants is taken as the radius and the buffer figure for each point of the site. Then the zone of the buffer including all the outside tangent parts is our ancestors, "living radiation zone". By approximating the radiation zone, clues can be provided about site predictions and changes in ancient surroundings such as the coastline changes of ancient rivers, lakes, and seas. By approximating the iso-curves of ruin's site distributions of different cultural periods in the Neolithic Period, further analysis of the regional features of ancestors' gathering centers and boundaries can be obtained. This can provide assistance for the settlement archaeological research and environmental archaeological research.

In addition, archaeologists have achieved nondestructive archaeological investigation to the surrounding areas by the use of detective archaeology technology. Detective archaeology is used to display the underground cultural artifacts on the screen through GIS and other digital technologies such as electric current, electromagnetic waves, and magnetic fields. On one hand, experts take hyper-spectral aerial photographs of the surrounding areas and try to discover large scale mausoleums and city ruin sites under the ground through the analysis of abnormal spectra. On the other hand, they attempt to identify the relationship between the locations of the underground sites by infrared flight data. Moreover, based on the above two detections, archaeologists will explore the "suspected" sites through geophysical prospecting. Therefore, the whole knowledge about ancient ruin sites is achieved through virtual reconstructing macroscopically natural, social environments, microcosmic food structures, and variety of crops.

Taking the research of the Sino-German Scientific and Technological Corporation in 2007, Museum of the Terracotta Warriors and Horses of Qin Shihuang and Darmstadt University of Architecture and Technology in Germany cooperated to implement the project "virtual explorations of emperor's mausoleums". In the project, Museum of the Terracotta Warriors and Horses of Qin Shihuang and Shanxi Archaeological Research Institute set up a research team. The team took advantage of the German's past rich experiences in successful reconstructions of many archaeological sites and theirstate-of-the-art technologies to try to implement virtual reconstructions of the Mausoleums in Xi'an based on relevant digital measurement technology. Based on the measured data of Emperor Qin's mausoleum, Terracotta Warriors Pits and Emperor Tang Taizong's mausoleum and archaeological information, the team adopted modern computer graphics and imaging technologies such as the 3D image modeling software Maya 6.5, integrated multimedia databases, 3D animation, and GIS technologies to create the surface structures and underground palace architectures of Qin's mausoleum. The creation of the Terracotta Warriors Pit structures and military array arrangements was reproduce to its splendid historic appearance of emperors' Mausoleums through the use of 3D animation and 3D imaging technology.

4.3 Dynamic Environmental Monitoring System

Most cultural heritage protection projects are faced with the challenges of natural disasters and human environment transformations. Therefore, a dynamic environmental monitoring system (DEM) should be adopted to achieve the real-time data collection and monitoring of the landscape environment and natural environment of cultural heritage sites. This allows recording of the data changes in each period so as to assess the protection for natural environment and artifacts. A dynamic environmental monitoring system can also monitor the construction planning and tourist activities in the reserves so as to provide the scientific basis for the protection and management of cultural heritage.

4.3.1 Application of Dynamic Environment Monitoring in China

Cultural heritage is the evidence of ancient civilizations to human beings. China has the third most cultural artifacts and historical sites, historic cities and natural landscapes, in the world currently, second only to Italy and Spain. Many sites have been listed among world heritage sites and their protection has achieved remarkable results. Some of the well-known sites are the Forbidden City, Chengde Summer Resort, and Dunhuang Grottoes in Gansu Province. However, China is experiencing various problems in their protection, such as the growing number of tourists, rapid development of the remote towns, and natural erosion because of wind, sandstorms, saline-alkali, and water damage.

In the convention protection of World Cultural and Natural Heritage proposed by UNESCO, monitoring and early-warning work is taken as one of the primary responsibilities of the World Heritage Committee. The Convention requests that all the member countries where the world heritage locations are should set up relevant monitoring systems and submit a report every six years. Prewarning and assessment of endangered heritage have been launched all over the world. Many national governments have carried out the tracking and monitoring of heritage protection, data accumulation and evaluation, and have achieved significant protective effects.

At present, the application of dynamic environmental monitoring systems in China is still in its initial period. There are various problems in heritage site preservation, such as the lack of digital information management and protection planning of basic information and data, backward security technologies, low capability of predicting disastrous risks, backward prewarning technology, lack of criteria for data accumulation and evaluation, and other issues. Compared with other countries, China is encountering a serious crisis in protecting cultural heritage resources [13].

Advanced international experience and modern technologies must be fully used to establish an efficient dynamic environmental monitoring and pre warning mechanism to achieve dynamic information management. China is in urgent need of building a dynamic information system and the Monitoring and pre warning system for world heritage management.

4.3.2 Objectives and Processes

The DEM system should achieve the following objectives:

(1) To establish an open, distributed database and information resources of the cultural heritage to achieve information acquisition, transmission, storage and management, and service network and intellectual management.

(2) To build a DEM center for cultural heritage to carry out the construction of standards, rules and regulations for dynamic information monitoring and prewarning work.

(3) To build the monitoring and prewarning model supporting the world cultural heritage management with a complete system with various indices and scientific contents, so as to achieve a series of monitoring of projects, including water quality monitoring, vibration monitoring, and mechanical and electrical equipment monitoring.

(4) To establish efficient mechanisms for protection, emergency and disaster reduction, so as to achieve remote management and joint operations.

(5) To establish a prevention-first protection mode to promote the regular study for the protection and management of world cultural heritage.

It can be summarized as “one platform, three management levels, and three supporting libraries”. The platform aims to establish a regional “cultural heritage management information system and dynamic monitoring and warning system”. Three level managements mean the management of departments of national, provincial, and heritage sites that are linked together. The goal is to realize integration of the national, provincial, heritage sites of dynamic information with Internet monitoring and warning work management. The three libraries are a real-time database, historical library, and an integrated library.

Choice of technical means

Monitoring means

A fixed monitoring station for acquisition and patrol acquisition is established.

Monitoring methods

Automated observation and control, labor reporting, remote sensing, telemetry, and network information sharing technologies are determined.

Monitoring data types

Data from automated observation and control, basic data from cultural artifacts' files and cultural artifacts' management data are confirmed.

Sources of monitoring information

Professional data from relevant departments and data from self-built monitoring stations need to be determined.

Processing of monitoring information

Various kinds of data, such as telemetry data and remote-sensing data are directly put into the historical archive library. The data from self-built monitoring stations, artifacts' management units, and the professional data from relevant local departments is automatically generated from the management and monitoring center of the heritage place that is then processed and indexed manually. The data is then loaded into a real-time database.

Setting the monitoring range

General monitoring scope

This includes monitoring the natural environment, landscape resources, environmental pollution, planned protected areas, ancient ruins and buildings, tourist numbers, and daily business management of the cultural heritage.

Key monitoring range

The key monitoring range covers monitoring the key management and protection work of the units of cultural artifacts, such as preventing fire, theft and accidents, and taking care of the moveable artifacts and archives.

Key prevention range

The key prevention range includes monitoring the security of the site, fire prevention, tourist security, and the preservation environment of the national cultural artifacts under different climate conditions.

Specifications of data formats in information acquisition

Data formats in information acquisition should conform to Extensible Markup Language (XML) description Language Specifications for Dynamic Data of the World Cultural Heritage in China.

4.3.3 Typical Application Analysis

Environmental remote sensing and monitoring and management information systems are widely used in cultural heritage protection.

Dunhuang grottoes with 1600 years of history are the largest grottoes in China, which reflect the rich Buddhist knowledge and art. However, constant natural erosions and human destruction have made the Grottoes aged and broken. After years of intense effort, Dunhuang grottoes now has a quality monitoring system to include broad environment monitoring, artifacts and caves monitoring, grottoes security monitoring, and visitor surveys [14]. Broad environment monitoring of Dunhuang grottoes started in the 1960s and a meteorological station was first established at the top of the Grottoes by Dunhuang Research Institute to monitor the temperature, relative humidity, rainfall, sunlight, wind speed, wind direction, and sandstorms. In the 1980s, monitoring work extended to the small environments of the caves. Artifacts and caves monitoring is the most important part in protecting and monitoring Dunhuang grottoes. At present, some monitoring jobs have been implemented, such as annual inspection of cave paintings, damage monitoring of cave paintings, analysis, and the monitoring of salt content cave paintings. All of these provide a scientific basis for the research of the damages, restoration, and preservation of cave paintings. After the 1980s, prewarning and monitoring facilities began to be built when the cave quantities and the protection ranges were considered. Currently, the combination of these technologies and artificial prevention serve to establish a relatively comprehensive security monitoring system.

The Leshan Giant Buddha has over 1,200 years of history. The world-famous Buddha in Sichuan Province is one of the Chinese natural and cultural heritages. However, its body suffers serious damage due to the weathering and the passage of time. Experts have detected reasons for the damage to the Buddha by using ultrasonic waves, geological surveys, and other modern scientific technologies. Experts have reinforced the dangerous rocks and selected the most suitable rock materials to restore the Buddha's original appearance. Looking at the Buddha's damage allowed China to think differently. China has devote resources to the study of the technology of the weathering of rocks, technologies of biological damages and biological weathering and the development and management of information system of tourist resources. The study will not only effectively protect the features of the Buddha, but also have meaningful insight for other cultural artifact preservation.

In the restoration of the cultural artifacts in Emperor Qin's mausoleum, aerial photogrammetry was applied to precisely survey and draws the map of the mausoleum's current status, the image map, the map of Warrior Soldiers' military array, and other features. Close-shot photogrammetry technology was applied to determine the elevation drawings of warrior soldiers and weapons. Aerial RS technology was applied to detect and discover the distributions of underground cultural artifacts, so as to understand the influence of geological phenomena on the underground cultural artifacts.

In the environmental monitoring and protection of the archaeological excavation of the Terracotta Warriors and Horses of Qin Shihuang with over 2,200 years of history, computer technologies were used to analyze the data of the air and soil. Microbiological analysis was used to understand how microscopic fungus damage affected the cultural sites. In the excavation phase, the researchers adopted modern technologies to carry out multi disciplinary research which served to achieve the comprehensive study on weather conditions in ancient times, especially in the spring and autumn periods of the Qin Dynasty and Han Dynasty. Scientific testing methods were applied to determine components of the unearthed bronze weapons from the pits, which serves to research the technologies of bronze smelting, casting and rust prevention in Qin Dynasty. This finding verified the component ration of copper, lead and tin in bronze smelting from historical records.

Protection methods based on science and technology are used in these world cultural heritages of China. For example, Jiuzhaigou Valley and the Forbidden City are equipped with atmospheric monitors, which enable experts to know the air quality of scenic areas so as to provide all-round protection for the precious world heritages.

4.4 Case Analysis of Archeological Site Space Information System

ASIS (Archeological Site-space Information System) is aimed at developing a practical platform based on Internet services. This platform can not only provide methods of managing, retrieving and analyzing the massive information in archaeological excavations for archaeological teams, but also provide the multi-dimension data platform for cultural and tourist visitors to have 3D virtual visualization tours of the archaeological sites.

4.4.1 Requirement Analysis

With the rapid development of network technologies, archaeological researchers and cultural tourist fans can easily access archaeological sites to obtain related information about some famous cultural sites and major archaeological excavations. Meanwhile, the increasing investments on the preservation of key cultural artifacts makes 3D laser scanning technologies and virtual reality-based technologies widely used in digital preservation of cultural sites. Some examples are the digital preservation and virtual tour of Dunhuang art and the reproduction of Beijing in Qing Dynasty. The application of GIS and VR technologies in analyzing and managing the information of archaeological excavations serves to achieve comprehensive, accurate, and rapid analysis of archaeological excavations and to provide visual and vivid information for archaeological researchers [15].

According to the above analysis, ASIS should have the following characteristics:

(1) Information expression: ASIS should introduce vector maps, 3D models, and other ways of expressing space information besides texts, images, and videos into the construction of a multi-dimensional information expression models.

(2) Information management: on the foundation of mature relational database technologies, ASIS should adopt space object management technologies to realize the storage, organization, and management of special objects information such as 3D models on the excavation sites.

(3) Information service: ASIS should provide the content-based retrieval method in addition the text-based retrieval, and should also provide the query results in more visual and vivid forms to users, such as texts, images, maps and model objects.

(4) System structure: within a three-tier structure mode, ASIS should store the information from excavation sites into database servers according to the information classifications so that users can achieve interactive access to Web servers by using extended browser software.

(5) Information management mode: on the basis of open and distributed modes, ASIS should use covert centralized management mode through user role access control.

(6) The selection of development technology: mainstream Internet services, geographic information services, and database services platforms should be applied. Common script languages (such as Java and C#) and third-party plugs (such as VRML and VRP) also should be used in the development procedure so that the complexity of 3D model's processing is low.

(7) Team Organization: the team is organized in terms of its knowledge. Experts are divided into three groups. Archaeologists are responsible for the level of demand analysis. Computer experts are responsible for digitalization. Digital media experts are responsible for rendering.

4.4.2 Framework of ASIS

ASIS (Archaeological Site space Information System) is designed to support the archaeological users for research and protection of cultural artifacts. ASIS also provides query services of the unclassified site information and the virtual display services of the excavation scene to the public. The Browser/Server (B/S) structure mode is a great choice and is shown in Fig. 4.5.

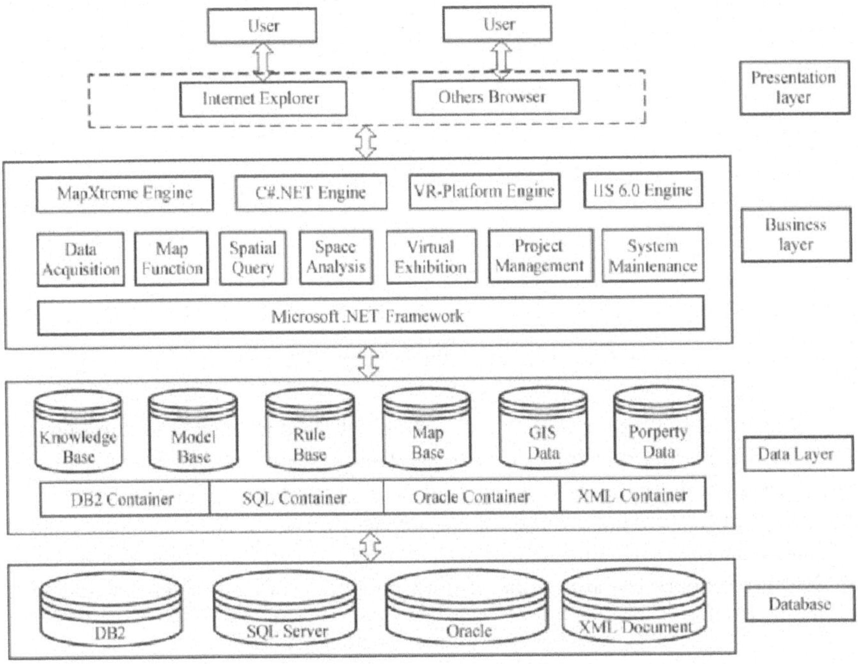

Fig. 4.5 Framework of ASIS.

With co-operation of Shanxi Archaeological Research Institute and Northwest University, the research team defined the data flow diagram of the digital aided measurement system for archaeological excavations, as shown in Fig. 4.6. The system consists of different function modules: data management, map management, heritage ruins site annotation, spatial analysis, system management, and other components.

The main modules are briefly described as follows: (1) the data management module, which implements the functions of collection, release, modification, and queries of the attribute information of the site; (2) map function module, which implements the functions of map capture, format conversion and network of the site; (3) site labeled, which implements the pixel-based interactive marking function of the site; (4) space analysis module, which implement the functions of distribution project chart drawing of the site and prediction on the distribution of associated sites; (5) statistical analy-

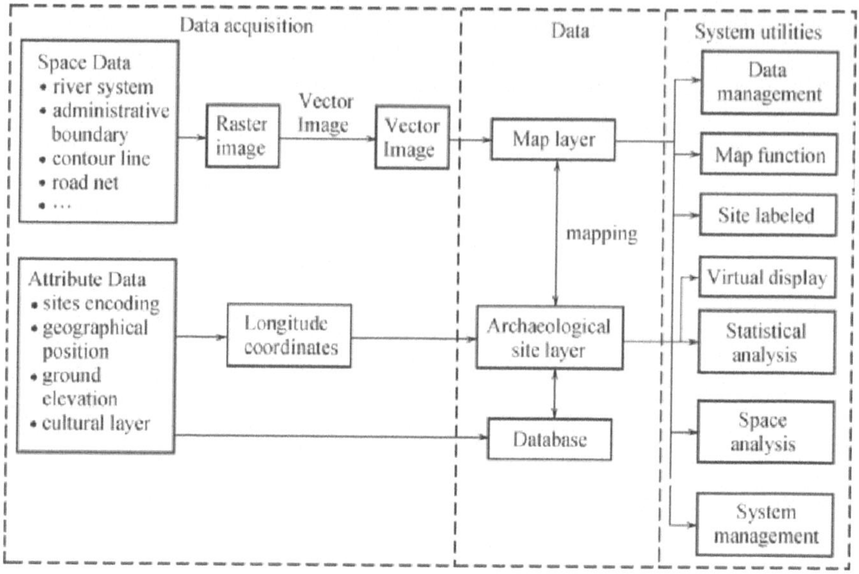

Fig. 4.6 System data flow diagram.

sis module, which implements the functions of classification and summary of the project engineering data, report printing and automatic drawing of cultural artifacts distributions; (6) virtual display module, which implement the functions of 3D virtual display of the excavation scene, and the function of 3D recovery of debris of cultural artifacts; (7) system management module, which implements the functions of data backup, work interface set and user access control.

4.4.3 Core Technologies

Open database design

Cultural sites excavation is a gradual process. The contents of relevant information will need exploration and arrangement that will be constantly updated with the progress of the excavation. The open characteristics require a digital aided survey platform to provide the following supports:

(1) setting various attributes;
(2) updating attribute structures according to the needs;
(3) reliably storing, loading, and modifying the attribute values;
(4) adding new types according to the needs.

Based on the above analysis, the information of archaeological excavation can be divided into static attribute information and dynamic attribute information. These attributes are described through an XML document, while, in the database, only one field is needed to store the XML document pointer, as shown in Table 4.1.

Table 4.1 Subset of attribute fields

Field Name	Type	Length(byte)	Memo
F_id	int	4	Key Word
F_key	nvarchar	50	Object ID
F_name	nvarchar	50	Name
F_memo	nvarchar	4000	Description
F_link	nvarchar	200	URL
F_other	nvarchar	4000	XML Attribute
F_owner	nvarchar	50	Owner
F_addtime	nvarchar	50	Time

The main advantage of this method is that the underlying storage file and the information of heritage sites are independent: (1) when the underlying data format stored in the system has major changes, and if information of heritage site has no change, the corresponding XML document needs not to be changed; (2) when information of heritage site changes, just the corresponding document type definition is changed and a small change to the original XML documents is needed.

Open XML-based attribute management

Definition of open attribute types

Consider the archaeology primitive collection of the distribution chart of the archaeological sites as a set of templates and XML template is adopted to give the definition of attribute types. The specific method is to define each custom attribute as an XML element and specify several attributes for each element.

Modification of the open attributes

Step 1: Generate the controls dynamically according to the templates.

The table of template data stores XML texts of many types of templates. The data frame needs to load the attributes of certain categories of data. The system first finds out the template of the category. The system then dynamically generates all the relevant attributes on the page according to the description of the template.

Step 2: Loading the attribute data to page controls.

The needed attributes to be displayed from the attribute data table are computed in the form of XML text. Parsing XML text, the corresponding attribute data can be loaded to the dynamic controls on the web page.

Step 3: Users modifying the attribute values.

Users can modify the control values through the operation of the web page.

Step 4: Parsing page data into XML text and then storing it.

When users need to store the modified results, the page populates the control values into the corresponding attribute positions in the XML template text respectively. A translation operation is performed to store the XML text into the attribute data table.

Modification of the open attribute structure

A category of pixels should match a corresponding open attribute template. When users need to modify the structure of custom attributes, they need to modify the appropriate template files and the system will automatically update the original attributes with the latest attribute structure.

The application of this mode enables users to easily achieve the addition of new attributes and the removal of the useless attributes. In addition, not only the values of each attribute but also the types and other ancillary information are stored in the XML document. This allows a diverse expression of each attribute on the Web page.

Map design of the excavation site

Visualization queries and space information analysis are key functions of a multi-dimensional data support platform in archaeological excavation. The access objects of the two functions are the space objects of the cultural artifacts marked out on the maps of the excavation site. The specific map design of the excavation site is as follows:

The map of the archaeological site consists of a base map and a distribution map. The base map defines the geographical information on the archaeological sites that includes mountains, waters, transportation, administrative boundaries, and other attributes. The base map can be expanded freely, such as adding the satellite remote sensing, aerial photography, ancient environment evolution, or other features. The distribution map of cultural artifacts defines the distribution of space information on the excavation site. The distribution map highlights a series of marking points of cultural artifacts according to space distributions. Each marking point matches the space object on the site which contains the 3D coordinate information. The marking of the space object serves to obtain mutual associations with attribute information of the site stored in the database (such as the level of protection, cultural identity, history etc.). The analysis of the site from the temporal and spatial distributions, and cultural attributes can be converted to a group of relational operators and the corresponding attribute field values loaded into the database.

GIS-based marking tools

Spatiality is the key feature of archaeological research. Pixels are the carriers of the space attributes. The association between the space information and the attribute information of the site can be achieved through pixels [16].

Since a product like MapXtreme does not provide the needed default tools, it is necessary to customize an interactive marking tool. Its creation process is as follows:

First, a custom tool such as JetPointMapTool from MapInfo is used. Other tools that can be used include: Web. UI, WebControls, and MapTool. Next, specify the attributes in the tools. Examples such as Client Code Source, Client Start Method, Client Stop Method, and Cursor Uniform Resource Locator (URL) are used to define the attributes. Add the event Point Found and event handler Point Found Handler.

Then, use this custom tool object on the system's Web page in the following manner:

```
JetPointMapToolca = new JetPointMapTool ();
MapControl1.MapTools.Add (ca);
ca.PointFound+=new JetPointMapTool.PointFoundHandler
(PointFoundHandler);
MapControl1.MapTools.CurrentTool=JetPointMapTool.Toolname;
```

When the tool processes the data, the coordinates are displayed in the following manner:

```
ca. PointFound+=new JetPointMapTool.PointFoundHandler
(PointFoundHandler);
MapControl1.MapTools.CurrentTool=JetPointMapTool.Toolname;
The function is processed in the custom event handler
PointFoundHandler.
```

When users use interactive tools to complete the label and click on the Web page, PointFound events are simulated to be processed in PointFoundHandler function. It should be noted that if custom label tools are used, the Execute method must be overlapped and the events must be simulated. An example follows.

```
    public override void Execute (string dataString, System.
acquireions.Array ListarrayList, MapInfo.Mapping.Map map)
    { MapInfo.Geometry.DPoint Point = new DPoint (0, 0);
    System.Drawing.Point [ ] points;
    points = ExtractPoints (dataString);
    System.Drawing.Point pt0 = points [0];
    map.DisplayTransform.FromDisplay (pt0,out Point);
    PointFoundEventArgs e=new PointFoundEventArgs (map,
Point);
    If (PointFound!=null) PointFound (this,e); }
```

Authority management

The spatial and attribute information of a Heritage site is populated into many database tables. A database engineer is in charge of collection, updating, and maintenance operations. Due to the turnover of staff and the complexity of the database engineer's role, problems maybe appear.

The visualization lab of Northwest University in China designed and developed a role-based access control operation, which has been applied in the ASIS system. The system defines various authority rights to people. A project leader can modify and assign the access rules between the staff and the project's database tables at any time. Various rules define various actions so that the data access can be easily controlled.

4.4.4 System Functions

Archaeological excavation projects need a multi-dimensional data supporting platform. ASIS can be designed to achieve the combination of the geographic information with the remains information of cultural artifacts. This can provide the 2D information, such as engineering data, pictures of the artifacts and the excavation video. This enables the release, management, retrieval, and display of the 3D information, such as point cloud models, solid models, and surface models.

Working mode of the system

In order to provide users with have more intuitive and convenient access to the system, ASIS offers two GIS working modes: the vector map mode and the satellite map mode. Users can set their own working mode through the mode tab, as shown in Fig. 4.7. Eagle Eye in the upper left corner of the working area enables users to achieve a rough selection of the concerned area and then achieve the precise positioning of the site through MapInfo-based technology.

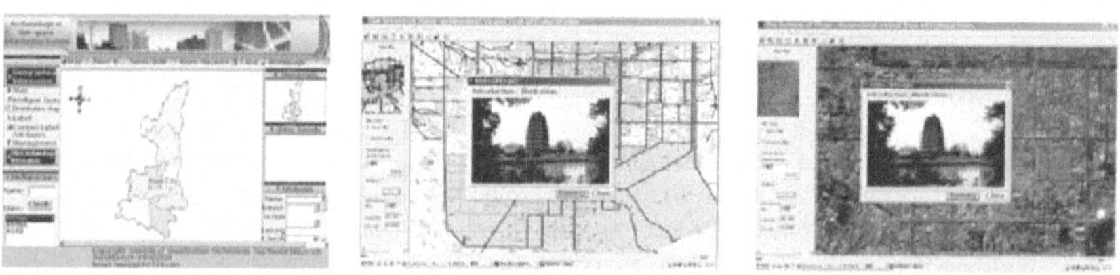

(a) Main interface (b) Vector map mode (c) Satellite map mode

Fig. 4.7 Working modes of ASIS.

Multi-dimensional data management function

The information of major archaeological excavations at different stages not only has massive data and diverse forms but also has complex associations between the time and the space. It is indispensible to carefully study the relationships between various data elements to establish a complete and accurate classification system and the form a multi-dimensional time and space database. This serves to achieve the multi-dimensional management of the information on the excavation site.

To efficiently manage the space data of the heritage site to meet the secure concurrent access of multi-users, ASIS uses a database server schema:

(1) Using the MapInfo space data server and Microsoft SQL Server, the use of ActiveX Data Objects (ADO). NET accesses the database and uses XML as a general data format. With the XML parser, data receptors can parse out the data.

(2) When using the server to handle requests, the metadata database is firstly accessed to make sure that the needed data is available and accessible. Then the server can accurately and quickly locate the geographical database and obtain the required 3D visualization data.

Querying and analyzing functions

From the perspective of archaeological study, archaeologists pay attention to both the attribute information and the space information of the cultural sites. The model of the virtual ancient environment is set up through the system. This model can help archaeologists study the distribution rules of the site communities and make scientific judgments and evaluations. These judgments guide the subsequent excavation and site protection. For the specific needs, ASIS adopts an ID code mechanism of geographic features to combine the space information with attribute information. The ID provides information pixel-based query and visualization analysis of the space information of the site.

ASIS uses GeoVRML-based node query and cluster analysis techniques. In order to support queries for space information, a GeoTouchSensor node is added to GeoVRML. The new addition extends TouchSensor in a VRML node. When users click the space node in a virtual ancient environment with the mouse, the node can transmit its geographic coordinates back to users. Users can send the captured coordinates to the two-dimensional view and through the view they can have access to the functionality of ASP.NET to achieve the query for attribute information of the site. Using the selection tools of the space objects in the system (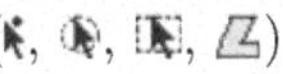), users can select one or more space objects, and then click the query button to obtain the space information and attribute information, as shown in Fig. 4.8.

3D Virtual exhibition function

Based on VRPlatform 8.0, the scene lighting, cameras, and roaming path are set to render and enhance the sense of reality of a scene. With VRP's External Authoring Interface (EAI) and by writing script code to achieve the interactive roaming between the 3D virtual scene and the external environment (clients), ASIS is designed to implement the 3D virtual display functions of the excavation. This ability provides the cultural and tourist fan with automatic guides, viewpoints selections, interactive roaming, intelligent roaming, and other enhancements, as shown in Fig. 4.9.

In its implementation, ASIS uses two nodes: GeoViewpoint and GeoPositionInterpolator of GeoVRML.

(1) GeoViewpoint node extends the standard node Viewpoint of VRML. GeoViewpoint is used for switching operations of the viewpoint. Event input

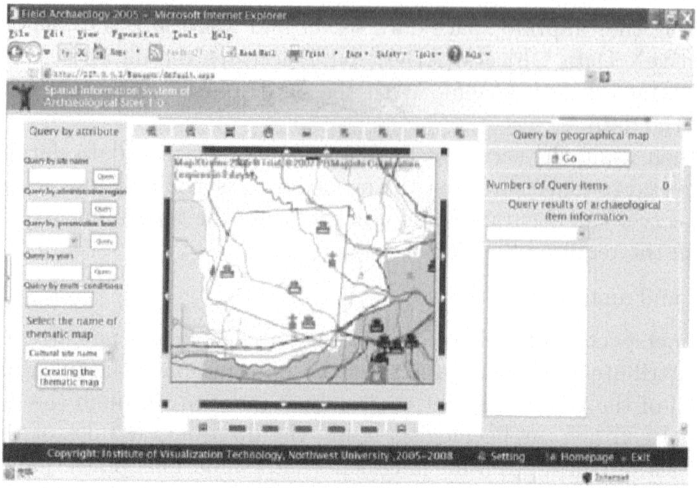

(a) Choosing the region by tools

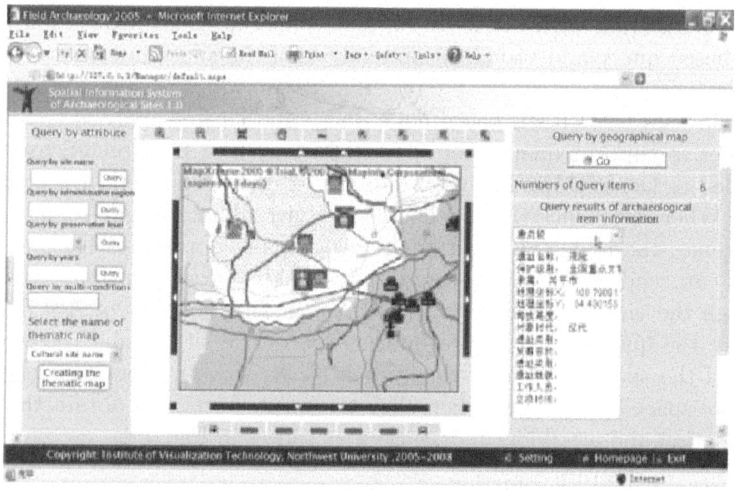

(b) Obtaining the property information

Fig. 4.8 Space querying and analyzing functions.

interface denoted by set_bind and event output interface denoted by isBound and bindTime of GeoViewpoint are the same with the standard Viewpoint node to change the viewpoint. These parameters are the same with the standardnode Vewpoint. The introduction of NavitionInfo's node domains headlight and navType provides the advantage of speed and can better achieve terrain and simulated flight and roaming.

(2) GeoPositionInterpolator node extends the standard node PositionInterpolator of VRML, and the eventOut can be used as the evenIn of GeoViewpoint or GeoLocation node to simulate the terrain or simulated flight and

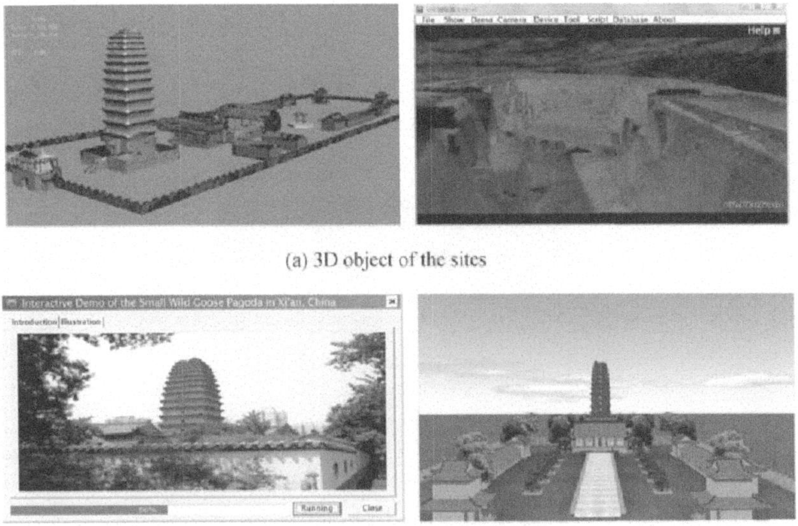

(a) 3D object of the sites

(b) Object loading interface

(c) Scene after rendering and baking

Fig. 4.9 Small wild goose pagoda virtual show.

roaming.

User access managing function

In archaeological excavation projects, the space and attribute information of the sites is located in dozens of data tables. Its modeling, updating, and maintenance are usually managed by the related staff responsible for site excavation, management, and research. Furthermore, the team members and their responsibilities often change when required. Therefore, the multi-dimensional data supporting platform of archaeological excavations is designed to be an open system platform and its B/S structure, on the one hand, it provides rapid deployment and implementation; on the other hand, it faces certain risks. Therefore, the research team uses "user's name + password + number verification code" to ensure the login security on the platform. The running interface is shown in Fig. 4.10.

In order to provide a reliable, efficient, and flexible access mode, ASIS uses a role-based access control scheme. The system administrator defines different roles, such as the project manager, the subproject manager, etc. to set the basic access rights of the system users. The project manager, according to the requirement, can adjust and set the access rules between project members and tables at any time, and set the access the behavior of the project members. The implementation of the interface is shown in Fig. 4.11.

System development environment

(1) The operating system is Windows 2000 Server and the Web server is IIS 6.0.

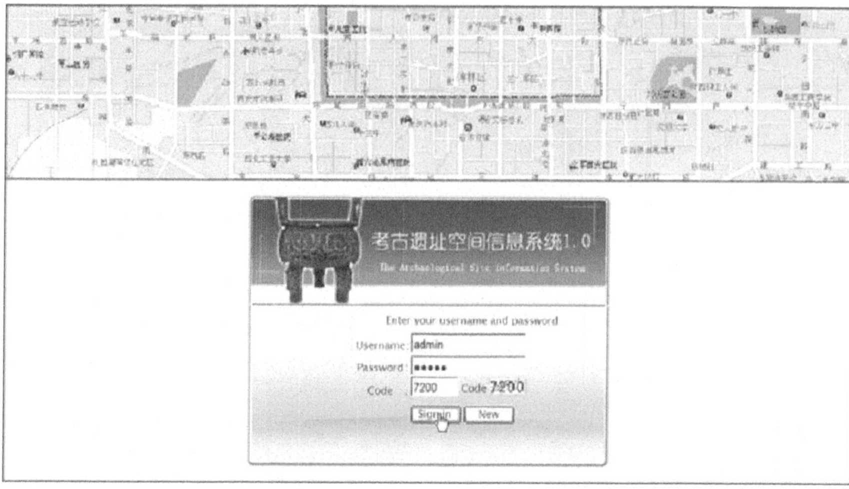

Fig. 4.10 User login interface.

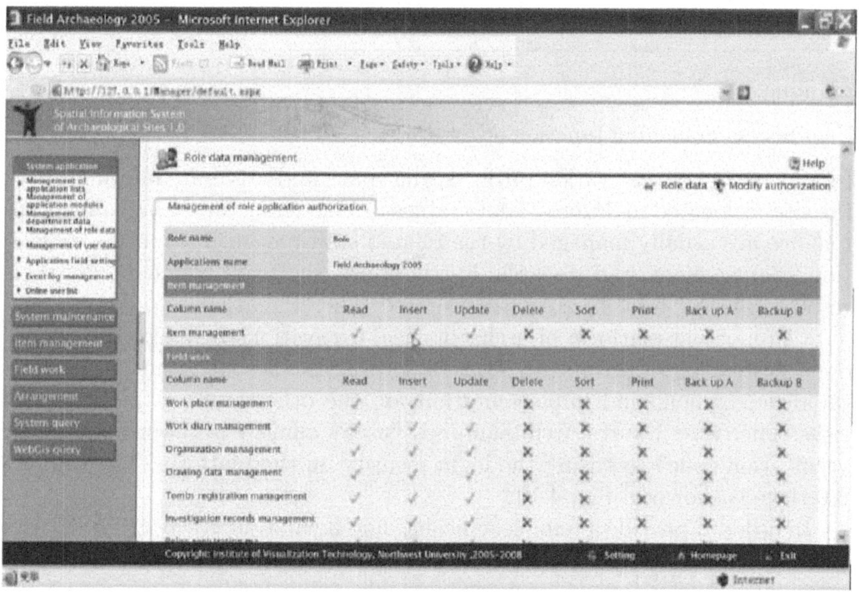

Fig. 4.11 User permissions interface.

(2) The development environment is Visual Studio 2005 (SP1) and the scripting language is C#.

(3) The database platform is SQL Server 2005, which supports multi-servers, data distribution, shared storage, SQL access, rights management, etc.

(4) The geographical information platform is MapXtreme 2005, which as-

sociates the site information with pixel objects, providing visual information analysis of the archaeological sites.

(5) The 3D modeling tools are 3Ds Max 9.0, allowing the rapid modeling of site buildings based on the 3D laser scanning data.

(6) The virtual display platform is VR-Platform 8.0, used to support the virtual roaming of the scene in the form of the third-party plug-in.

(7) Clients have access through the Internet Explorer (Flash 6.0 above) and other browsers.

For the actual needs of archaeological excavation projects, the ASIS system provides not only 2D information, such as engineering data, cultural pictures, excavation video, and the multi-dimensional data platform to explore the scene, but also the release, management, search, and display services of the multi-dimensional information, such as the point cloud models, solid models, and surface models. The platform uses the B/S structure, which has the characteristics of cross platform, low cost, easy deployment and implementation. Its pixels-based interactive markings and space query function provide archaeologists with a visual management and analytical tool of site information. Its virtual display of the site scene based on the middleware technology features provides cultural and tourist fans with quite realistic virtual roaming environment. It can be expected that, with depth research, the system will add intelligent functions, such as virtual recovery, and expansion of simulations of the site.

4.5 Summary and Prospects

It can be predicted that the construction of digitization, information management, grid, and intellectualization of cultural heritage protection will follow the integration of 3S, GIS, and VR technologies. The comprehensive application of 3S technology can explore the trends or patterns of archaeological multi-source information in the space system and expand and improve non-destructive detection technology solutions. The computer-aided quantitative analysis method and various mathematical models can be adopted to reproduce rules of human behaviors and environmental factor configurations. Currently, 3S technology in archaeological practice is still in a relatively independent application stage. Most studies still focus on spatial data acquisition and primary levels of spatial analysis. The academic integrity and comprehensive studies are not sufficient. Therefore, integrated use of 3S technology for comprehensive exploration research is a new trend. Integrations of multi-source information and method integrations are problems that need to be urgently solved.

The main archaeological results of GIS technology in China are in the application of RS technology. The goal of this technology is to accurately grasp the spatial distribution rules of the artifacts' locations from the macroscopic view. The use of GIS for archaeological research focuses primarily on constructing archaeological databases. An example is the development of an "electronic map" of artifacts' distributions in Three Gorges Reservoir area. The focus of GIS technology in the above archaeologies is on the management of cultural artifacts and archaeological data. There are three main trends in archaeological applications of GIS technology. The first one is to apply virtual reality technology and visual range analysis in archaeological research to resolve how to quickly obtain massive 3D spatial data of the studied area. The second one is examining the existing scattered, one-sided and partial 3D spatial data to apply the 3D visualization technology in archaeological researches and to build a 3D spatial model of the studied area. The goal is to restore the ancient terrains and surroundings of the ancient human activities. The third one is to apply RS and GIS technologies in archaeological research, and to use RS technology to solve large scale and macroscopic archaeological problems.

References

[1] Zhou M, Geng G, Wei N (2007) Content-based Image Retrieval. Tsinghua University Press, Beijing

[2] Liu J, Geng G (2010) Research on 3D Reality-Based Modeling and Virtual Exhibition for Cultural Sites. In: Proceedings of the ICCASM, (15): 307–313, Shanxi, China, 22–24 October 2010

[3] Li A, Bi S, Pei A, et al (2004) Research and Construction of GIS for Field Archaeology. Geography and Geo-Information Science, 20(1): 39–42, 72

[4] Lu M, He Y (2008) Organization and Indexing Method for 3D Points Cloud Data. Geo-Information Science, 10(2): 190–194

[5] Chen Z, Guevara J (1987) Systematic Selection of Very Important Points (VIP) from Digital Terrain Model for Constructing Triangular Irregular Networks. In: Chrisman N (ed) Proceedings of the AUTO-CARTO 8, ASCSM, Baltimore, America, pp 50–56

[6] Hoppe H (1998) Smooth View-dependent Level-of-Detail Control and Its Application to Terrain Rendering. In: Proceedings of the IEEE Visualization, 10: 35– 42, Microsoft Res, USA, 24 October 1998

[7] Zhai W, Chi Z, Fang F, et al (2003) Research on Spatial Data Organization for Large Scale Scene. Computer Engineering, 29 (20): 26–27, 139

[8] Zhang Z, Wu K, Hao L, et al (2005) On Some Issues of Digital Environmental Archaeology. Henan Social Sciences, 13(3): 101–103

[9] Kan A, Wang X (2008) The Archaeological Detection Methods Supported by 3S Technology: A Review. Remote Sensing for Land & Resources, 77(3): 4–9

[10] Chen S, Huang C (2005) Perspectives on the Cultural Heritage Conservation and Development. Geographical Research, 24(4): 489–498

[11] Xia Z, Deng H, Wu H (2000) Geomorphologic Background of the Prehistoric Cultural Evolution in the Xar Moron Reiver Basin, Inner Mongolia. Acta Geographica Sinica, 55(3): 329–336

[12] Hu J, Cui H (2002) Cultural Landscape Pattern During the Early Historic Period in the West Liaohe River Basin. Geographical Research, 21(6): 723–732

[13] Chen S (2005) The Protection of Cultural Heritage and Environmental Remote Sensing Monitoring. Scientific Chinese, (2): 34–36

[14] Pan Y, Lu D (2003) Digital Protection and Restoration of Dunhuang Mural. Journal of System Simulation, 15(3): 310–314

[15] Liu J, Geng G (2009) Design and Implementation of Archeology Site Spatial Information System Based on .NET. Computer Engineering and Design, 30(23): 5404–5407

[16] Gao Y, Geng G, Dong L (2007) A Study of Spatial Objects Processing Method in Rational Database. Computer Application and Software, 24(6): 12–13

5 Virtual Rigid Artifact Restoration Technology

China has a rich history filled with timeless relics such as pottery, porcelain, bronze, and pottery figurines that highlight many dynasties and eras of unique culture. These relics have undergone thousands of years of weathering, erosion, war, and historical change. Among these artifaces, many have become fragmented or incomplete. Using traditional manual methods to restore these broken or incomplete artifaces is slow, and the cost is high. Information technology has many advantages, such as large capacity storage, high-speed computing, multimedia display, and remote transmission. The use of modern science combined with technology is a necessary and effective ways for the protection of cultural heritage.

5.1 Fragment Classification

Ancient porcelain is a "living fossil" of human life. Porcelain provides extremely valuable archaeological information that reflects the prevailing social and cultural life of the era. In artifacts excavation, a lot of ancient porcelain is found. Various porcelain pieces are often mixed together. Therefore, it's very difficult to restore broken procelain and manage records. The application of information technology into heritage restoration and management is an important task in digital cultural heritage protection. According to the geometric features, color, decoration, and other characteristics the classification of ceramic fractures from the large mixed fragments is the first key step.

Porcelain's exterior features are reflected in the form of texture, color, edging, lines, composition, layout, decoration, and shape [1]. Based on visual perception, all of these characteristics in the human perception are represented as an image. Different visual characters are represented in the brightness of an image's pixels, color changes, or an overall relationship which in the local area within the image pixel brightness or color change. We extract the color porcelain, texture, and other characteristics which represent visual features. The values of the extracted features are not the same for different porcelains. We can use these features for the basis of categorization and identification.

Application of digital image processing technology involves using image color and texture analysis methods, extracting the significant color of porcelains, texture feature information, and the porcelain characteristic parameters. This results in porcelains as output. We can establish porcelain classifiers to achieve automatic classification of scattered porcelains, as shown in Fig. 5.1. Through this method, we can effectively speed up conservation efforts. An added benefit of the method is it provides preparation for computer-aided conservation, stitching and recovery.

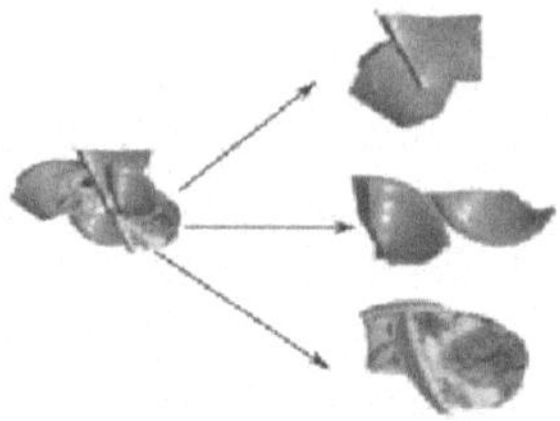

Fig. 5.1 Classification.

The porcelain image classification principle is based on different porcelains (Fig. 5.2) in an image's color space showing its different characteristics. The colors of porcelains have certain rules to follow. The color of the image of porcelains can be a basis for classification. In addition, the variation of visible pixel brightness or color in an image could be represented by extracting the texture-related features. Different types of porcelains have different extracted texture features. The texture can also be the category standard of porcelains. The porcelain pieces texture classification's task is to put the porcelains with the similar texture into one class from the various, mixed porcelain. According to the results of various porcelain pieces, the same class has a similar texture.

Fig. 5.2 Difference of porcelain pieces' image colors and texture features.

Two stages of porcelain classification:

Stage one: feature extraction.

Based on an known classified ceramic sample set, we can use color features to do preclassification. Samples are selected of the same color class of porcelains with different texture feature extraction methods. The image texture features matrix would be established by using the k-nearest neighbor method to do comparison and analysis, calculating the similarity of different image of porcelains, and to find a better way, making the distance which represents texture features minimized in the same class, maximized among various classes. The processing of the effective classification is shown in Fig. 5.3.

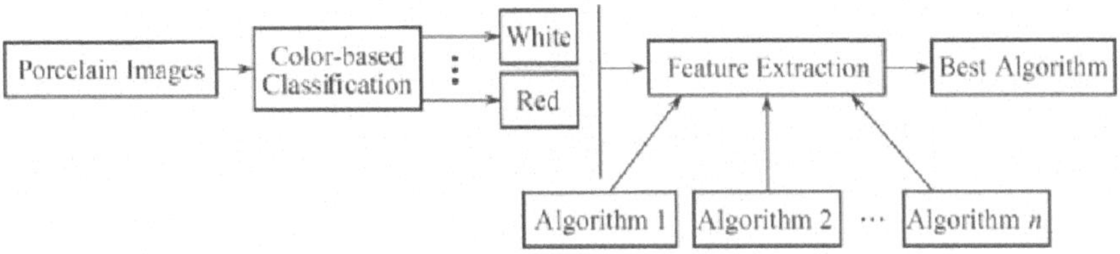

Fig. 5.3 Image feature extraction.

Stage two: classification algorithm.

Applying the first stage's method performs feature extraction. A feature database for classification of porcelains is established next. Based on feature database information, complete Bayesian, fuzzy clustering, and neural network classification methods are used to calculate the similarity between the expected porcelains and various classifications. According to different classification algorithm's accuracy, a misdiagnosis rate and classification efficiency of the porcelains is used to determine the best method of classification, as shown in Fig. 5.4.

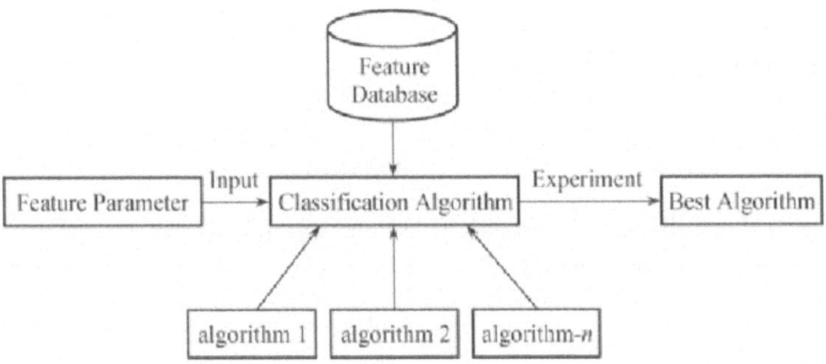

Fig. 5.4 Image feature classification.

5.1.1 Gabor Transform Feature Extraction

Gabor transform is a specific feature extraction method based on Gabor transform porcelain classification. Gabor wavelet transform can be used in straight edge detection with changes of direction and scale. It can make a better description of the biological neurons in visual experience problems. The important features of the texture analysis and extraction would be also achieved. The method has been widely used in texture analysis, image recognition and other fields. In the space domain, Gabor filters can be seen as a Gaussian function modulated by a sinusoidal plane wave [2]. A two-dimensional Gabor function has the form:

$$g_{uv}(x,y) = \frac{k^2}{\sigma^2}\exp\left(-\frac{k^2(x^2+y^2)}{2\sigma^2}\right)\left[\exp\left(ik\cdot\begin{bmatrix}x\\y\end{bmatrix}\right)-\exp\left(-\frac{\sigma^2}{2}\right)\right], \tag{5.1}$$

where $k = \begin{pmatrix}k_x\\k_y\end{pmatrix} = \begin{pmatrix}k_v\cos\varphi_u\\k_v\sin\varphi_u\end{pmatrix}$ with $k_v = 2^{-\frac{v+2}{2}}\pi, v = 0,1,2,3,4,\ldots,$ $\varphi_u = u\frac{\pi}{K}$ (K is the total number of directions), $u = 0,1,2,\ldots,K$.

Marcelja [3] used Gabor filters to do a simulation of visual cell reception field, pointing out that it can analyze on a local aspect-spatial frequency of the signal. Daugman [4] made a further analysis on the uncertainty relation within many fields like the signal spatial frequency and direction, to prove that the Gabor filter is the only function to place lower bound of time-frequency uncertainty principle.

A two-dimensional Gabor filter has the ability of distinguishing direction and frequency selectivity in both spatial and frequency domains. The structural parameters of Gabor filter is the frequency k_v and the rotation angle φ_u. A Gabor filter in the frequency change can handle images in different frequency bands of information. The change in direction can handle images with different directions information.

The parameter σ determines the bandwidth of the filter. The mutual relationship between the two is

$$\sigma = \sqrt{2\ln 2}\left(\frac{2^\phi+1}{2^\phi-1}\right), \tag{5.2}$$

where ϕ is the half-peak bandwidth. When ϕ is 0.5 octave, $\sigma \approx 2\pi$.

A Gabor filter's wavelength λ_v can be expressed by center frequency:

$$\lambda_v = \frac{2\pi}{k_v}.$$

For example, when the direction of the filter parameters is $\varphi_0 = 0$, the center frequency $k_{0,1,2,3,4} = \frac{\pi}{2}, \frac{\sqrt{2}}{4}\pi, \frac{\pi}{4}, \frac{\sqrt{2}}{8}\pi, \frac{\pi}{8}$, corresponds to the filter's wavelength: $\lambda_{0,1,2,3,4} = 4, 4\sqrt{2}, 8, 8\sqrt{2}, 16$.

A Gabor filter's effective radius can be approximated as

$$r_v = \frac{2\sqrt{2}}{k_v}\sigma. \tag{5.3}$$

When the filter bandwidth is of 0.5 octave, the filter center frequency is the maximum of $\frac{\pi}{2}$. Experiments show that to achieve the best filtering effect [5], the time parameter is calculated by using $\sigma \approx 2\pi$. The filter window radius is calculated with $r_v = 2\sqrt{2}\ \lambda_v$. Each window contains four complete wavelengths. This is enough to describe the frequency characteristics of the image in local area.

A Gabor filter for the direction of the parameter range is $[0, 2\pi]$. With the symmetry characteristics of the Gabor filter itself, the direction of the parameter values only need to take $[0, \pi]$ into account.

The porcelain image convolutes with each filter, with the parameters of the filtered image as $I_{u,v}(x, y)$:

$$\mu_{u,v} = \frac{\sum_{x=1}^{M}\sum_{y=1}^{N} |I_{u,v}(x,y)|}{M \times N}, \tag{5.4}$$

$$\sigma_{u,v} = \frac{\sqrt{\sum_{x=1}^{M}\sum_{y=1}^{N} (|I_{u,v}(x,y)| - \mu_{u,v})^2}}{M \times N}. \tag{5.5}$$

The output produces texture feature of porcelain [6], as shown in Fig. 5.5. The left picture is the sampling image of the porcelain. The middle part shows the waveforms of real part of the Gabor filter. The right image shows the convolution transformation result with the orientation parameters equaling to 2 and frequency parameter equaling to 0.

(a) Sample (b) Gabor filter waveform's real part (c) Transformation result

Fig. 5.5 Gabor filter orientation parameter $u = 2$ and frequency parameter $v = 0$.

5.1.2 SVM Classification

Support Vector Machines (SVM) is based on structural risk minimization criteria. SVM aims to promote the generalization ability of classifier, assume the error of classified result for the training sample minimum. The core principle equals to solve the problem of quadratic programming with linear constraint so that a hyper plane is constructed to generate a decision plane.. This allows the feature space distance between the two models maximum, and it guarantees the global optimal solution [7]. The following describes the process:

Training sample set

$$T = \{(x_1, y_1), \cdots, (x_l, y_l)\} \in (xy)^l x_i \in R^n, \quad y_i \in y = \{1, -1\}, i = 1, 2, \cdots, l.$$

Construct and solve the optimization problem:

$$\min_{\alpha} \frac{1}{2} \sum_{i=1}^{l} \sum_{j=1}^{l} y_i y_j \alpha_i \alpha_j K(x_i, x_j) - \sum_{j=1}^{l} \alpha_j,$$

$$s.t. \sum_{i=1}^{l} y_i \alpha_i = 0, \quad 0 \leqslant \alpha_i \leqslant C, i = 1, \ldots, l$$

where $K(x_i, x_j)$ is the kernel function, C is penalty parameter. The optimal solution is $\alpha^* = (\alpha_1^*, \alpha_2^*, \ldots, \alpha_l^*)^{\mathrm{T}}$, calculating $w^* = \sum_{i=1}^{l} y_i \alpha_i^* K(x_i, x)$, and select $0 < \alpha_j^* \in \alpha^*$, compute $b^* = y_j - \sum_{i=1}^{l} y_i \alpha_i^* K(x_i, x_j)$, structure the partition hyperplane $(w^* \cdot x) + b^* = 0$. According to the hyperplane, we can get classification decision function: $f(x) = \mathrm{sgn}((w^* \cdot x) + b^*)$.

The way we use the classification of pairs is according to M samples of porcelains constructed by class $M(M-1)/2$ decision functions $f_{i,j}(x), 1 \leqslant i, j \leqslant l, i \neq j$, using a voting mechanism to decide on the samples that belong to the category.

5.2 The Representation of Space Contour Curve

In this section, chain code, Spline, polygonal approximation, based on scale space feature points and based on invariant variety technologies are introduced to represent space contour curve.

5.2.1 Chain Code

Chain code is a very common way of representing shape, and that means it does not simplify shape but can represent shape effectively.

Using chain code to represent shape was introduced by Freeman [8] in 1961. Freeman [9] used chain code to extract the key points to generate a relative translation, rotation, scale-invariant representation of the rotation, and summarized the various methods and algorithms of chain codes.

Figure 5.6 describes all the nodes around node A, whose orientation is from inside to outside following clockwise. Connection a_i is a straight line. A chain is an ordered table where $A = a_1, a_2, \ldots, a_z$. Freeman used chain code to describe the boundaries and to identify key points to the formation of the boundary description with the right translation, rotation, and scaling invariance. He also described another chain code method that focuses on the shape of the contours. The focus outline is a structure of the distance from the centroid to boundary points.

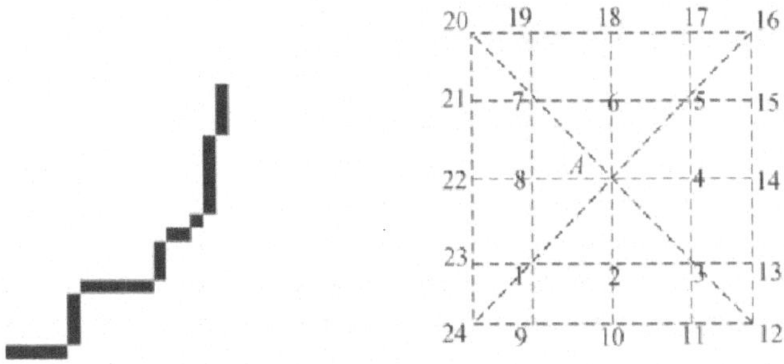

Fig. 5.6 General representation of chain code.

Parui and Majumder [10] used an improved chain code for symmetry analysis. The shape of the boundary is represented by a hierarchical structure. The polygon is used to represent the highest point and the axis of symmetry is the connection from the highest point to the lowest point.

5.2.2 Spline

Spline is very popular in the area of function interpolation and curve approximation. Ikebe and Miyamoto described in detail the spline application for the shape of the design, presentation, and restore in the literature [11].

The mathematical description of spline can be referenced and found in various literatures [12, 13]. Spline has the advantage of minimum curvature. Using the minimum average curvature of the curve approximates the given function curve [14]. Figure 5.7 is a uniform cubic B-spline curve. The shortcoming of spline in interpolation problems is that the changes of a local function value will affect the entire spline. B-splines are proposed in order to not to spread the changes of local function values to other intervals. It

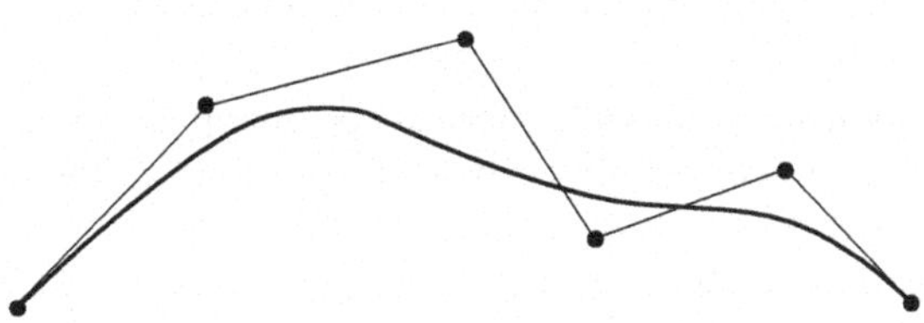

Fig. 5.7 Uniform cubic B-spline.

can also be used as the interpolation between plane curves determined by the parametric equation so that each parameter can be independent of the interpolation equation. Cohen and Zhuang [15] proposed a B-spline based curve representation and matching method.

5.2.3 Polygonal Approximation

Polygonal approximation approximates the shape of an edge by using polygon segments. Using the minimum error, minimum perimeter polygon, minimum internal area of a polygon, or an external area of the smallest polygon can provide the approximation criteria. In these errors, the most commonly used measure is the largest error and the integral square error. The most commonly used method is the split and merge method proposed by Pavlidis [16]. In this method, the curve divided is represented by the number of line segments until the error can be accepted, while there maybe mergence between the split lines. If the error between the merged line and the original curve is not beyond the maximum error allowed, the line is merged. Pavlidis [17] used the square and the partial derivative of error function to guide Newton descent method to search for the best breakpoint. Wu and Leou [18] proposed a different criterion to obtain the polygon approximation. The polygon approximation criteria they used are the largest internal area, the smallest external area, and the minimum area deviation. Bengtsson and Eklundh [19] proposed a hierarchical polygon approximation method. The split and combined method is often used in polygon approximation while the scale space method is often used to track feature points on the curve. The feature that does not change with scale is the most stable shape feature. Witkin [20] used polynomial approximation to estimate the tangent direction of points on an edge, thus generating multi-scale representation of a curve. Chung and Tsai [21] developed a polygonal approximation method based on the Hopfield neural network. This method defined polygonal approximation as a minimization problem of a neural network energy function. Chung's goal was to minimize the arc and chord deviation between the curves and the polygons.

5.2.4 Feature Extraction Based on Scale Space

Feature extraction based on scale space is one of popular methods for feature extraction. The most commonly used scale spaces are Gaussian scale space, wavelet scale space, and shape scale space. The method which is based on Gaussian scale space by high lighting the target was proposed by Witkin [20]. Tracking the location of feature points at different scales gives the simplified form of the shape. The points that still exist in the simplified representation are considered to be a significant feature of the target. Babaud et al. [22] proved that Gaussian kernel is the only linear kernel, which has very good characteristics of retaining the intrinsic features of points. When the scale increases, that is, the filter bandwidth increases, the intrinsic characteristics of those points still exist. Gaussian filter is the only filter with this feature. Asada and Brady [23] proposed a new method called the curvature graph. After the profile passes through the Gaussian filter with different bandwidths, it can gain the multiscale representation of the edge shape. Curvature graph method then calculates the curvature at different scales to obtain the curvature map. Mokhtarian and Mackworth [24] applied the scale space method in shape descriptors. Along the outline of the shape, smooth contours using the Gaussian core with different bandwidths are used to calculate the curvature. Curvature function is used as a multishape descriptor in the scale space image. Curvature function has translation, rotation and scale invariance. The concept of multi-scale is also proposed in morphology. Simplified method based on morphological is divided into two categories. One category is morphological decomposition and the other is morphological refinement. Chen and Yan [25] performed various operations on images using variable-size structure of the primitives. Anelli et al. [26] used the genetic algorithm, and attempted to solve the problem of selecting the structure primitives. Laganiere [27] successfully extracted corners using form decomposition. Moisan [28] proposed affine morphological scale space for simplifying shapes. Reinhardt and Higgins [29] compared the difference between shape decomposition and refinement. Relative to four different cost functions, shape decomposition is four times more efficient than shape refinement. The wavelet scale space method and Gaussian scale space method have the same principle: filter curve with different scales. The difference is that wavelet scale space is not linear scale space. Wavelet scale space cannot guarantee causality and produces strange corners. This is the reason it is not widely used.

5.2.5 Representation of Space Curves Based on Various Invariant

Fourier descriptors

Fourier descriptors are the classic method of describing shape. Zhan and Roskies [30] gave a detailed definition of Fourier descriptors and Persoon and Fu [31] have improved it. Fourier descriptors are a function, which first represents shape boundary by using a cumulative angular function. The cumulative angular function is performed by Fourier transformation and the coefficients can be calculated to describe the shape. The coefficients are Fourier descriptors. Under certain conditions, it will have displacement, rotation, size, and starting point invariance. Zahn used the shape boundary representation with tangent angle and arc length. The boundary rotates in a clockwise direction and generates a rotation angle relative to the starting point. After Fourier transformation, the local information of the shape is assigned to all the factors which do not exist in the frequency domain. The tangent angle and arc length in the method maybe disturbed by noise. It is difficult to determine the scope of noise of the tangent angle. After Fourier transformation of the boundary function, the results of the factors are used to describe the shape. Because the arc length is standardized, the description of the shape invariance for changes is in proportion. The shape description for the position change is also invariant. The rotation of the object can cause phase changes in the Fourier transformation. However, the coefficient magnitude of the Fourier transform of this method can guarantee rotation invariance. Fourier descriptors can encode, reconstruct, and classify a 2D curve. Its main advantages are that it is easy to implement and it is based on the mature theory of Fourier analysis. Its drawback is that the Fourier transformation does not provide local shape information and the angle cumulative function is very sensitive to noise.

Wavelet descriptor

Many computer vision applications often use multi-resolution analysis methods in order to improve accuracy and decrease noise. In the shape wavelet representation method, the global in formation of the shape is given in the coarse scale and the local information is given in the fine scale. Wavelet transformation provides a multi-resolution representation, so the function of matching or identification can be flexible to adjust according to the input images and the targets. The biggest drawback of wavelet transform is that it depends on the starting point of the target curve. The wavelet representation of the same object with two different samples maybe very different because of the difference in starting points. In pattern recognition applications, the starting point may cause serious problems, but in technical or other literature this issue is not explained. Chuang and Kuo [32] assumed that the input image has been corrected. Li and Kuo [33] gained the starting point using the centroid of a simple function of the minimized amplitude of the curve. Tieng and Boles [34] used the zero crossing point of the wavelet coefficients to match the model with the unknown object. They used redundant wavelet transform, namely, nondecimal wavelet transform to overcome the dependence on the starting point. The nondecimal representation of the wavelet requires a large amount of computations and the number of coefficients are very large, so nondecimal wavelet shape matching is very slow. Chen and Tien stated [35] the shape was transformed to polar coordinate system firstly. Next, extraction of the Fourier coefficients by Fourier transformation and extracting the wavelet coefficients from the amplitude of the Fourier coefficients as features for classification. Yang and Lee [36] introduced a method to determine the starting point, thus ensuring the wavelet transformation is independent of the starting point constraints.

5.3 Repair Method Based on Matching Fracture Lines

In this section, basic principles, extracting fracture line, special contour noise elimination, matching of fragments and fragments assembly technologies are discussed.

5.3.1 Basic Principles

The repair method in practice has the issue of different fragments with thickness inconsistent. This issue can be taken as a rigid matching and assembly for fragments based on complex curve and surface. This problem can be resolved with three focus areas: (1) the shape descriptor defined by geometry features (contour line, cross line, curvature user, torsion, length, angle, and direction); (2) the matching algorithm based on the representation of model; (3) the smooth and complete assembly between two objects [37].

Ideal fragmentation can be defined as follows: when a broken object that has a smooth surface and a thickness of 0, then the surface is split into two or more parts. Their boundaries are usually irregular curves and we define the following notations for easy description:

Φ denotes the complete object; ϕ_1, ϕ_2, ..., ϕ_n denote the ideal fragments; f_1, f_2, ..., f_n denote the fragments' feature set, $f_i(i = 1, ..., n)$ is an ordered structure composed by discrete geometry features (string structure), φ_1, φ_2, ..., φ_m represent the actual model of fragments, with corresponding features f'_1, f'_2, ..., f'_n; Θ represents fully or partially matched model.

Their relationship can be expressed as follows: if ϕ_i, ϕ_j are two parts adjacent on Φ, then they must be complementary matched. In other words, f_i, f_j are partially matched; if f'_i, f'_j are partially matched, then φ_i, φ_j are not always complementary matched. Therefore, it is necessary to introduce other constraint mechanisms for automatic recovery of broken objects.

The condition whether two fragments can be matched or not is defined as

$$M(\varphi_i, \varphi_j) = \begin{cases} m(f'_i, f'_j, T) = \text{TRUE} \\ m(f'_i, f'_j, T) = \text{FALSE} \end{cases}. \tag{5.6}$$

If $M(\varphi_i, \varphi_j)$ is positive it means φ_i, φ_j matched each other, otherwise it cannot be matched.

After a successfully match, we need to assembly φ_i, φ_j. By iteration of the process, we finally obtain the recovered model Θ.

In the actual process of virtual recovery, it is not enough to repair the model by matching and merging. The process discussed above should be done under the following assumptions:

(1) Two fragments ϕ_i, ϕ_j should be broken away from Φ.

(2) f_i, f_j should be extracted from φ_i, φ_j and with no noise.

(3) The boundary of φ_i, φ_j should be complete or without deformation.

The realization of computer-aided recovery includes: data capture, 3D object modeling and feature extraction, complementary shape matching, reassembly, and model repair. The process is shown in Fig. 5.8.

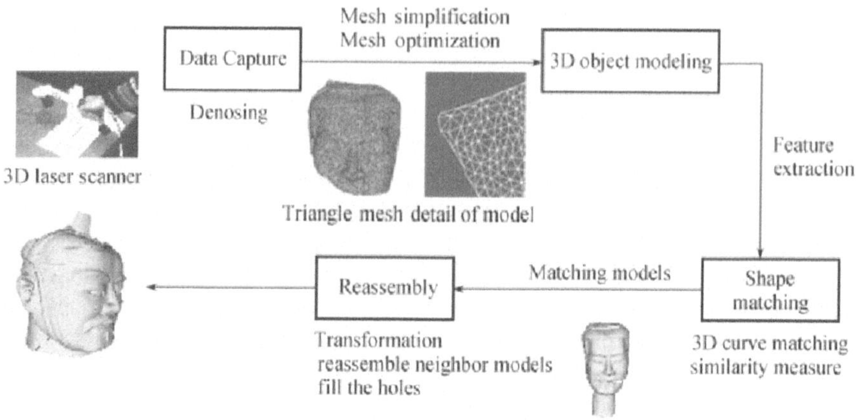

Fig. 5.8 Virtual recovery process of broken objects.

5.3.2 Methods of Extracting Fracture Line of Artifact

Method of boundaries extraction based on triangle meshes

For each vertex P and triangle mesh T of the 3D model, $U_P = \{T|P \in T\}$ denotes the sets of triangle meshes and $V_P = \{Q|\exists T, P \in T\&Q \in T\}$ denotes the adjacent vertices sets of vertex P. It is easy to conclude the following relationship between U_P and V_P:

(1) If Q $\in T$, and Q $\in V_P$, then there is $T \in U_P$.

(2) There are only two cases for point(s) in V_P: belongs to an element in the U_P, or belongs to two elements in the U_P.

According to the relationships, V_P might have two cases: all elements in V_P belong to two elements in U_P; at least one element in V_P belongs to one element in U_P. Both of these cases exactly fit into the two scenarios of point P on the curved surface: interior and boundary points. As shown in Fig. 5.9, $U_A = \{\Delta AGH, \Delta AHI, \Delta AIB\}, V_A = \{G, H, I, B\}$. As G and B only belong to an element of $U_A(\Delta AGH$ and $\Delta AIB)$ respectively, A is a boundary point. $U_H = \{\Delta AGH, \Delta FGH, \Delta EFH, \Delta EJH, \Delta IJH, \Delta HIA\}, V_H = \{A, G, F, E, J, I\}$. As any point in V_H belong to two elements in U_H, H is an interior point.

Based on the above relationship(s) of points on a curved surface, a search occurs and results of the set of boundary points of the curved surface are produced. In practice, however, the boundary points are a small proportion of all points in the curved surface, therefore it is not necessary to check all points.

The following facts also exist: if P is a boundary point, then the points in V_P only belong to one element; if U_P is also a boundary point, and moreover, it is the boundary points adjacent to P. It can get the boundary points which are adjacent to the current check point. The best way to find out the border of a curved surface is to use the following steps. Perform a search and get one boundary point. Obtain the new boundary point based on the known boundary point, and so forth until the end point is reach for the first boundary point, and all these boundary points are arranged sequentially. Such as point A in the above Fig. 5.9, while checking points G and B. Both G and B are adjacent to the boundary point A. While checking point G, point F is the adjacent boundary point. Therefore, the points which need to be checked are greatly reduced and performance is improved.

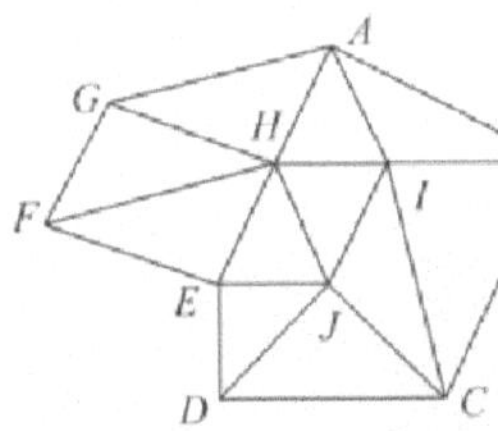

Fig. 5.9 Inner-points and boundary points

If only there is one boundary edge on the curved surface, the above mentioned method can produce it directly. However, if there are many boundary edges on the curved surface, we need to check all points on the curved surface. The above method does not increase performance, but the advantage is that all the boundary points are ordered so there is no need to perform sorting. One situation that one needs to notice is that if two curved surfaces are connected by one point or two holes on the curved surface are separated by a point, exceptions will happen using the above method. In Fig. 5.9, if you remove ΔAHI and ΔIJC, except for the outer with thickness inconsistent boundary edge, it might extract a boundary edge $AHICJIA$, rather than $AHIA$ and $IJCI$. This case would require special handling.

Contour extraction in regards to thickness

The major consideration of the above-mentioned method is that the artifact is thin without fracture surface. Other considerations are to extract and match the contours of each model based on the contour lines and stitching the successful matching contour model to achieve the virtual restoration purposes. In practice, however, many objects have a layer of thickness. Using a three-dimensional input device, the discrete geometric data of a three-dimensional object shape with thickness is captured. It is possible to scan data of the fracture surface, so some processing should be done to detect feature curve.

In practice, some of the fracture surfaces will be captured. Specific models will occur the following cases: If the fracture surface has not been scanned, the outer curve of the object model is the contour, named the outer contour. If the fracture surface is scanned, there are two cases—one is formed by the outer contour line, another is formed by the inside edge of the object model consisting of characteristic curves which is named curve contour. The greater the curvature is, the more the curve changes.

If the 3D model of fragment is with fracture surface after data capture, the boundary curve of model (outer curve) is not taken as the feature curve to achieve fragments match. The research of this section assumes that the surface of the objects has partly or totally fracture surfaces. The purpose is to correctly extract the characteristic contour lines of the triangle mesh surfaces (might be the inner contour, might be the outer contour, also parts of the inner contour, and parts of the contour). An example is shown in Fig. 5.10.

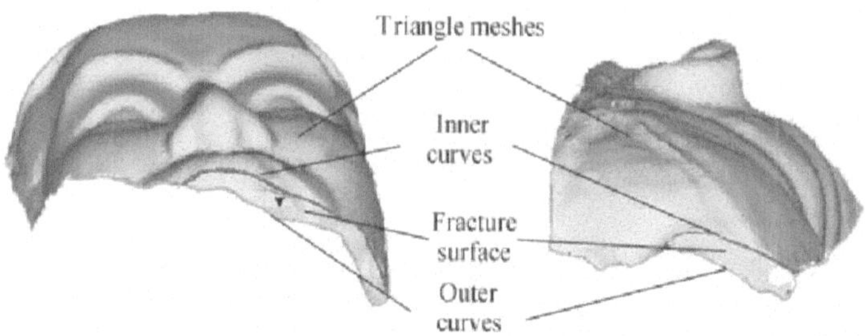

Fig. 5.10 Contour extraction in different conditions.

This project uses the combination of edges and surfaces methodology. It also uses the normal vector distribution of vertices to construct a function for correctly extracting the rigid object's contour lines (the inner contour):

Calculate the angle between normal vectors

Figure 5.11 calculates the relationship of the edges and its adjacent triangles, where u and v are normal vectors separately

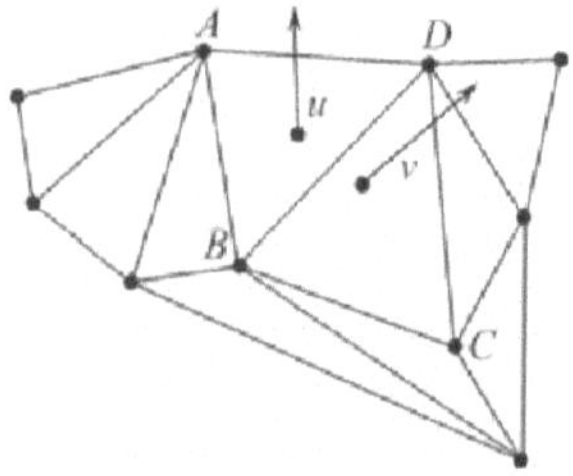

Fig. 5.11 Angle of normal vector between two adjacent triangle meshes.

The triangle ABD of normal vector $n_1 = AB \times BD$, The triangle BCD of normal vector $n_2 = DB \times BC$, based on the vector inner product to get

$$n_1 \cdot n_2 = |n_1||n_2| \cos < n_1, n_2 > .$$

Inner contour extraction algorithm

If the object model contains a fracture surface, it is very important to understand the contour matching methodology. It will be difficult on the final matching and stitching procedures if the analysis is based only on the outer boundary lines. Therefore, this paper will discuss the formation and nature of the contour lines of object models. A defined method to extract the contours will be explained based on boundary lines. If the fracture surface exists, then there is a point of intersection between inside and outside contours of the object model. The intersection be taken as a seed point for inner contour. In Fig.5.12, the contour consisting of A, B, C, D, E, A is the outer contour, and the contour consisting of A, F, G, C, D, E, A is the inner contour. The contour consisting of C, D, E, A is the overlapping contour of inner and the outer contour. The region consisting of A, B, C, G, F, A is the fracture surface. The region consisting of A, F, G, C, D, E, A is surface of the model. On the contour consisting of A, F, G, C, the angle of the normal vectors correspondence to neighbor triangle meshes is usually greater than angle of the normal vectors correspondence to other neighbor triangle meshes.

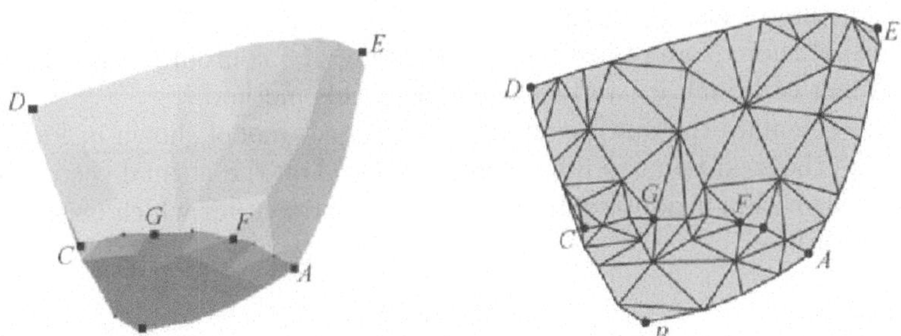

Fig. 5.12 Inner and outer contours of fracture surface.

Based on the above idea, the seed-point search algorithm is shown as follows:

Step1: Calculate all the points in outer contour for its adjacent edges, and then obtain the adjacent triangles normal vector angle sorting by descending order.

Step2: Calculate the 2-nearest neighbor vertices, whose angle is greater than a certain threshold.

Step3: Calculate each set of points adjacent to each side of the triangle normal vector angle.

Step4: If the angle is greater than a certain threshold, the edge is taken as the candidate seed edge.

Step5: In candidate seed edges, if there is a common point, then the common point is used as the seed point.

While applying this algorithm the result can be one or more seed points. This condition can serve as the terminal condition for the characteristic curved line extracting algorithm. In the triangle meshes model, the characteristic lines exist between intersections surfaces. Both the triangle's edges and characteristic line are in the same direction. At this point, the triangle normal vector angle which is adjacent to the characteristic line is greater than the triangle normal vector angle which is adjacent to the flat areas. This forms a supplementary angle between triangle surfaces. When the normal vector angle is greater than the value set by a user, it can be identified as the two vertices of the edge feature points, the edge of the characteristic line.

The characteristic curve extraction algorithm described as follows:

(1) The seed point as the current point.

(2) Calculate the set of points adjacent to the current point. Calculate the adjacent edges of adjacent triangles normal vector angle.

(3) If the angle is greater than a certain threshold, the edge is added to the list of characteristics.

(4) The adjacent point of the current point is known as the current point.

(5) If the current point is the seed points or boundary points then end the algorithm or else go to (2).

Thus, if there is an object model consisting of a contour within the inner edge (inner contour), it can be extracted by this method.

First calculate the outer contour of the object model shown in Fig. 5.13. Calculate the seed point in inner contour. Based on the normal vector, inner contour algorithm is adopted to extract the inner contour which exists in the fracture surface.

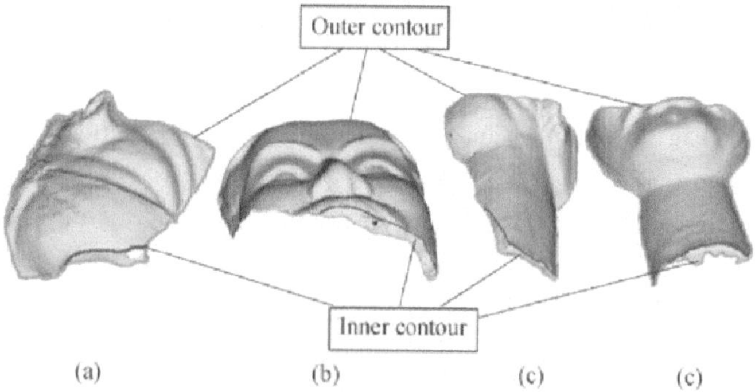

Fig. 5.13 Inner and outer contour extraction results for fracture surface.

5.3.3 Special Contour Noise Elimination

The filtering stage is used to observe the processing of the extraction results of the contours and to achieve contours smooth. Filtering provides two purposes. The first is to filter out irregular curves, which are due to artifacts of the excavation, digital process errors, fragments of many years of cultural material erosion, weathering and impact. For this purpose, we must filter out those high frequency parts of the curve, because they are the largest of these adverse factors, as shown in Fig. 5.14. Second, the curve filter is used to reduce the complexity of the curve. This makes it possible to match quicker and to identify similar segments of the curve. The curve can be considered a simple one-dimensional signal. The larger part of the curve of the mutant is the high frequency signals. A filter can reduce the high frequency components to reduce the error part of the curve.

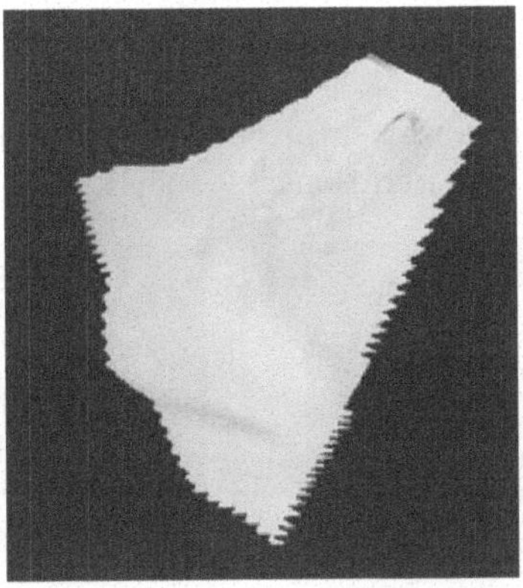

Fig. 5.14 Edge of a digital surface.

A Gaussian function can constitute a time-domain and frequency domain. It has a smooth performance of the low-pass filter [38], three-dimensional curves for each direction vector convolution, and generates a discrete Gaussian function, which constructs a low-pass filter.

The contours of the filtered curve are expressed as $L'(t,\sigma)$. The original contour curve is expressed as $L(x(n),y(n),z(n))$, then

$$L'(t,\sigma) = L(x(t),y(t),z(t)) \otimes g(t,\sigma) = (X(t,\sigma),Y(t,\sigma),z(t,\sigma)),$$

where $\otimes$ is a convolution:

$$\begin{cases} X(t,\sigma) = x(t) \otimes g(t,\sigma) \\ Y(t,\sigma) = y(t) \otimes g(t,\sigma) \\ Z(t,\sigma) = z(t) \otimes g(t,\sigma) \end{cases} . \tag{5.7}$$

Its impulse response is

$$g(t) = \frac{1}{\sigma\sqrt{2\pi}} e^{-\frac{t^2}{2\sigma^2}}, \qquad -\infty < t < \infty, \sigma > 0. \tag{5.8}$$

Gaussian distribution parameter σ determines the width of Gaussian filters. When σ is a large value, high frequency signals that needs to be filter out are less.

We use the following iterative processes:

First, let P as a curve passes through multiple vertices $p_0, \ldots, p_{n-1}$ that represent a closed polygon. Initialization data through the parameters t_i (the arc length between p_0 and p_i in polygon) to represents each point p_i.

Then, repeat as follows: compute a continuous curve $u(t)$ when $t = t_i, u(t) = p_i$. The Gaussian low-pass filter used in $u(t)$, and you will have a smooth curve $v(t)$. Each t_i will be redefined as $v(t)$, which is the arc length between $t = t_0$ and $t = t_i$. In the next iteration, the curve $u(t)$ will be recalculated by using the original point p_i and the modified parameters t_i and so forth.

Usually after a few iterations, the curve will tend to be consistent. Figure 5.15 is the result after two iterations.

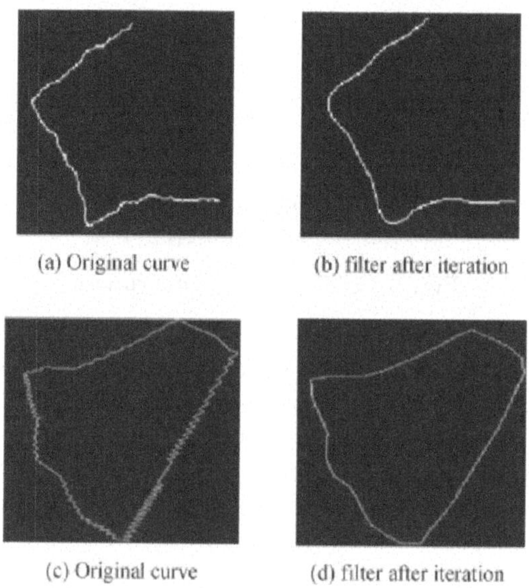

Fig. 5.15 Contour curve filter result.

5.3.4 Matching of Fragments

Fast matching technique of space curves base on Fourier transformation

After contour curves are extracted, the point on the boundary of a region has been identified. We can extract information from these points. This information can be used to identify the shape of a different area. If a boundary contour has M points that can be used, we can treat this area as complex plane, vertical axis is the imaginary axis, and abscissa is the real axis.

Assume there is a plane xy with a boundary that consists of N points; each point can be represented by coordinate (x_k, y_k). From any point (x_0, y_0), traverse the entire boundary counter-clockwise, and then obtain such coordinates $(x_0, y_0), (x_1, y_1), \ldots, (x_{N-1}, y_{N-1})$.

These coordinates can be represented in the form $x(k) = x_k, y(k) = y_k$. The boundary can be represented by $S(k) = [x(k), y(k)], k = 0, 1, 2, \ldots, N-1$, each coordinate can be treated as plural, as follows:

$$s(k) = x(k) + \mathrm{j}y(k), \quad k = 0, 1, 2, \ldots, N-1. \tag{5.9}$$

In other words, we treated x-axis and y-axis as a plural sequence of the real-axis and imaginary-axis. We give a new explanation to the coordinate, but the characteristic of boundary do not change.

This explanation has obvious advantages that it makes a two-dimensional problem into a one-dimensional problem. The discrete Fourier transformation of $s(k)$ can be written as follows:

$$a(u) = \frac{1}{N}\sum_{k=0}^{N-1} s(k)\exp\left(-\frac{\mathrm{j}2\pi uk}{N}\right), \quad u = 0, 1, 2, \ldots, N-1. \tag{5.10}$$

We named the Complex Coefficient $a(u)$ as the boundary's Fourier Descriptors (FDs). Do inverse Fourier transform to $a(u)$, we can reconstruct $s(k)$:

$$s(k) = \sum_{u=0}^{N-1} a(u)\exp\left(\frac{\mathrm{j}2\pi uk}{N}\right), \quad k = 0, 1, 2, \ldots, N-1. \tag{5.11}$$

Suppose we use the first M Fourier coefficients, rather than all Fourier coefficients, which means $a(u)$ takes 0 when $u > M-1$ in the equation above. Thus we obtain the approximate value of $s(k)$:

$$\hat{s}(k) = \sum_{u=0}^{M-1} a(u)\exp\left(\frac{\mathrm{j}2\pi uk}{N}\right), \quad k = 0, 1, 2, \ldots, N-1. \tag{5.12}$$

Although we just take the first M coefficients to calculate weights of $\hat{s}(k)$, k is still from 0 to $N-1$, which means the approximate boundary contains the same number of points, but not all the items are used to reconstruct each point. M is usually chosen as an integer power of 2 when there are a large number of points on the boundary, thus we can accelerate the calculation speed of boundary descriptor by FFT. Because the DFT is a reversible linear transformation, there can be no information lost or gain during this process. For the frequency domain representation of shape, simple processing can avoid the dependence on location, size, and direction. When given an arbitrary FD, a number of steps can make it normalized regardless of the original shape's size, location, and direction.

Conclusions can be draw directly from nature of DFT about issues of normalization. For instance, to change the size of the contour as long as the FD component is multiplied by a constant. As the Fourier transformation is linear, its inverse transform will be multiplied by the same constant. In another example, make a rotation angle to the contour as long as each coordinate is multiplied by $\exp(j\theta)$. Due to the nature of DFT, every time it makes a rotation angle θ in space, the same happens in the frequency domain. By nature of DFT the movement of the starting point outline, produces a finite numbers of sequences in space that actually represent a period of periodic function. The coefficient of DFT is the coefficient of periodic function in form of Fourier expression. When the contour point starts moving in space, it is equivalent to multiplying the kth frequency coefficient in the frequency domain. In fact, it is results are by the nature of translation of Fourier transformation. When T changes from 0 to 2π, the starting point will traverse the entire contour.

Given an arbitrary FD and a series of steps of the normalization, we can obtain a standard size, orientation and starting point of the contour.

In actual implementation we should take into account the following questions: First, nonuniform sampling will bring trouble in matching. Therefore, we take a measure of uniform spaced sampling instead of traditional sampling. Second, the algorithm of FFT requires the array length to be an integer power of 2. Thus before using FFT, we should adjust the length of expression to the smallest integer power of 2 but longer than then length of expression.

In fact, the contour extracted from the sample image will be treated as input for shape analysis algorithms. This contour's perimeter is approximately equal to the actual contour's perimeter. If the original data has high sampling density, the sequence will be the extreme approximation of original data.

We consider that a contour line is formed by a sequence of points. A space contour can be represented as follows:

$$P = (p_1, p_2, \ldots, p_n).$$

p_i expresses the vector make-up of the number i point on the contour and centroid of contour.

RMS (root mean square) is calculated by the least square method. We define $P = (p_1, p_2, \ldots, p_n)$ and $Q = (q_1, q_2, \ldots, q_n)$ for two space contour curves. Suppose P after translation, and the centroid $\left(\frac{1}{n}\sum_{i=1}^{n} p_i\right)$ coincides with the origin. Perform the same translation to Q. Then we can define $d(P,Q,R,a)$ as follows:

$$d(P,Q,R,a) = \sqrt{\frac{1}{n}\sum_{i=1}^{n}||Rp_i + a - q_i||^2}, \tag{5.13}$$

where R is the rotation matrix, a is the translation vector, $\|x\|$ represent the length of vector x. The RMS $d_{rms}(P,Q)$ between P and Q can be defined as

$$d_{rms}(P,Q) = \min_{R,a} d(P,Q,R,a).$$

We define the problem of searching the contour as follows.

Input: a template contour $P = (p_1, p_2, \ldots, p_m)$, a real number $\delta > 0$, a set of contour $QS = \{Q^1, Q^2, ..., Q^N\}$.

Output: Q^j, for each Q^j, contains at least one sub-section that makes $d_{rms}(P, Q^j_{i,i+m-1}) \leqslant \delta$.

$Q_{i,j}$ represents a subsection $(q_i, q_{i+1}, ..., q_j)$ of contour $Q = (q_1, q_2, ..., q_n)$

The searching algorithm of the subsection can use the original algorithm by calculate all RMS of $Q^j_{i,i+m-1}$, which takes time complexity of $O(Nmn)$, with n represents the length of Q^j.

Using the algorithm above, we obtain the result shown in Fig. 5.16. During our research, we prove that the smaller distance between two curves, the distance of the hash vectors is smaller. Based on Fourier transformation on discrete contour points, we adopt the hash technique to search matching curve sections proved to be fast and stable.

Matching connection points of 3D polygonal arcs

The problem of polygonal arcs matching is one of the basic issues in computer vision, image analysis and pattern recognition. This problem can be expressed as: for any two polygonal arcs, the matching problem is to find their longest common subpolygonal arc, in other words, to determine the part they have in a common shape.

The representation and matching method of polygonal arcs is based on the analysis of the polygonal arc's geometry shape. We introduce the concept of a connection point. At the same time, by establishing local Cartesian coordinates on a connection point, we can obtain each point's spherical coordinates. Because rotation and translation is invariant under this condition, we use such a coordinate to represent polygonal arcs. This coordinate can also be used for a feature set of polygonal arcs, which maintains geometry and topology. Thus, the matching of 3D polygonal arcs turns into matching of a 1D value string, to accelerate the matching process.

For two given polygonal arcs C and D, if the local Cartesian coordinates have already been established and the parameters have been calculated, C and D can be represented by such a feature set:

$$\Gamma_C = \{S_0, S_1, \ldots, S_n\}, \quad \Gamma_D = \{T_0, T_1, \ldots, T_m\},$$

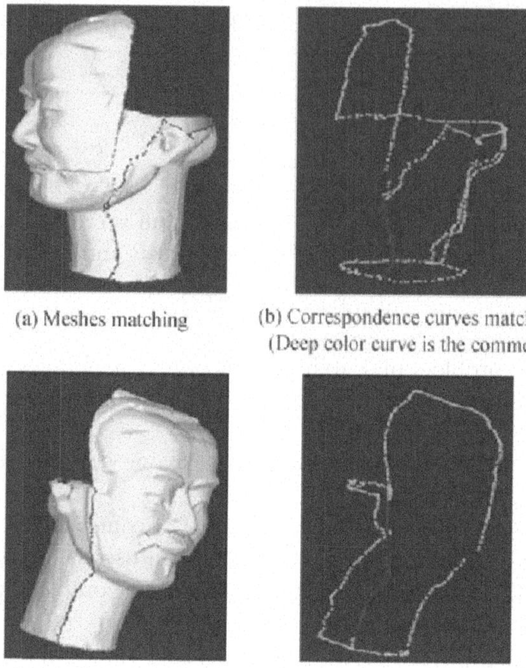

(a) Meshes matching
(b) Correspondence curves matching (Deep color curve is the common)
(c) Meshes matching
(d) Correspondence curves matching (Deep color curve is the common)

Fig. 5.16 Matching between neighbor contours.

where $S_0, S_1, \ldots, S_n, T_0, T_1, \ldots, T_m$ describe connection points for two polygonal arcs respectively.

We can match these two connection points by comparing the component values of connection points S_i and T_j in Γ_C, Γ_D, only if each component has the same value. Otherwise, the matching fails. This shows that if one component is unequal the matching fails. Only three components satisfy the condition, we can get a matched result. But such condition is just ideal, actual data is usually not ideal. Therefore, tolerance should be considered into matching algorithm for robustness. For judging two conditions, we define two measurement functions:

$$\begin{cases} MSE_1(S_i, T_j) = (S_{i+k}^{(\lambda)} - T_{j+k}^{(\lambda)})^2, \\ MSE_2(S_i, T_j) = \dfrac{1}{l+1} \displaystyle\sum_{k=0}^{l} \sum_{\lambda=1}^{3} (S_{i+k}^{(\lambda)} - T_{j+k}^{(\lambda)})^2 \end{cases} \tag{5.14}$$

where $S_i^{(\lambda)}$ is the number λ component value of S_i, $T_j^{(\lambda)}$ is the number λ component value of T_j, $\lambda = 1, 2, 3$, $l = \min\{m, n\}$.

When $MSE_1(S_i, T_j)$ is bigger than a given threshold, the corresponding two compared polygonal arcs $S_{i+k}, T_{j+k}, k = 0, 1, \ldots, l$ cannot be matched.

Otherwise, the matching is a success.

As the matching of polygonal arcs is often according to the order of the connection point, different orders can cause different match results. Choose clockwise or counter-clockwise for two-dimensional to ensure the consistency of the match. For three-dimensional, we can use a twice matching process with order or reverse sequence on the feature set of polygonal arcs.

For a given two polygonal arcs matching, the calculation time complexity of local Cartesian coordinates is $O(n)$, the calculation time complexity of connection point's spherical coordinate is $O(n)$. Define n as the number of points on polygonal arc. If it is equal for two polygonal arcs, then the matching time complexity is $O(n^2)$. If one is n and another is m, the time complexity can be $O(n \times m)$. But if S_i and T_j are matched, then whether S and T are matched depends on whether S_{i+k} are $T_{j+k} (k = 0, 1, \ldots, l)$ matched $(i + k = (i + k) \bmod (n + 1), j + k = (j + k) \bmod (m + 1))$. In such condition, the matching time complexity can be linear.

The algorithm is as follows:

Input: given two polygonal arcs.

Output: matched connection point and transformation of rotation and translation.

Step1: For each connection point on each polygonal arc, establish local Cartesian coordinates

Step2: For each connection point, calculate its spherical and Cartesian coordinates corresponding to its local Cartesian coordinates.

Step3: Calculate matching measurement functions $MSE_1(S_i,T_j)$ and $MSE_2(S_i,\ T_j)$, then determine whether matched or not. If matched, then calculate transformation of rotation and translation.

For the boundary of fragments partially matching, do space transformation. Suppose there exists l matching items, and should sufficient two surfaces G^1 continuous after transformation. Thus such problem can be turned into a Bi-objective programming:

$$\begin{cases} \text{Min}: \sum_{i=1}^{l} |v_{1i} - v_{2i}| \\ \text{Min}: \sum_{i=1}^{l} (p_{1i} - p_{2i})^2 \\ s.t \begin{cases} M_1 A = M_2 \\ V_1 A = V_2 \\ A = A_T A_R \end{cases} \end{cases}, \tag{5.15}$$

where A is the transformation matrix of a spatial location from fragment 1 to fragment 2. A_T represents the translation matrix. A_R represents the rotation matrix. M_1 and M_2 represent the corresponding points on boundary which can be successful matched. V_1 and V_2 represent a corresponding sequence of a cross-cut vector on a boundary which can be successfully matched. Note that if the cross-cut vector of fragment 1 points to the external border, those of the fragment 2 should point to the opposite direction.

An object's surface can be captured by a three-dimensional scanner to generate the triangle mesh model correspondingly. After the pipeline of data is preprocessed, arc string matching and space transformation are performed. We give the successful matching result shown in Fig. 5.17 ((a) and (c) are the representation boundary of fractures and (b) and (d) are the result of matching).

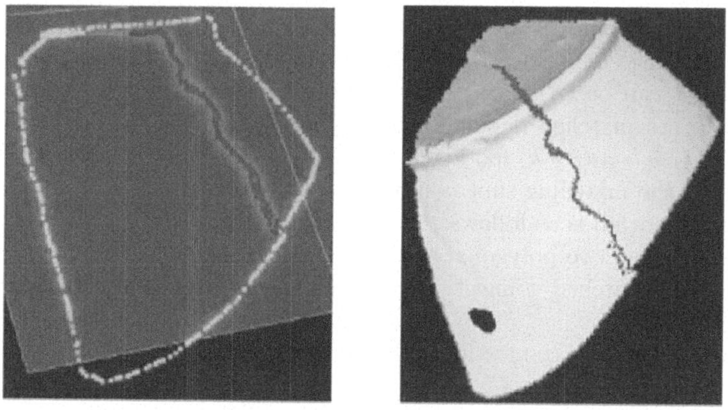

(a) Curves of fractures (b) Result of matching

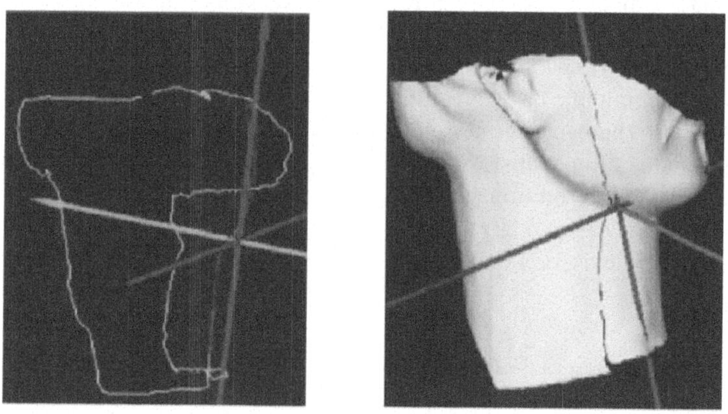

(a) Curves of fractures (b) Result of matching

Fig. 5.17 Complementary shape matching result.

5.3.5 Fragments Assembly

In general, recovery of cultural fractures is manual. When two pieces can be matched, they will be assembly and considered as a new one. When we find the two profile curves that closely match from a large number of fragment contour curves, we need to characterize the two contour curves corresponding to the fragments and join them together. The joined fractures will replace the two original fragments.

The curve sections can be unified and jointed together using the potential matching curve section in the two contour curves. The rigid body motion between two surfaces (rotation and translation) is used until the curve sections tend to overlap.

Establish a local coordinate system

To find the relationship between the two potential matched surfaces, we need to define the local coordinate system. The coordinate system is defined by the matching curve sections. Each surface has matching curve sections. A local coordinate system can be constructed for each surface respectively. Calculations of the rotation matrix and translation vectors between two local coordinate systems, such matrices and vectors can be used in the world coordinate system to matches the curve between two surfaces.

Take p_ip_j for example. Two points p_i, p_j on p_ip_j, a straight line $\overline{p_ip_j}$ connecting two points. Find the midpoint of the curve, labeled p_k, then p_ip_k and p_kp_j has an equal arc length. Obviously, there exists only one p_k (we assume p_k is not on $\overline{p_ip_j}$). Then, find a point o' on $\overline{p_ip_j}$ making $o'p_k$ and $o'p_j$ are perpendicular, of course, o' is unique. o' will be the origin of the local coordinate system. The vertical local coordinate system of the three basis vectors are defined as follows:

$$\begin{cases} e_1' = \dfrac{p_j - o'}{\|p_j - o'\|} \\ e_2' = \dfrac{p_k - o'}{\|p_k - o'\|} \\ e_3' = e_1' \times e_2' \end{cases}, \tag{5.16}$$

where $\|\ \ \|$ and $\times$ represent Euclidean norm and the cross product. These three vectors in the world coordinate system have unit length, and relative to the three-dimensional curve p_ip_j are rotation and translation invariant. The definition of these three vectors is based that p_k do not locate on $\overline{p_ip_j}$.

These three vectors in the old coordinate system are unit length, and relative to the three-dimensional curve $\overline{p_ip_j}$ are rotation and translation invariant, the definition $l^o = \|p_i - p_j\|$ is the Euclidean distance between p_i and p_j. Transform the scalar l^o in old coordinate system to the unit length in new coordinates to achieve the scale invariance, we choose them for an example:

$$e_1 = l^o e_1^o, e_2 = l^o e_2^o, e_3 = l^o e_3^o.$$

Use $\{o, e_1, e_2, e_3\}$ to form a new coordinate system. In this coordinate system, point p is expressed as

$$p = o + u_1e_1 + u_2e_2 + u_3e_3,$$

where $u=(u_1, u_2, u_3)$ is the coordinate in new system coordinates of point p.

Transformation of a space coordinate

Define the global and local coordinate system as follows:

$$\mathrm{I}: \{o, e_1, e_2, e_3\} \qquad \mathrm{II}: \{o', e_1', e_2', e_3'\}$$

The coordinate of e_j' in I is (x_j, y_j, z_j), $j = 1, 2, 3$. Because II is a Cartesian coordinate system, so $|e_j'| = 1 (j = 1, 2, 3)$ and $e_j' \perp e_i'$ when $i \neq j$. I is also Cartesian coordinate system, so the conditions above can be written as

$$x_j^2 + y_j^2 + z_j^2 = 1, \quad j = 1, 2, 3;$$
$$x_i x_j + y_i y_j + z_i z_j = 0, \quad i \neq j.$$

So the transition matrix from I to II can be defined

$$A = \begin{pmatrix} x_1 & x_2 & x_3 \\ y_1 & y_2 & y_3 \\ z_1 & z_2 & z_3 \end{pmatrix}. \tag{5.17}$$

The transition matrix from II to I can be defined by $A^{-1} = A'$.

Define the coordinate of o' in I is (x_0, y_0, z_0), and then the point coordinate transformation formula can be defined as follows:

$$\begin{pmatrix} x \\ y \\ z \end{pmatrix} = A \begin{pmatrix} x' \\ y' \\ z' \end{pmatrix} + \begin{pmatrix} x_0 \\ y_0 \\ z_0 \end{pmatrix}. \tag{5.18}$$

Merge of the surfaces

For different p_i, p_j, there can be an inconsistent local coordinate. Two surfaces can be merged into one only if their contour curves have potential matching curve section. Considering the matching curve section can be approximately taken as the boundary and shared by two broken objects, the two fragments then will be put into a same local coordinate system. According to each p_i, p_j, we can determine a local coordinate system. After calculation we can get the transformation formula between two coordinates, and then make the matching curve sections consistently in a same local coordinate system. Therefore, the rotation matrix and translation vector in this formula are what we need most.

In order to merge the two surfaces or curves, we need rotation and translation to make two surfaces glue in a world coordinate system coordinate, and also for the matching curve sections overlap.

Suppose two surfaces S_A, S_B, their local coordinate system are expressed as

$$\mathrm{I}_A: \{(o_A', e_{A1}', e_{A2}', e_{A3}')\} \qquad \mathrm{I}_B: \{(o_B', e_{B1}', e_{B2}', e_{B3}')\}$$

The point coordinate transformation formula between local coordinate system and world coordinate system is

$$A_A \begin{pmatrix} x'_A \\ y'_A \\ z'_A \end{pmatrix} + \begin{pmatrix} x_{A0} \\ y_{A0} \\ z_{A0} \end{pmatrix} = A_B \begin{pmatrix} x'_B \\ y'_B \\ z'_B \end{pmatrix} + \begin{pmatrix} x_{B0} \\ y_{B0} \\ z_{B0} \end{pmatrix}, \tag{5.19}$$

where A_A, A_B are the transition matrix from the coordinates of I_A, I_B to the world coordinate system. From the equation above, the point coordinate transformation in this relationship:

$$\begin{pmatrix} x'_A \\ y'_A \\ z'_A \end{pmatrix} = A_A^{-1} A_B \begin{pmatrix} x'_B \\ y'_B \\ z'_B \end{pmatrix} + A_A^{-1} \begin{pmatrix} x_{B0} - x_{A0} \\ y_{B0} - y_{A0} \\ z_{B0} - z_{A0} \end{pmatrix}. \tag{5.20}$$

Set the rotation matrix R and translation vector β:

$$R = A_A^{-1} A_B, \quad \beta = A_A^{-1} \begin{pmatrix} x_{B0} - x_{A0} \\ y_{B0} - y_{A0} \\ z_{B0} - z_{A0} \end{pmatrix}. \tag{5.21}$$

Then

$$\begin{pmatrix} x'_A \\ y'_A \\ z'_A \\ 1 \end{pmatrix} = \begin{pmatrix} r_{11} & r_{12} & r_{13} & \beta_1 \\ r_{21} & r_{22} & r_{23} & \beta_2 \\ r_{31} & r_{32} & r_{33} & \beta_3 \\ 0 & 0 & 0 & 1 \end{pmatrix} \begin{pmatrix} x'_B \\ y'_B \\ z' \\ 1 \end{pmatrix}. \tag{5.22}$$

Here the $r_{ij}(i, j = 1, 2, 3)$ is an element in R, $\beta_i(i = 1, 2, 3)$ is the number i component in β.

After calculation of the rotation matrix R and translation vector β, we merge the surface S_A, S_B, perform ing transformation on S_B in order to make the two curve sections match, as shown in Fig. 5.18.

It is sufficient to show and provide an observation while merging two surfaces. For curve S the merged contour curves will be considered as a new curve for next matching step. The matching between the two curves must be tight and without any gap.

The optimal curve matching depends on the strategy in the matching process. Considering the edges of fractures maybe lost, choose the longest matching curve sections that may consist of several small sections of the curve, or an outline of the curve (Fig. 5.19). Figure 5.20 gives some examples of neighbor fractures matching.

The new contour curve is merged with the condition of assuming the matching point error can be omitted. The error range is ε, which we defined

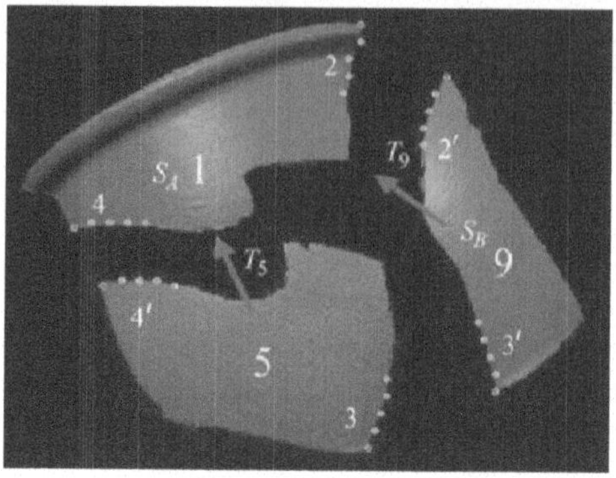

Fig. 5.18 The Motion of reassembled surfaces.

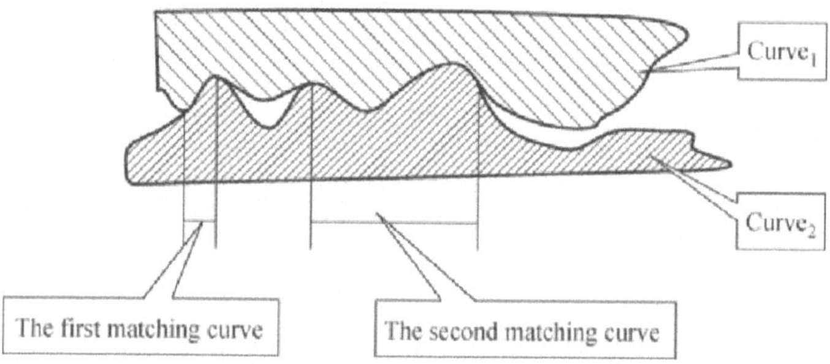

Fig. 5.19 Matching of curves.

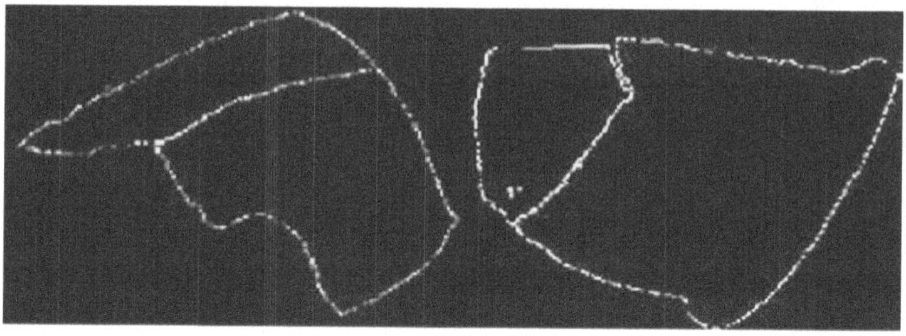

Fig. 5.20 Matching of fractures.

in the process of curve matching. Therefore, it is impossible that the error is greater than ε, otherwise the point cannot be the matching point in a contour curve. So we can get the assumption that the matching point error is absolutely less than the error range ε.

After joining the surfaces, the new fragment will replace the old one. For the original contour curves by merging them together, we can get the new contour curve of jointed fragments.

5.4 Repair Holes

During the processing of digital artifacts, we generally cannot obtain complete geometric information. It will have holes. This is caused by two reasons:

(1) The influence of the passage of time, soil erosion and human activities, forces the continued destruction of artifacts, resulting in their damage.

(2) During the digital capture process the existing equipment is restricted by work and the acquisition environment. This leads to the obtained three-dimensional data that is not complete. These holes not only affect the generation of visual effects, but also have important implications on the future application of three-dimensional data. Hole repair can be divided into three steps: (a) identify the hole of the cultural model; (b) insert the discrete points and triangulation; (c) optimize the model. Carr [39] used the RBF (radial basis function) to achieve surface reconstruction and hole repair based on scattered point cloud. Wang and Oliveira [40] proposed an automatic method of holes' identification. He achieved the hole repair using the moving least squares. Verdera et al. [41] proposed a method using the partial differential equations (PDE) to achieve hole repair. Pernot et al. [42] achieved hole repair by using minimum curvature flow to insert a new grid. Li et al. [43] used edge-based expansion to project the holes' boundary to the least-squares plane and then split them. Cheng et al. [44] achieved hole repair by using the method of moving least squares. Zhang et al. [45] achieved the algorithm based on anisotropic hole repair. The hole is repaired by splitting and then doing mesh subdivision. Wang et al. [46] first classified the holes, then used RBF (radial basis function) to achieve hole repair.

5.4.1 Hole Boundary's Projection and Internal Point's Insertion

For the hole boundary contour vertex set $Boundary = \{V_i = (x_i, y_i, z_i)|i = 0, 1, 2, ..., n-1\}$, the least squares plane needs to fit with these boundary vertices and project the holes' boundary onto this plane to get the projection polygon to determine the scope of the hole. The least squares plane is recorded as $s(O, normal)$, and O is the border center, $O = \frac{1}{n}\sum_{i=0}^{n-1} V_i$. The covariance matrix of the boundary vertices is $C = \sum_{i=0}^{n-1}(V_i - O)(V_i - O)^{\mathrm{T}}$. The eigenvalues are $\lambda_1, \lambda_2, \lambda_3$. It shows that normal is the eigenvector corresponding to the smallest eigenvalue. We can calculate the range of holes by projecting the vertices of the hole to this plane.

A series of points on the holes bordary are $p = \{p_1, p_2, \ldots, p_n\}$. We can get a polygon with these points as the boundary. The set of points q is used to store the inserted discrete points. Below are the steps to insert discrete points into the polygon [44].

Step 1: Clear the temporary target point set q. For the current boundary contour point p_i, its neighbors are p_{i-1}, p_{i+1}. Calculate the average length of two adjacent sides $L = (\overline{p_{i-1}p_i} + \overline{p_i p_{i+1}})/2$.

Step 2: Calculate internal angle a of two adjacent edges which are the edges of current point p_i. In order to avoid a deformity triangle, making the final triangle similar to an equilateral triangle, let $n = \lfloor a/60 \rfloor$, if n is equal to 0 go to Step 3. Then calculate $\beta = a/(n+1)$ and split the angle a to $n+1$ copy of β. With the intercepting point on corner point line by length L, we can get a candidate insertion point r, its coordinate formula is

$$r = \frac{p_{i+1} - p_i}{|p_{i+1} - p_i|} \times \begin{pmatrix} \cos n\beta & \sin n\beta \\ -\sin n\beta & \cos n\beta \end{pmatrix} \times l + p_i. \tag{5.23}$$

Step 3: Traverse each point q_i in the target set q. Calculate the distance between q_i and the current candidate insertion point r by $d_i = |q_i r|$. If $d_i \leqslant$ the threshold, merge q_i and r denoting $q_i = (q_i + r)/2$. If not, join candidate point r into target set of q.

Step 4: If there are more than 3 points in the point set of q, make the target set q as the new boundary contour point set. Find the new insertion point from Step 1. Repeat the above process till the number of points in q is less than or equal to 3.

Figure 5.21 is a discrete point set generated by this algorithm.

Fig. 5.21 Discrete point set inserted into the hole boundary.

5.4.2 Hole Repair Technique Based on Radial Basis Function

The hole boundary vertex and its k-adjacent vertex set is known as the *Hole Point*. The corresponding value for the *HolePoint* is $\{h_0, h_1, \ldots, h_{n-1}\}$. We can create function f by RBF (radial basis function) that for $\forall q_i$ there is a $f(q_i) = h_i$. Scattered points implicit surface equation can then be constructed.

Seminorm is used to measure a surface's energy and smoothness. The seminorm is defined as

$$\|f\|^2 = \int_{R^3} \frac{\partial f(x)}{\partial x^2} + \int_{R^3} \frac{\partial f(x)}{\partial y^2} + \int_{R^3} \frac{\partial f(x)}{\partial z^2} \\ +2\left(\frac{\partial^2 f(x)}{\partial x \partial y}\right)^2 + 2\left(\frac{\partial^2 f(x)}{\partial x \partial z}\right)^2 + 2\left(\frac{\partial^2 f(x)}{\partial y \partial z}\right)^2 \mathrm{d}x. \tag{5.24}$$

Seminorm is smaller then the surface is smoother. Duchon [47] pointed that the simple representation of the smoothest surface interpolation is

$$f^*(x) = p(x) + \sum_{i=1}^{N} \lambda_i |x - x_i|. \tag{5.25}$$

Radial basis function is defined as

$$f(q) = \sum_{i=1}^{k} \overline{\omega}_i \phi(\|q, q_i\|) + \pi(q), \tag{5.26}$$

where $\|q, q_i\|$ represents the Euclidean distance between two points, $\overline{\omega}_i$ is weight; ϕ is the basis function; π is a polynomial function $\pi(q_i) = \pi_0 + \sum_{j=0}^{k-1} \pi_i q_i^{(j)}$, it is divided into constant and linear combination of vectors, $q_i^{(j)}$ is the jth component of vector q_i. Commonly a basis functions have the following forms:

$$\begin{aligned} \phi(r) &= r; \\ \phi(r) &= r^3; \\ \phi(r) &= r^2 \log(r); \\ \phi(r) &= \exp(-cr^2). \end{aligned} \tag{5.27}$$

We can see from the definition of implicit surfaces that if $f(q_i) = 0$, q_i is on the surface, else if $f(q_i) \neq 0$, q_i is not on the surface. Further analysis shows: if $f(q_i) > 0$, q_i is in the external surface; if $f(q_i) < 0$, q_i is in the internal surface, so the *HolePoint* in the vertex set meets $f(q_i) = 0$.

To avoid presenting a trivial solution of RBF, we should insert points that $f(q_i) \neq 0$. So we can insert the points in the vertex set *HolePoint* that the distance of each vertex along the normal direction is d_i. Therefore, the input of the radial basis functions can be divided into two parts:

$$f(q_i) = 0 \,(i = 0, 1, \ldots, n-1) \text{ and } f(q_i) = d_i \,(i = n, \ldots, N).$$

With the orthogonal constraints:

$$\sum_i \omega_i = \sum_i \omega_i \pi_1 = \ldots \sum_i \omega_i \pi_n = 0, \tag{5.28}$$

we can get linear equations:

$$Ax = b, \tag{5.29}$$

where $A = \begin{bmatrix} \phi_{ij} & P^{\mathrm{T}} \\ P & 0 \end{bmatrix}$, ϕ is n-matrix, $\phi_{ij} = \phi(\|p_i, p_j\|)$, $x = [\overline{\omega}_1, \overline{\omega}_2, \ldots, \overline{\omega}_1,$ $\pi_1, \pi_2, \ldots \pi_n, \pi_0]^{\mathrm{T}}$, $b = [h_1, h_2, \ldots, h_k, 0, 0, \ldots 0]^{\mathrm{T}}$.

Specific form of equations is as follows:

$$\begin{pmatrix} \varphi_{11} & \cdots & \varphi_{1N} & 1 & x_1 & y_1 & z_1 \\ \vdots & \ddots & \vdots & \vdots & \vdots & \vdots & \vdots \\ \varphi_{N1} & \cdots & \varphi_{NN} & 1 & x_N & y_N & z_N \\ 1 & \cdots & 1 & 0 & 0 & 0 & 0 \\ x_1 & \cdots & x_N & 0 & 0 & 0 & 0 \\ y_1 & \cdots & y_N & 0 & 0 & 0 & 0 \\ z_1 & \cdots & z_N & 0 & 0 & 0 & 0 \end{pmatrix} \begin{pmatrix} \overline{\omega}_1 \\ \vdots \\ \overline{\omega}_N \\ \pi_0 \\ \pi_1 \\ \pi_2 \\ \pi_3 \end{pmatrix} = \begin{pmatrix} h_1 \\ \vdots \\ h_n \\ 0 \\ 0 \\ 0 \\ 0 \end{pmatrix}. \tag{5.30}$$

The concrete steps of hole repair are as follows:

Step1 : Let the hole boundary vertex, its k-nearest neighbor vertex set the *HolePoint*, and the points whose distance is d_i along each vertex's normal as the input of the radial basis functions. Calculate the radial basis function implicit equation of hole area.

Step2 : With the radial basis functions, use the gradient descent to adjust the new inserted vertices into the new constructed implicit surface, and remain the topological relation of inserted vertices, the result is shown in Fig. 5.22.

(a) Meshes with hole (b) Hole-filling (c) Meshes with hole (d) Hole-filling

Fig. 5.22 Hole-filling results.

5.4.3 Technique of Hole Repair Based on Moving Least Square Method

Moving Least Square (MLS) was first introduced in early 1980s by Lancaster, and mostly applied to surface and curve fitting. This allows us to take the advantage of the calculated local approximation to get a global approximation, and has been achieved useful result in many areas. Compared with traditional least square methods, MLS has two significant improvements [48]:

(1) Different ways to create the fitting function. This method does not take traditional polynomial or other functions, but the function consisted of a coefficient vector $a(x)$ and a basis function $p(x)$ where $a(x)$ does not take a constant, but a function of coordinate x.

(2) Introduction of the concept of compact support. Consider the value y at point x that is only influenced by nodes in subdomain near x, this subdomain is what we call the influence domain of x, points outside this domain have no effect to value of x. To denote the weight function $w(x)$ in the influence domain, if $w(x)$ takes a constant in this whole domain, we achieve the traditional least square method.

These improvements can bring many advantages such as mitigation or solving the difficulties in traditional curve and surface fitting process. We can take different basis functions for different accuracy, and take different weight functions to obtain different smoothness of surface (curve) fitting, this is what other methods cannot achieve. In this paper, the smooth surface can be fitted by points near the holes or discrete points inserted in the holes.

Suppose that unknown function $u(x)$ gives its n function values of node $x_i (i = 1, 2, \ldots, n)$ in solution domain Ω as $u_i = u(x_i)$. $u(x)$ can be defined approximately as follows:

$$u(x) \approx u^h(x) = \sum_{i=1}^{m} p_i(x) a_i(x) = p^{\mathrm{T}}(x) a(x). \tag{5.31}$$

In Eq. (5.31), $a(x) = [a_1(x), a_2(x), \ldots, a_m(x)]^{\mathrm{T}}, a_i(x)$ is the undetermined coefficient.

$p^{\mathrm{T}}(x) = [p_1(x), p_2(x), \ldots, p_m(x)], p_i(x)$ is basis function, m is the number of basis function. Usually we choose monomials as the basis function. We give the definition of one order basis function, and quadratic basis function in two-dimensional:

$$\begin{aligned} P^{\mathrm{T}}(x) &= [1, x, y], & m &= 3, \\ P^{\mathrm{T}}(x) &= [1, x, y, x^2, xy, y^2], & m &= 6. \end{aligned}$$

Undetermined coefficient $a_i(x)$ is the function of $x = [x, y]$. In the moving least square approximation, $a_i(x)$ can be determined by minimizing the weighted square of errors generated in neighborhood Ωx of x by approximate function $u(x)$, which is

$$J = \sum_{t=1}^{m} w_t(x)[u^k(x) - u(x_t)]^2 = \sum_{t=1}^{m} w_t(x) \left[\sum_{i=1}^{m} p_i(x_t) a_i(x) - u_t \right]^2, \tag{5.32}$$

where $u^k(x)$ is the function value at node x, $w_t(x)$ is the weight function corresponding to node x, and the function of compact support centered as

x_t. Due to the minimal value of J,

$$\frac{\partial J}{\partial a_j(x)} = 2\sum_{t=1}^{m} w_t(x)\left[\sum_{i=1}^{m} p_i(x_t)a_i(x) - u_t\right] p_j(x_t) = 0, \quad j = 1, 2, ..., m. \tag{5.33}$$

According to the equation above, we can calculate the coefficient to $a_i(x)$, and then derive the surface fitting formula as follows:

$$s\,(u, v) = a_0 + a_1u + a_2v + a_3u^2 + a_4v^2 + a_5uv, \tag{5.34}$$

where

$$\begin{aligned} a(x) &= A^{-1}(x)B(x)u, \\ A &= P^{\mathrm{T}}W(x)P, \\ B &= P^{\mathrm{T}}W(x). \end{aligned}$$

After obtaining s, transform parameter coordinate system (u, v, s) to Cartesian coordinate system (x, y, z). Figure 5.23 gives the example of skull repair where (a) is the skull model with some holes and (b) is the complete model after hole-filling following above algorithm.

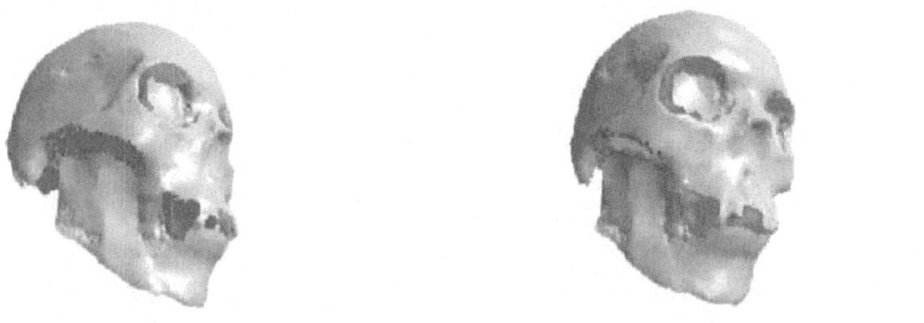

(a) Skull models with hole (b)Complete models after hole-filling

Fig. 5.23 The result of holes repair of a skull.

5.5 Restoration of Revolution Surface

A large number of pottery-shape artifacts unearthed are symmetric and special in the shape, as shown in Fig. 5.24. Such artifacts are nearly symmetric in the shape, and also their inner and outer surfaces of containers are of a revolution surface. For the restoration of such cultural fractures, we record its shape, color, texture, and texture measurements. Then all fragments are compared to classify the fragments into groups, each of which belonged to the same containers. The fragments of each group are matched and assembly by experience, however, this method needs all the fragments are excavated. Wars, earthquakes, natural disasters, fires, water, and many other factors make the vast majority of these excavated artifacts not complete. This reason makes that a large number of cultural relics unearthed that cannot be restored by matching and assembly the fragments. At the same time, cultural workers in the repair activities may also cause secondary damage to cultural relics. As a result, the problem of how to both avoid the destruction of cultural fractures and restore the pieces that will be unable put together is worthy studying and solving. With continuous improvements of the digital, development of computer graphics, machine vision, and reverse engineering this section will study computational ways for digitizing the symmetric cultural fragments and the shape information (axis, generatrix) in detail and use the fragments of such artifacts to restore virtually original shape. It not only provides the basis for virtually restoring realistic artistic heritage, but also makes the appreciation of artifacts online possible [49].

Fig. 5.24 Incomplete pottery-shape artifacts.

The SHAPE Laboratory of Brown University produces detailed work in the field of digital preservation of cultural heritage. Its STITCH project mainly focuses on the problem of stitching and restoring of heritage virtually. The project has similar study objects, which are symmetry and broken pottery-shape artifacts. However, this project studies how to automatically and validly stitch these pottery fragments virtually. The STITCH [50] project briefly introduces the framework of its restoration system in the literature. The framework is highly scalable, and the basic foothold is to make a pairwise comparison of the fragments. Then "try (proposal)" comparison and "assessment (evaluation)" are done repeatedly. After this process, computation of similarities for each pair of fragments is performed, and it will be as the input of the next step which is greedy selection method in stitching (assembly) module. The articles [51] and [52] proposed a restoration method based on a fracture curve of pottery fragments, the symmetry axis and generatrix information, Bayesian probability model, and the random variables for the relationship between each fragment. These are defined, and finally brought back to the problem of the maximum likelihood estimation or maximum posteriori probability. The curvature needs to be calculated in the calculation of the symmetry axis and the generatrix of pottery fragments.

The Pattern Recognition and Image Processing group at Vienna University of Technology has also performed a great deal of pottery restoration work [53 – 55]. These projects focus on how to effectively help the archaeologists quickly classify the pottery fragments with axial symmetry. The group obtains three-dimensional information on pottery fragments using the method of structured light technique, and estimates symmetric information of the pottery with a three-dimensional Hough algorithm. Then they calculate the fractures information and split automatically the characteristics of each part of the fractures. Next they calculate the characteristic curve segments to classify the whole fractures. The automatic classification process actually mimics the manual classification process done by archaeologists. In addition, the group also proposed auto-matching method of symmetric pottery-shape cultural fractures in the literature [56]. As these fragments are considered as a part of the revolution surface, the matching algorithm has been simplified. When each axis of each fragment to be matched are aligned, the matching search space has only two free degrees, namely the translation on axis and rotation around the axis. The matching method achieves satisfactory results used in both an ideal model and an real model built by the author in the literature.

Radim and Jan [57] proposed a method that estimated the generatrix of axisymmetric pottery-shape artifacts fractures. It needs to calculate curvature, but the efficiency is not high. For point cloud data, there is a lot of literature on how to rebuild the surface of the revolution. Elsasser and Hoschek [58] uses NURBS surfaces to define surface of revolution, and discusses the reconstruction for the two cases (the symmetry axis known and symmetry axis unknown). The method [59] needs adjustment manually and measured objects to normal posture. Pottmann [60] uses the Line Geometry method to solve the reconstruction of a revolution surface.

5.5.1 Workflow

The workflow starts with the digitalization of internal and external surfaces of the cultural fractures. Then compute in reverse the geometry of the fractures and restore the lost part. Last, paste the texture information. This is the restoration process of the pottery-shape cultural fractures. The general steps are as follows. First is fractures digitization. Capture digital data of fractures, including converting it into a certain format data and storing it. Next, preprocess the fractures data. Because of the requirement of the reverse algorithm, the model data needs to be pre-processed such as simplification or noise reduction, and so on. Third, provide geometric information extraction of the internal and external surface. The extraction of geometric information for fragments includes computation of the symmetry axis and the generatrix information. Fourth, calculate the restoration model. According to the geometric information, repair or restore the original model of cultural relics. Fifth, texture mapping is used to map the texture for the restoration model. The Sixth step is the output of restoration results. The restoration results of the artifacts are outputted in a specified format.

5.5.2 Incomplete Pottery-shape Artifact Restoration

Calculation of the relic's symmetric axis

Symmetric axis describes the basic geometric information of the rotation surface. Anti-calculated symmetric axis from 3D point cloud data discussed in this paper is the key step of the recovery method. Currently, the literature research can be divided into three categories. The first is curvature method, which needs to calculate the average intersecting lines curvature between the cluster and surface of model. The second is Hough algorithm, which converts normal vector of the sampling points on model surface to the Hough space, then find symmetric axis. The third is calculating line geometric method, this method boils down to the generalized eigenvalue and eigenvectors of the matrix problem. Based on the actual requirements, this paper gives another possible method of optimal symmetric axis.

Algorithm based on curvature

The core idea of these methods comes from the special nature of the surface of revolution. There exits the intersection curve between the plane which takes the axis of the surface of revolution as the normal vector and the surface of revolution. If a curve can be generated, then the curve is an arc. As shown in Fig. 5.26, m is a unit vector parallel to the symmetric axis. In the figure m is also the normal vector of the plane A. A intersects the rotary surface to form an arc. To calculate the exact direction of symmetric axis surface of revolution, our goal is to find a normal vector which enables the intersecting curve be an arc or as much an arc as possible.

Literature [61] gives a solution which is one of the best ways to view the issue. The algorithm first interpolates the scanned point cloud data, then reconstructs piecewise linear surfaces to select some vectors N_i uniformly from the unit ball as the center of axis origin. For each vector N_i, establish a plane cluster as the normal vector of N_i. Then intersect this set with the surface to get a piecewise linear curve cluster $C_i(j), j = 1, 2, \ldots, s$. Set k_j as the average curvature of the curve $C_i(j)$, the $\bar{k}_i = \sum_{j=1}^{s} k_j$ represents the mean curvature derivative of the curve cluster $C_i(j), j = 1, 2, \ldots, s$. k_j is smaller which means the shape of the curve $C_i(j)$ is more like an arc. The direction of vector N_i is more close to the symmetric axis.

The algorithm efficiency is very low. In fact, assume that the size of the

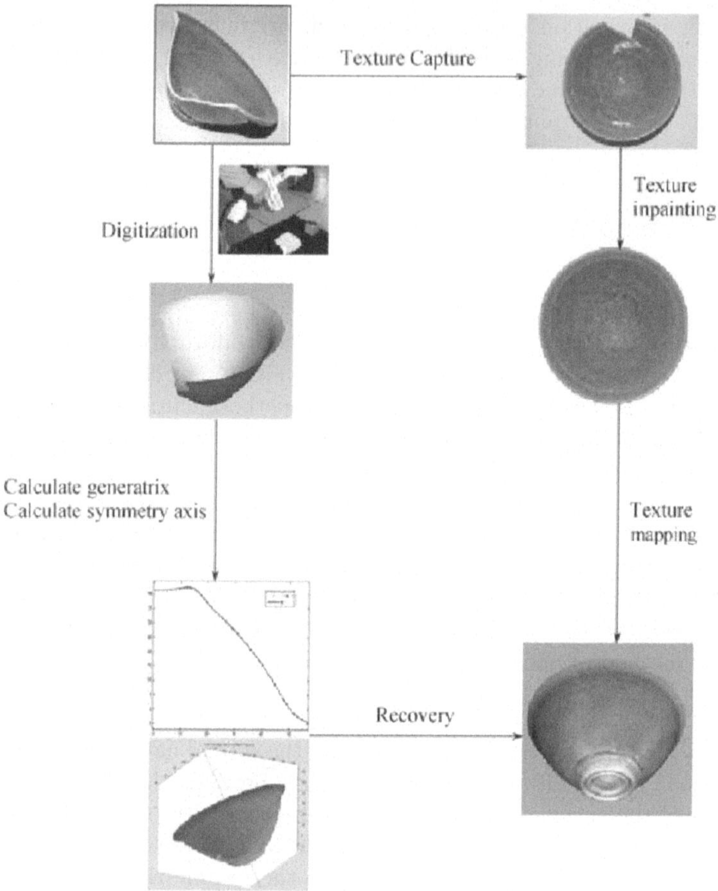

Fig. 5.25 Technology roadmap.

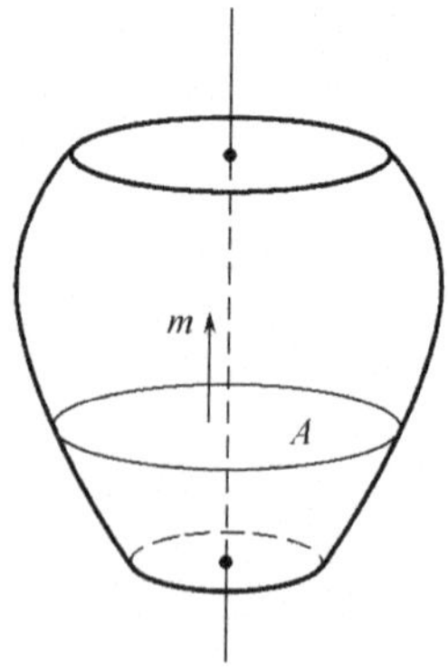

Fig. 5.26 Intersecting curve between the plane and rotation.

input data is n, the time complexity of curve intersection algorithm and the curve curvature are $O(n)$, then the algorithm's time complexity is $O(n^4)$. The results are obtained with the density of the uniform normal vector select. The more dense it is, the more accurate the solution. A lot of unnecessary operations are processed in the solution especially the derivative calculation of the solution that impacts the accuracy of the algorithm.

The STITCH project [62] gives another curvature-based computing solution program. The algorithm uses the special nature of the surface of revolution to avoid solving the curvature values by calculating the derivative. Also a known sample of m points on the surface of revolution can be defined as the sampling points and corresponding to the diameter p_i and the normal vector n_i. Assuming the symmetric axis is L which is determined by p_0 and the unit direct vector will be v. Limit this to $p_0 \cdot v = 0$, the symmetric axis turns into four degrees of freedom, as shown in Fig. 5.27. The radius of curvature of point p is equals to $|b \cdot p|$. Therefore, curvature is determined as follows:

$$|b \cdot p| = \frac{|a \cdot p|}{\sin \alpha} = \frac{|(p - p_0) \times v|}{|n \times v|}, \quad k = \frac{1}{|b \cdot p|}. \tag{5.35}$$

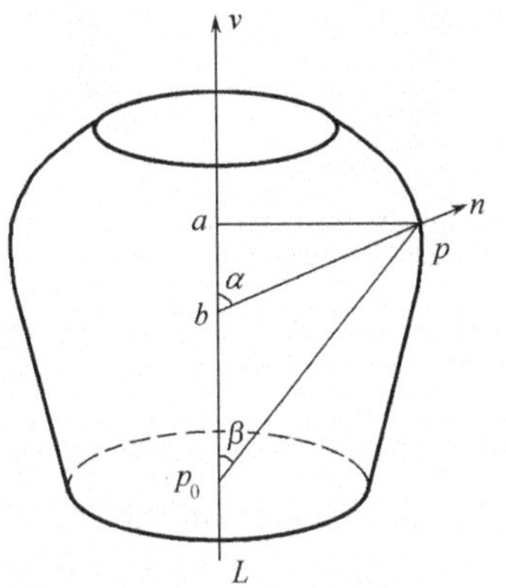

Fig. 5.27 Calculate axis of surface of revolution.

The circle center can be expressed as $c_i = p_i - n_i \cdot \frac{1}{k}$. As the center of each sampling point should be close to the symmetric axis, thereby minimizing the following formula, the axis of symmetric can be derived as

$$\begin{aligned} f(p_0, v) &= \sum_{i=1}^{m} |(c_i - p_0) \times v|^2 \\ &= \sum_{i=1}^{m} \left| (p_i - p_0) \times v - \frac{|(p_i - p_0) \times v|}{|n_i \times v|} (n_i \times v) \right| \end{aligned} \tag{5.36}$$

and subjected to $p_0 \cdot v = 0$, $|v| = 1$. In order to enhance the robustness of the algorithm, the literature also proposes a weighted optimization.

Algorithm based on Hough space

The normal vector at each point on a rotary surface should intersect with the symmetric axis. All intersections should be in the symmetric axis of the rotation plane. Before estimating the symmetric axis, you need to calculate the normal vector value at the point on the surface. In order to keep calculation stability use the principal component analysis to calculate the normal vector n_i, and then all lines (p_i, n_i) are clustered in 3D Hough space. For all points (p_i, n_i) on each line vote based on the points numbered in this 3D Hough space. The largest set of points form the candidate axis of rotary surface symmetric axis. Through searching optimization, find the optimal solution. The following diagram is computed for a symmetric axis using the Hough algorithm. Figure 5.28 shows the result of axis estimation by Hough algorithm.

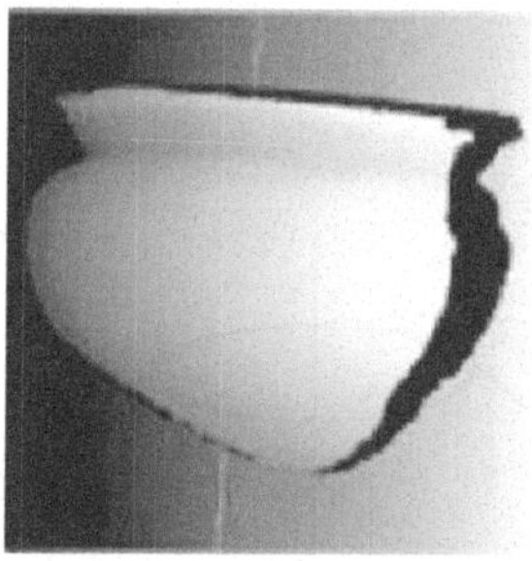

Fig. 5.28 Computed symmetric axis (with permission from Kampel).

Algorithms based on computational line geometry

The method regarding the space points on the surface are two kind of movements. One is rotation around the axis, as shown in Fig. 5.29. Another is a translation motion along the axis. For the points of the helix surface with an axis Z, the motion parameter equation is expressed as

$$x(t) = \begin{cases} x_0 \cos t - y_0 \sin t \\ x_0 \sin t + y_0 \cos t \\ z_0 + pt \end{cases}.$$

The starting point is at $X(0)$, p_t is the translation speed along the axis. Assume that the motion vector at m is (x, y, z), its velocity vector is $(-y, x, p_t)$, all the vertical direction of the velocity vector constitutes the path normal cluster of this point, as shown in Fig. 5.30.

Make the $L(l, \bar{l})$ as the normal vector in $v(m)$, L meets

$$l \cdot v = 0. \tag{5.37}$$

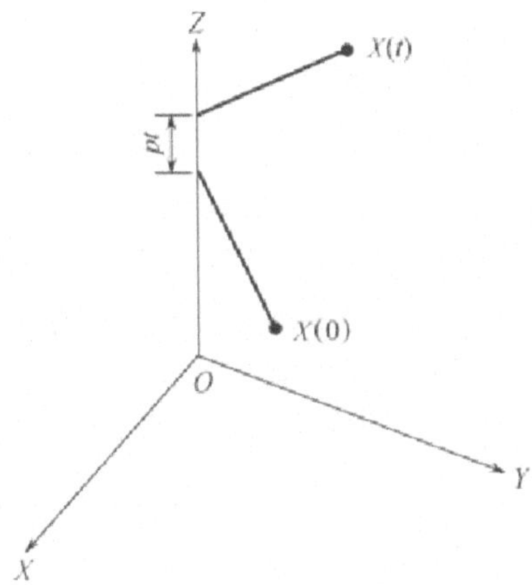

Fig. 5.29 Point x performing a helix movement.

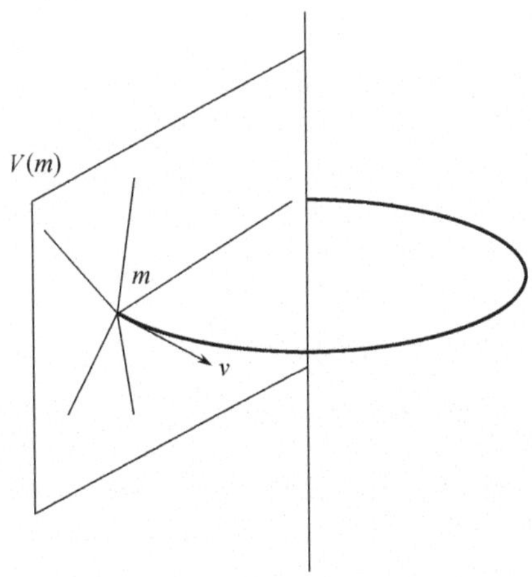

Fig. 5.30 Path normal cluster.

In addition, according to the nature of the Plucker coordinates

$$\bar{l} = p \times l \tag{5.38}$$

from Eqs. (5.37) and (5.38) can be obtained

$$\bar{c} \cdot l + c \cdot \bar{l} = 0, \tag{5.39}$$

where $C(\bar{c}, c)$ is constant vector, notice that $\lambda \cdot C$ that can make Eq. (5.39) establish. So, $C(\bar{c}, c)$ can be used as a normal cluster of any spiral movement. The literature [60] gives calculation the rotation of the screw axis $(a, \bar{a})$ and translation motion velocity p of the spiral movement using $C(\bar{c}, c)$:

$$a = \frac{c}{\|c\|}, \quad \bar{a} = \frac{\bar{c} - pc}{\|c\|}, \quad p = \frac{c \cdot \bar{c}}{c^2}. \tag{5.40}$$

If $p = 0$, this spiral movement represents the points on the spiral plane. That is, if we find $C(\bar{c}, c)$ through $L(l, \bar{l})$, we can calculate the symmetric axis. The deviation between $L(l, \bar{l})$ and a linear cluster $C(\bar{c}, c)$ are defined:

$$m(L, C) = \frac{|\bar{c}l + c\bar{l}|}{\|c\|}. \tag{5.41}$$

Assuming the normal vector of k sampling points on the rotary surface are $N_i(n_i, \bar{n}_i), i = 1, 2, \ldots, k$, then the solution process of the symmetric axis turns into the process of minimizing the following formula:

$$F(x) = \sum_{i=1}^{k} (\bar{x}n_i + x\bar{n}_i)^2 = X^{\mathrm{T}}NX, \quad \|X\| = X^{\mathrm{T}}DX = 1. \tag{5.42}$$

In this formula, $X = \begin{bmatrix} \bar{x} \\ x \end{bmatrix}$, $D = diag(0, 0, 0, 1, 1, 1)$, $N_{ij} = \mu_i \cdot \mu_j$, $\mu_i = (n_{1i}, n_{2i}, \ldots, n_{ki})$, $1 \leqslant i, j \leqslant 6$.

At this point, the problem boils down to solving a generalized matrix eigenvalue problem. If we have a vector X make $NX = \lambda DX$, then $F(x) = X^{\mathrm{T}}NX = \lambda X^{\mathrm{T}}DX = \lambda$. Therefore, the eigenvector of smallest nonnegative eigenvalue corresponding to D is the solution of the linear line cluster which we are looking for. After the solution is obtained we can use Eq. (5.40) to estimate the value of the symmetric axis.

Generatrix line calculation of rotary relics

The generatrix line defines the contour of surface of revolution. This book chooses the artifacts which must have complete generatrix line information. If it is a small portion of shape-like artifact, you cannot restore the original appearance of the relics. You must make the necessary matches in order to get the complete generatrix information. In general, automatic generatrix calculation is nothing more than using a series of the plane intersects symmetric axis to fractures model to obtain a series of intersecting lines, known as the candidate generatrix. Then use make combination, which refers to select a good candidate as the best generatrix information. Existing methods use iterative methods to calculate the generatrix with longest rotary surface. The first step is to change the rotary surface to coincide with the symmetric axis of the coordinate axis Z. Set a series of axial plane formed clusters e_i. As shown in Fig. 5.31, intersect with the revolution surface to generate a series of intersecting lines.

Since all intersection planes are parallel to the symmetric axis, you can calculate each of the intersection line projection on a symmetric axis (axis Z). To define the height of an intersection line h_i, find the corresponding projection along the length direction and calculate the maximum value of intersecting lines h_i regarded it as the final generatrix. In practice, the literature [52] avoids the intersection between cross-sectional plane and all triangular

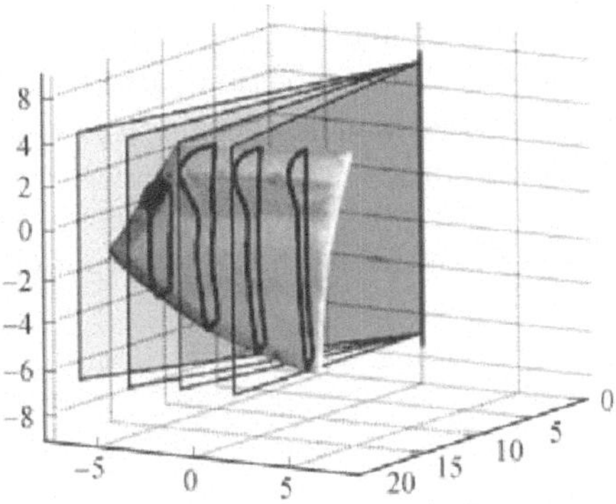

Fig. 5.31 Intersecting curves with the revolution surface (with permission from Kampel) [53].

facets. It first filters out the triangular patches that may intersect with the intersecting plane if possible and then it finds the intersection. However, this method does not consider the case of fractures that have holes, in that case the calculated generatrix has incomplete information.

As Fig. 5.32 shows, if you choose to take the longest line as the generatrix, then only an incomplete generatrix can be found.

This book improves on the method in the literature [53] according to the specific needs of relics' recovery and adds a fitting process of the intersection to adapt to the case of the hole on fractures.

Define the bounding box center of fractures that has a projection O in the symmetric axis, defined the symmetric axis as $I(O, d)$. Here is the section plane selection method. First, find the boundary contour fragment $S(s_1, s_2, ..., s_r)$. Assume the contour lines have been uniform sampled, as shown in Fig. 5.33.

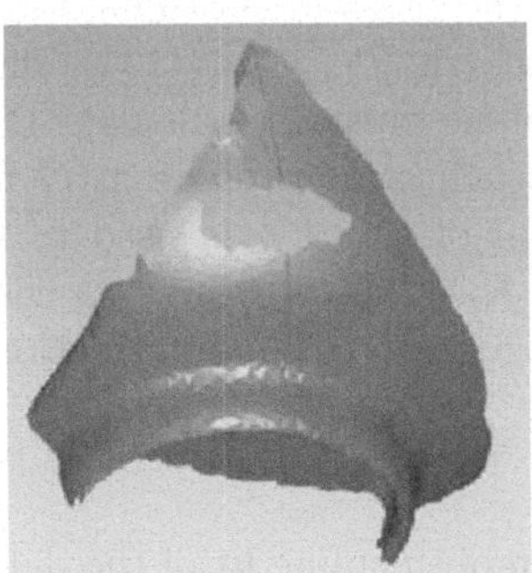

Fig. 5.32 The case of fracture with hole.

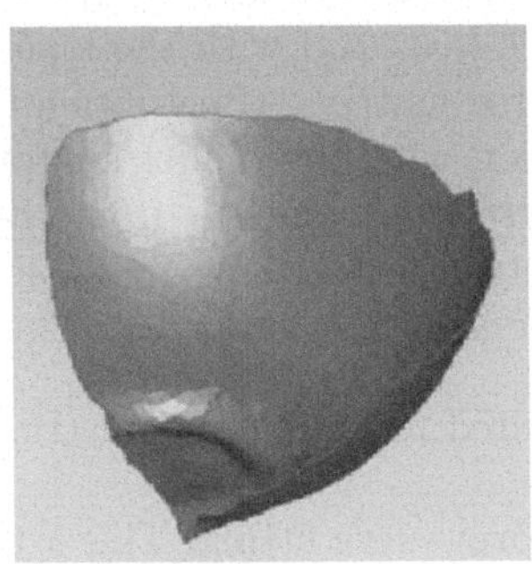

Fig. 5.33 Contour line.

Building a cross-sectional plane $\pi_t(O, n_t)$ start from a point along the boundary line S_b to direction Ψ_1, as shown in Fig. 5.34. Here $n_t = \text{norm}(d \times$

s_t), whenever a new cross-sectional plane was built, calculate the direction change between n_t and n_{t-1}. If the direction turns to the opposite Ψ_1, stop generating a new cross-sectional plane and begin to establish the section plane along Ψ_2 which is opposite direction Ψ_1 at S_b, until no more section plane can be created. As Fig. 5.35 shows, when the change of direction between n_t and n_{t-1} are opposite to Ψ_1, it means that the section plane no longer needs to be created.

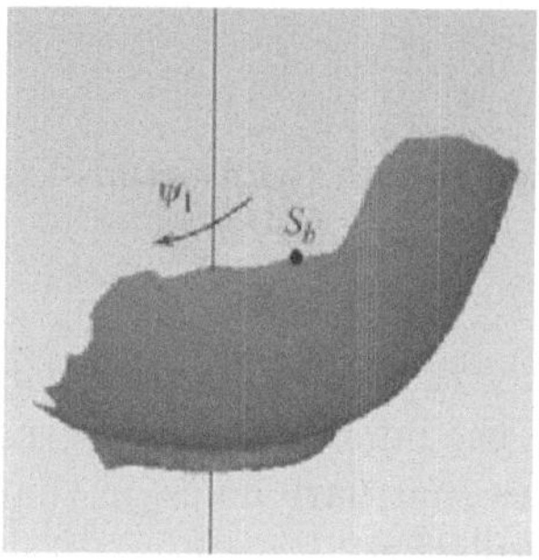

Fig. 5.34 Building cross-section plane along axis.

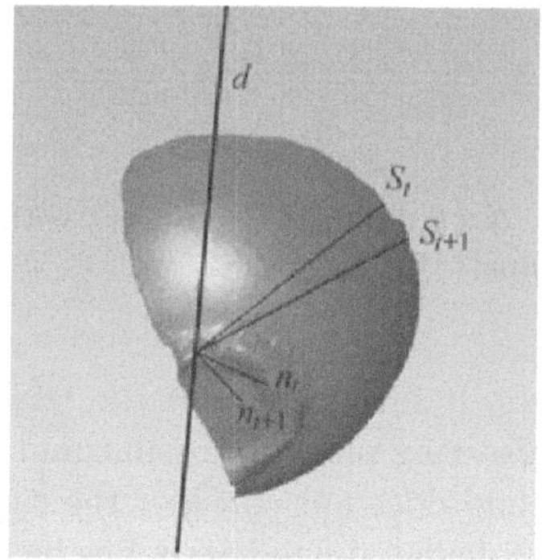

Fig. 5.35 Cross-sectional plane intersection.

Whenever a section plane $\pi_t(O, n_t)$ is built at s_t, we can carry out intersection operations. The first step is to construct the local coordinate system $\chi_t(O, I_t, J_t, K_t)$, and we make J as the same direction with symmetric axis. Then $J = d$. Set the direction K the same direction with $d \times (s_t - O)$, that is $K = \text{norm}(d \times (s_t - O))$. Finally, $I = J \times K$. Next, calculate the old and the new coordinate transformation matrix. Set the coordinate system $\chi_t(O, I_t, J_t, K_t)$ to the original coordinate system with the transformation matrix $Tr_t, Tr_t = [I_t, J_t, K_t]$. From the original coordinate system to $\chi_t(O, I_t, J_t, K_t)$ with the transformation matrix $Tr_t' = \text{Inv}(Tr_t)$, Inv means inverse matrix. After obtaining section plane clusters, calculate the intersection with the model for fractures, for each section plane $\pi_t(O, n_t)$. The intersection resulting from the intersection of sets U_t, is used to sort the points in U_t as x coordinate in $\chi_t(O, I_t, J_t, K_t)$. Delete points of x coordinate value less than zero point. This is because generatrix line information is only required to be half symmetrical. Find the set $U = \bigcup_{i=1}^{k} U_t$ of these points to perform curve fitting. This article uses a smooth spline fit of the data to get the generatrix profile. Smoothness is set to $p = 0.2$.

Table 5.1 shows the calculation results to the outer surface generatrix of fractures using Matlab 7.0

Table 5.1 Generatrix fitting results of fractures model

No.	3D Model	Generatrix	Smoothness
1	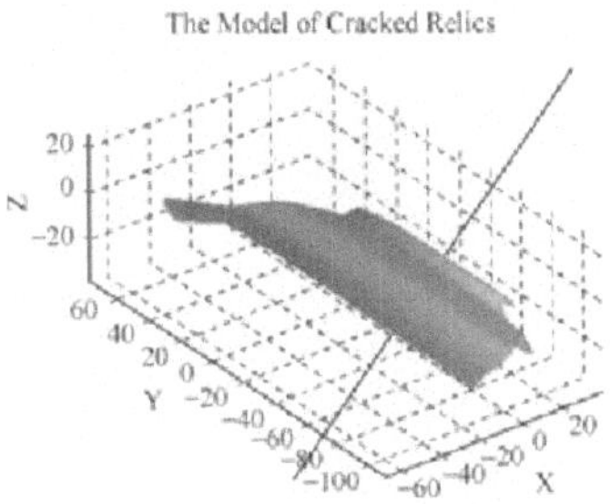	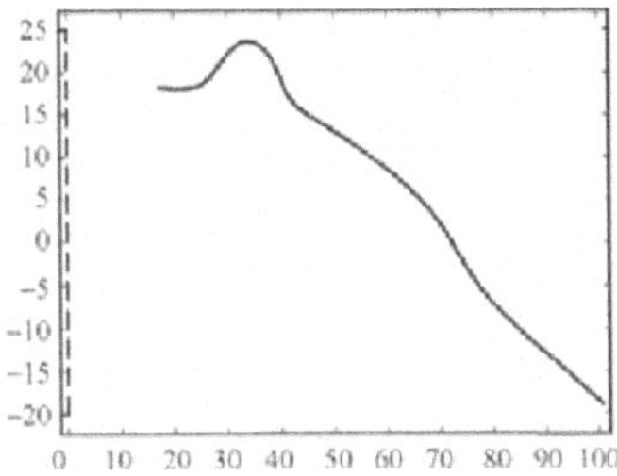	4.851
2	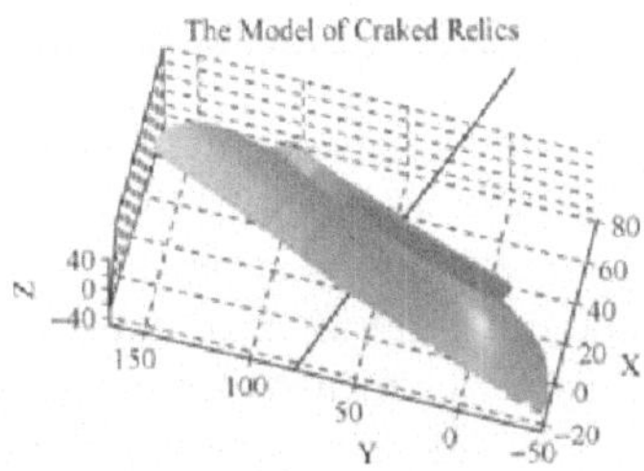	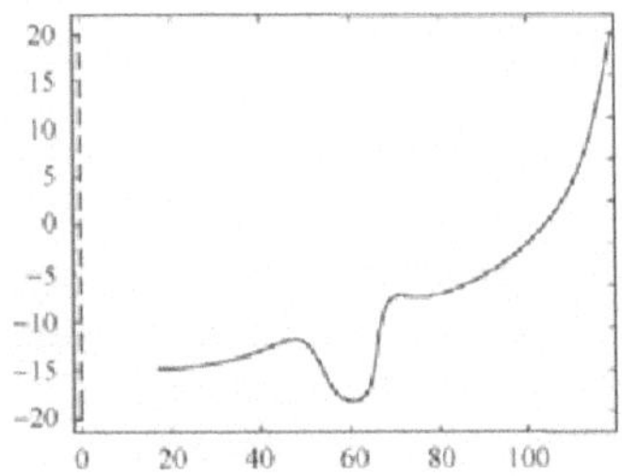	3.273
3	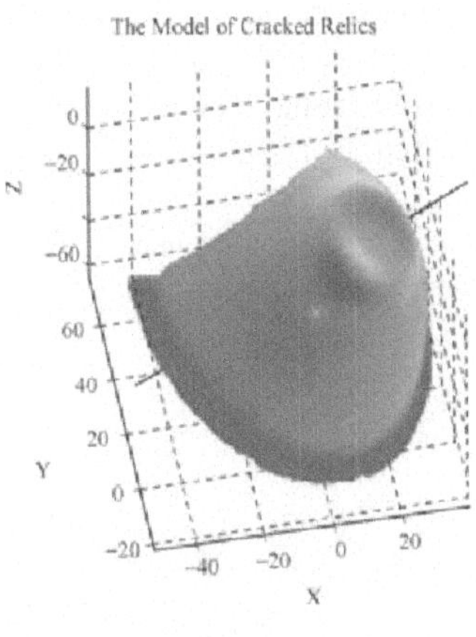	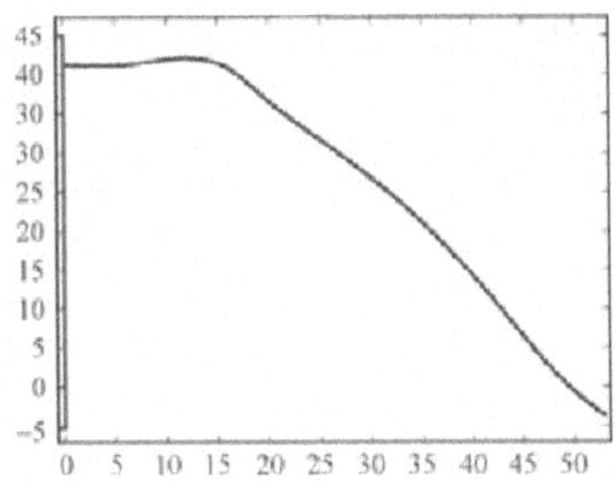	0.168
4	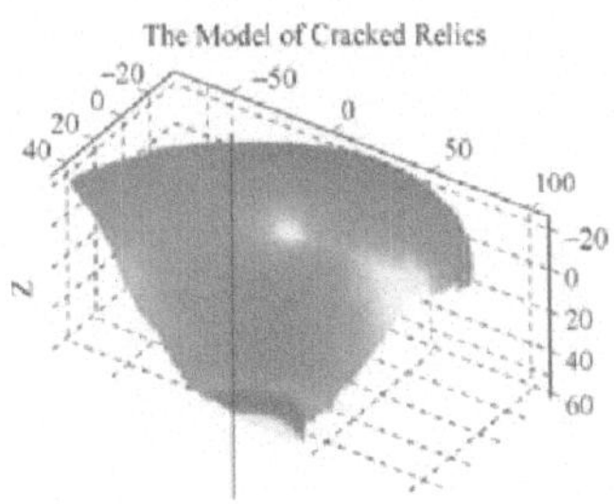	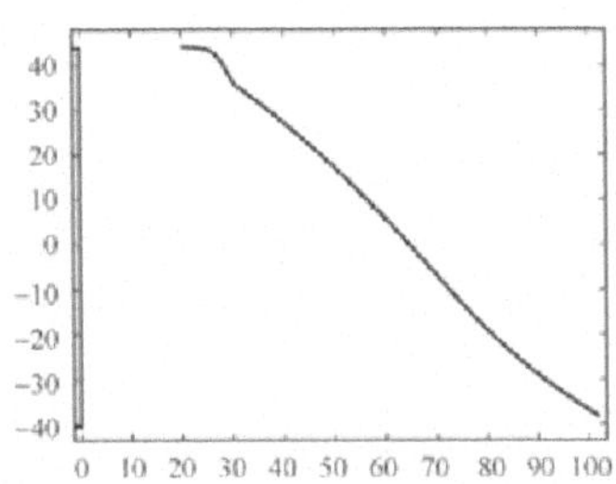	5.369

(to be continued)

(Table 5.1)

No.	3D Model	Generatrix	Smoothness
5	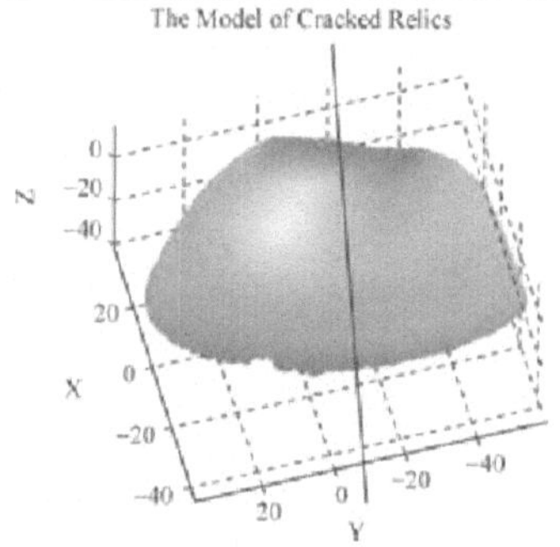	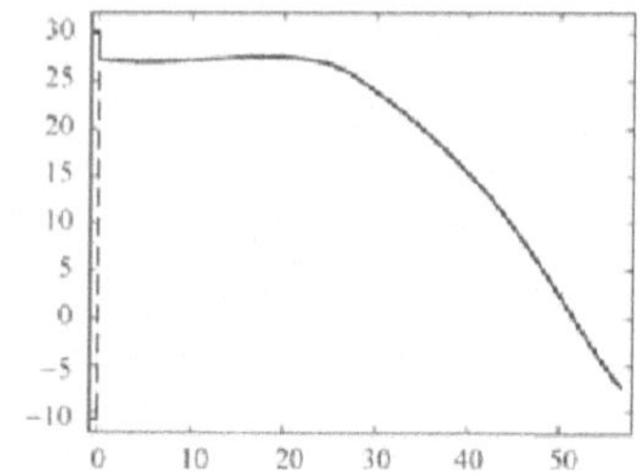	0.024

In the actual repair process, we often encounter the generatrix calculation not connected with the symmetric axis using the fragmentation of 1, 2, 4 on Table 5.1. If use such generatrixes directly, holes will appear on the bottom of model after the recovery. In order to get the full generatrix we must connect the generatrix with the symmetric axis. This paper regards the missing part as a plane, which is the plane part of the bottom bowl. Thus, generatrices start from the bottom last point of the generatrix line along the direction perpendicular to the symmetric axis to generate a new point on the generatrix. Figures 5.36 and 5.37 plot the generatrix through the extension. Figure 5.38 shows the repair result of broken porcelain.

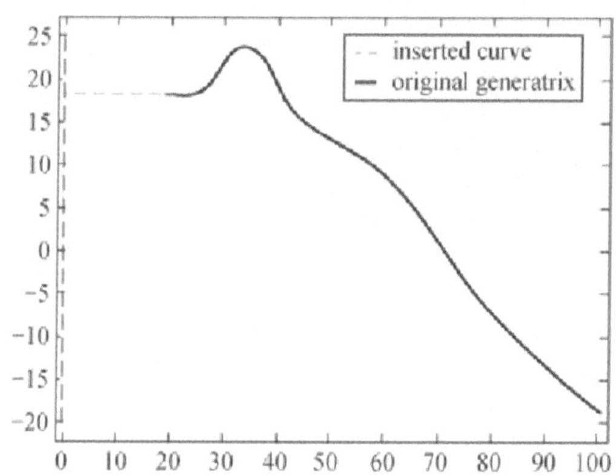

Fig. 5.36 Extended generatrix.

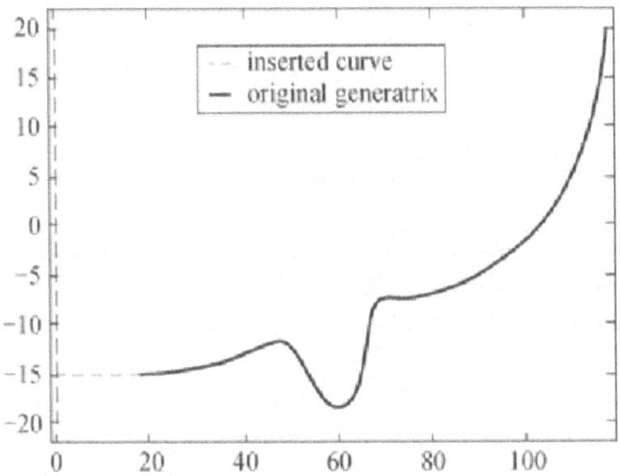

Fig. 5.37 Extended generatrix.

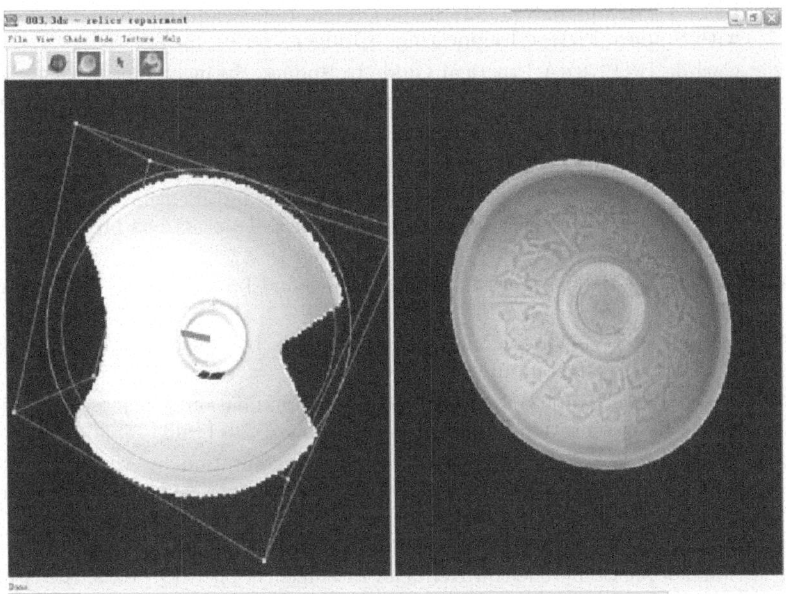

Fig. 5.38 Left is broken porcelain, right is restored model.

References

[1] Feng X (2001) Chinese Ceramic. Shanghai RareBooks Publishing House, Shanghai

[2] Lee T (1996) Image Representation Using 2D Gabor Wavelets. IEEE Transactions on Pattern Analysis and Machine Intelligence, 18(10): 959 – 971

[3] Marcelja S (1980) Mathematical Description of the Response of Simple Cortical Cells. Journal of the Optical Society of America, 70 (11): 1297 – 1300

[4] Daugman JG (1985) Uncertainty Relation for Resolution in Space, Spatial Frequency, and Orientation Optimized by Two-dimensional Visual Cortical Filters. Journal of the Optical Society of America (A), 2 (7): 1160 – 1169

[5] Lades M, Vorbruggen J, Buhmann J, et al (1993) Distortion Invariant Object Recognition in the Dynamic Link Architecture. IEEE Transactions on Computers, 42(3): 300 – 311

[6] Wei N, Geng G, Zhou M (2005) Content-based Image Retrieval Using Gabor Filters. Computer Engineering, 31(8): 10 – 11

[7] Yang D, Tian Y (2003) The New Data Mining Method: Support Vector Machine. Science Press, Beijing

[8] Freeman H (1961) On the Encoding of Arbitrary Geometric Configurations. IRE Transactions on Electronic Computers, EC – 10: 260 – 268

[9] Freeman H (1974) Computer Processing of the Line Drawing Images. ACM Computing Surveys, 6: 57 – 97

[10] Parui S, Majumder D (1983) Symmetry Analysis by Computer. Pattern Recognition, 16: 63 – 37

[11] Ikebe Y, Miyamoto S (1982) Shape Design, Representation, and Restoration with Splines. Picture Engineering. Springer, Berlin, pp 75 – 95

[12] Carl de B (1978) A Practical Guide to Splines. Springer, Berlin

[13] Shi F (1994) The Computer-Aided Geometric Design and Non-uniform Rational B-spline. Beijing Aerospace University Press, Beijing

[14] Mortenson M (1985) Geometric Modeling. Wiley, NewYork

[15] Cohen F, Zhuang Z (1995) Invariant Matching and Identification of Curves Using B-splines Curve Representation. IEEE Transactions on Image Processing, 4(1): 1 – 10

[16] Pavlidis T (1982) Algorithms for Graphics and Image Processing. Springer, Berlin

[17] Pavlidis T (1977) Polygonal Approximations by Newton's Method. IEEE Transactions on Computers, 26: 800 – 807

[18] Wu J, Leou J (1993) New Polygonal Approximation Schemes for Object Shape Representation. Pattern Recognition, 26: 471 – 484

[19] Bengtsson A, Eklundh J (1991) Shape representation by Multiscale Contour Approximation. IEEE Transactions on Pattern Analysis and Machine Intelligence,13(1): 85 – 94

[20] Witkin A P (1983) Scale-space Filtering. In: Proceedings of the International Joint Conference on Artificial Intelligence, pp 1019 – 1022, Karlsruhe, West Germany, 8 – 12 August 1983

[21] Chung P, Tsai C, Chen E, et al (1994) Polygonal Approximation Using Competitive Hopfield Neural Network. Pattern Recognition, 27: 1505 – 1512

[22] Babaud J, Witkin A, BaudinM, et al (1986) Uniqueness of Gaussian Kernel for Scale Space Filtering. IEEE Trans PAMI, 8: 26 – 33

[23] Asada H, Brady M (1986) The Curvature Primal Sketch. IEEE Transactions on Pattern Analysis and Machine Intelligence, 8: 2 – 14

[24] Mokhtarian F, Mackworth A (1986) Scale-based Description and Recognition of Planar Curve Sand Two Dimensional Shapes. IEEE Transactions on Pattern Analysis and Machine Intelligence, 8: 34 – 43

[25] Chen M, Yan P (1991) A Multiscaling Approach Based on Morphological Filtering. IEEE Transactions on Pattern Analysis and Machine Intelligence, 11(7): 694 – 700

[26] Anelli G, Broggi A, Destri G (1998) Decomposition of Arbitrarily Shaped Binary Morphological Structuring Elements Using Genetic Algorithm. IEEE Transactions on Pattern Analysis and Machine Intelligence, 20(2): 217 – 224

[27] Laganiere R (1998) A Morphological Operator for Corner Detection. Pattern Recognition, 31 (11): 1643 – 1652

[28] Moisan L (1998) Affine Plane Curve Evolution: A Fully Consistent Scheme. IEEE Transactions on Image Processing, 7(3): 411 – 420

[29] Reinhardt J, Higgins W (1996) Comparison Between the Morphological Skeleton and Morphological Shaped Decomposition. IEEE Transactions on Pattern Analysis and Machine Intelligence, 18(9): 951 – 957

[30] Zahn C, Roskies R (1972) Fourier Descriptors for Plane Closed Curves. IEEE Transactions on Computers, 21(3): 269 – 281

[31] Persoon E, Fu K (1977) Shape Discrimination Using Fourier Descriptors. IEEE Transactions on Systems, Man, and Cybernetics, 7(3): 170 – 179

[32] Chuang G, Kuo C (1996) Wavelet Descriptor of Planar Curves: Theory and Application. IEEE Transactions on Image Processing, 5(1): 56 – 70

[33] Li J, Kuo C (1996) Automatic Target Shape Recognition via Deformable Wavelet Templates. SPIE: Automatic Object Recognition VI, vol 2756, pp 2 – 13, Orlando, USA, 8 – 12 April, 1996

[34] Tieng Q, Boles W (1997) Recognition of 2D Object Contours Using the Wavelet Transform Zero-Crossing Representation. IEEE Transactions on Pattern Analysis and Machine Intelligence,19(8): 910 – 916

[35] Chen G, Tien D (1999) Invariant Fourier Wavelet Descriptor for Pattern Recognition. Pattern Recognition, 32(7): 1083 – 1088

[36] Yang H, Lee S (1998) Recognition of 2D Object Contours Using Starting Point Independent Wavelet Coefficient Matching. Journal of Visual Communication and Image Representation, 9(2): 171 – 181

[37] Fan S (2005) Complementary Shape Matching and Stitching Method of BrokenRigid. Dissertation, Northwest University

[38] Leitão HCG, Stolfi J (1998) A Multi-scale Method for the Re-assembly of Fragmented Objects. Technical Report IC – 98 – 06, Institute of Computing, University of Campinas

[39] Carr J, Beatson R, Cherrie J, et al (2001) Reconstruction and Representation of 3D Objects with Radial Basis Functions. In: Proceedings of the 28th Annual Conference on Computer Graphics and Interactive Techniques, pp 67 – 76, Los Angeles, USA, 12 – 17 August 2001

[40] Wang J, Oliveira M (2007) Filling Holes on Locally Smooth Surfaces Reconstructed from Point Clouds. Image and Vision Computing, 25 (1): 103 – 113

[41] Verdera J, Caselles V, Bertalmio M, et al (2003) In Painting Surface Holes. In: Proceedings of the International Conference on Image Processing, pp 903 – 906, 14 – 18 September, 2003, Barcelona, Spain

[42] Pernot J P, Moraru G F, Veron P (2006) Filling Holes in Meshes Using a Mechanical Model to Simulate the Curvature Variation Minimization. Computers & Graphics, 30: 892 – 902

[43] Li G, Chen Z, Zhang S, et al (2007) Auto Repair Algorithm of Complex Holes for Mesh Surface. Journal of Zhejiang University (Engineering Science), 41 (3): 407 – 411

[44] Cheng X, Zhou M, Geng G, et al (2006) Filling Methods of Space Triangular Mesh Surface. Application Research of Computers, 23(06): 158 – 159

[45] Zhang J, Yue W, Wang N, et al (2007) Repair Algorithm of Anisotropy Holes in Triangular Mesh Modal. Journal of Computer Aided Design and Graphics, 19 (7): 892 – 897

[46] Wang H, Du J, Liu S, et al (2005) Various Types of Holes Repair Algorithm Based on Radial Basis Function. Mechanical Science and Technology, 24 (6): 744 – 747

[47] Duchon J (1977) Splines Minimizing Rotation-invariant Semi-norms in Sobo- lev Spaces. In: Schempp W, Zeller K (eds) Constructive Theory of Functions of Several Variables, Lecture Notes in Mathematics, 571: 85 – 100, Springer, Berlin

[48] Lancaster P, Salkauskas K (1986) Curve and Surface Fitting: An Introduction. Academic Press, USA

[49] Li C (2006) Research on Axial Cracked Relics Recovery. Dissertation, Northwest University

[50] Stuart A, David H (2002) Toward a Framework for Assembling Broken Pottery Vessels. In: Proceedings of the Eighteenth National Conference on Artificial Intelligence, pp 945 – 946, Edmonton, Canada, 28 July – 1 August, 2002

[51] Willis A, Cooper D, et al (2002) Bayesian Pot-assembly from Fragments as Problems in Perceptual-Grouping and Geometric-Learning. In: Proceedings of the 16th International Conference on Pattern Recognition, 3: 297 – 303, Quebec Convention Center, Canada, 11 – 15 August 2002

[52] Willis A, Cooper D, et al (2001) Assembling Virtual Pots from 3D Measurements of their Fragments. In: Proceedings of the International Symposium on Virtual Reality Archaeology and Cultural Heritage, pp241 – 252, Glyfada, Greece, 28 – 30 November 2001

[53] Mara H, Martin K (2003) Automated Profile Extraction of Archaeological Fragments for Classification. In: Proceedings of the 8th Computer Vision Winter Workshop, pp 67 – 72, Valtice, Czech, 3 – 6 February 2003

[54] Kampel M, Melero F J (2003) Virtual Vessel Reconstruction from a Fragment's Profile. In: Proceedings of the 4th International Symposium on Virtual Reality, Archaeology and Intelligent Cultural Heritage, pp 79 – 88, Brighton, UK, 5 – 7 November 2003

[55] Martin K, Robert S (2003) Profile-based Pottery Reconstruction. In: Proceeding of the Conference on Computer Vision and Pattern Recognition Workshop, pp 4 – 4, Madison, USA, 16 – 22 June 2003

[56] Martin K, Robert S (2004) 3D Puzzling of Archaeological Fragments. In: Proceeding of the 9th Computer Vision Winter Workshop, pp 31 – 40, Piran, Slovenia, 4 – 6 February 2004

[57] Radim H, Jan F (1997) Estimation of Profiles of Sherds of Archaeological Pottery. In: Proceeding of the Czech Pattern Recognition Workshop, pp 126 – 130, Milovy, Czech, 17 – 20 February 1997

[58] Elsasser B, Hoschek J (1996) Approximation of Digitized Points by Surfaces of Revolution. Computers & Graphics, 20(1): 85 – 94

[59] Franca C, Edie M, Giovanni M, et al (2003) A Particular Class of Spline in Reconstruction of Revolution Surfaces From 3D Data Measured by CMM. Robotics and Computer Integrated Manufacturing, 19(1 – 2): 219 – 224

[60] Pottmann H, Randrup T (1998) Rotational and Helical Surface Approximation for Reverse Engineering. Computing, 60(4): 307 – 322

[61] Qian X, Huang X (2004) Reconstruction of Surfaces of Revolution with Partial Sampling. Journal of Computational and Applied Mathematics, 163(1): 211 – 217

[62] Yan C, David M (2002) Geometric Structure Estimation of Axially Symmetric Pots from Small Fragments. In: Proceedings of the International Conference on Signal Processing, Pattern Recognition and Application, pp 92–97, Crete, Greece, 25–28 June 2002

6 Virtual Restoration Techniques of Calligraphy and Painting

Calligraphy and painting have been highly valued throughout the history of China and recognized as a typical expression of Chinese traditional arts. Calligraphy and painting in China have their pursuits in exterior beauty and a focus of the inner lyrical mood that are stressed collectively. However, due to temperature, humidity and other natural conditions and human factors, calligraphy works and paintings, made on paper, silk or other delicate materials, are rarely kept well. With the development of computer and data acquisition technology using computer image processing to achieve efficient restoration of paintings has great research and application values. This chapter firstly describes the different types of incomplete paintings, and then shows the image segmentation and contour tracing technology areas to be achieved, and finally show how to use the Bertalmio Sapiro Caselles Batlester (BSCB) model, Total Variation (TV) model, and curvature driven diffusions (CDD) to realize the implementation of defective areas.

6.1 Issues of Calligraphy and Painting Restoration

Archaic calligraphies and paintings appear with natural aging, damage, fading, stains, mildew, and other imperfections. Restoration is needed to recover the original appearance. The traditional manual restoration methods include several steps: cleaning the core of the paintings, repairing the silk and liner paper, mending the holes, and repairing color. All processes are quite complex and difficult. An inappropriate mistake can lead to irreparable damage [1]. With the rapid development of computer technology, especially the digital image processing technology, virtual restoration of calligraphy and painting can come true. Even if the restoration is a failure, the original calligraphy and painting are not affected. The restoration can be repeated until satisfaction. This virtual restoration of calligraphy and painting technology causes no harm itself, and also reduces the workload for heritage experts.

Image restoration techniques are originated in the repair of ancient valuable artworks which are done by skilled craftsmen. However, because of the irreversible repair process, the repair works of artworks require highly skilled craftsmen. With the development of science and technology, repair work can be done by a computer, the cost of repair is reduced greatly, artificial repair experience is simulated, and the efficiency of the repair is largely improved compared to the artificial repair.

The existing problems of calligraphy and painting include: dirt, crease, color diffusion, damage, and other factors, which can influence the quality of calligraphy and painting. The incomplete paintings are shown in Fig. 6.1. Virtual restoration of calligraphy and painting can be achieved by information technology.

Crease

Because the size of calligraphy and painting can be large, creases will emerge

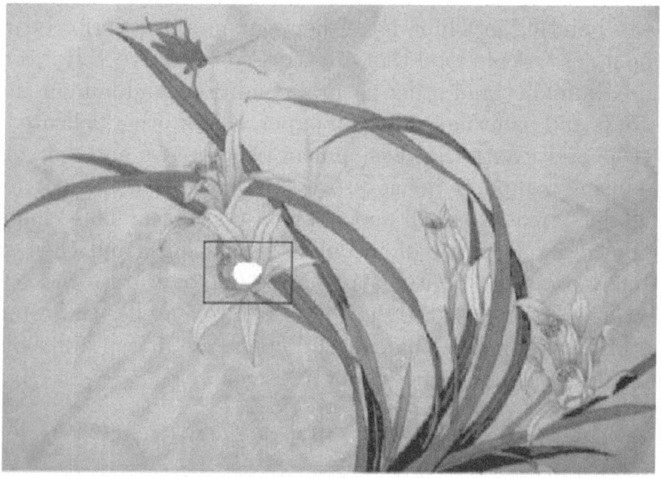

(a) Incomplete painting with large area

(b) Incomplete painting with small area

Fig. 6.1 Incomplete paintings.

when it is folded to store. Furthermore, incorrect mounting can lead to creases.

Defacement

There is a big difference between the fouling of calligraphy and painting and natural images or pictures. The fouling of natural images or a picture is usually caused by a small stain or other issue. The fouling of traditional calligraphy and paintings is often a large blemish area on the background, which is caused by slow spread of ink influenced by humidity in the air with time passing.

Dirt

After a long time, the color in the painting turns darker which leads to the obscurity in the picture. Because of smoke, oil, mildew spots, and human factors, the pictures appear to have some additional attachments.

Broken and incomplete

A serious problem existing in calligraphy and painting restoration is the incompleteness of the calligraphy and painting, which is caused by inappropriate or long storage.

Improper previous restoration

As the constraints of repair techniques and the different understanding of calligraphy and painting, the process of restoring itself may cause damage to the original calligraphy and painting.

The purpose of calligraphy and painting restoration is to extend storage time and restore the original appearance of the calligraphy and paintings. The traditional methods of calligraphy and painting restoration include remounting and decoration which consists of exposing the old patching, full color, and other methods.

6.2 Defaced Calligraphy and Painting Restoration

Recognition of damaged region and restoration of damaged regions are the key technologies of virtual restoration of calligraphy and painting, which are introduced in this section.

6.2.1 Recognition of Damaged Region

Image segmentation

Image segmentation is an important imaging technology which has widely drawn the attention of people in theoretical study and practical applications.

There are many methods of image segmentation. Some split operations can be directly applied to any image while others only apply to specific categories of images. Some algorithms need rough segmentation of the image first and then use the extracted information for accurate segmentation.

Image segmentation means the image is decomposed into a number of specific parts, which have a similar nature (region or object). With those parts, we can analyze and describe the image. An image often contains many different types of regions, such as objects, environments, backgrounds, and so on. In the research and application of images, people often show their interest in certain parts of the image. These parts are frequently referred to as goals or prospects (as other parts of image are backgrounds), which are generally corresponding to the specific nature of the region of an image. In order to identify and analyze the target, we have to separate these related regions. On the basis of this, we can make further use of the target such as feature extraction and measurement. Image segmentation refers to the technology and process that cuts the image into specific regions and extracts the interesting target. This specific feature can be gray level, color, texture, etc. The target can correspond to a single region or multiple regions.

The common segmentation methods contain threshold, region growing, edge detection algorithms, and other specific theory segmentation algorithms.

Threshold method

In this case the image is composed of two parts. The histogram of gray level often appears two peaks. The gray value of the valley between two peaks of histogram is always taken as the threshold. All pixels greater than or equal to the threshold will be taken as one category and the others will be taken as the new category. In order to improve the reliability of classification in practical applications, we can use some additional information (such as the area ratio of two regions) to make the choice of threshold more reasonable.

Region growing

This is a sequential image segmentation method that extracts regions or entities from the image. According to the criteria of the gray level, uniformity of texture, contrast with the same background, region, shape, size and so on, a segmentation region can be formed by combining the adjacent pixels with a similar nature.

Edge detection

This is a method used to obtain the contour curve of the images. The basic idea of this method is to detect the edge points of the image, and then connect the points to an outline according to some strategies, which constitutes a segmentation region. Generally we obtain the object boundaries by using the techniques of curve fitting, contour tracking, or connection of the edge points.

Segmentation based on specific theories

A number of new image segmentation algorithms have been formed by inspired from other disciplines, including wavelet transform, fractal theory, morphology, genetic algorithms, and artificial intelligence research.

Edge detection

Edge [2] is the set of pixels around which the gray area changes. Edge is an important feature in image segmentation. The common types of edges include ladder-like edge, pulse-like edge, roof-like edge, as shown in Fig. 6.2.

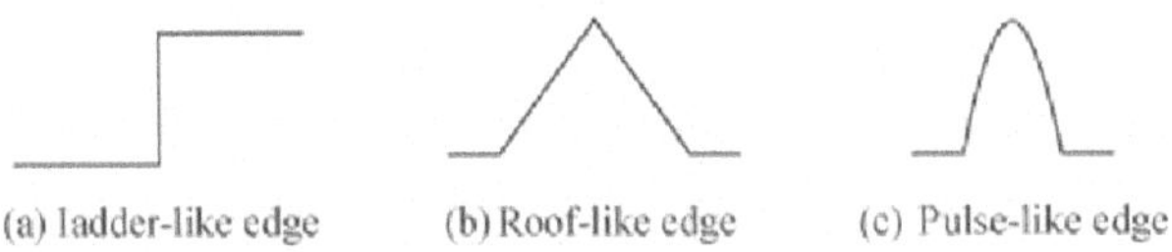

Fig. 6.2 Edge schematic diagrams.

Contour edge detection emphasizes the edge of the image. The edges that are outside the image area are usually reduced or even completely removed. This is a more prominent contour of the image processing method. A classical edge detection method is to examine the gray-scale changes of each pixel in the image in a neighborhood, according to the variation of the adjacent first or second order directional derivative of the edge, to detect the edge with a simple method. Edge detection is often supported by a differential operator, using the directional derivative convolution masks-based method to complete the detection. In fact, derivation in digital images uses the difference operator.

Edge in the case of the images is reflected by the discontinuity of gray. For a pixel on the edge of the image, its neighborhood is a band of gray-scale changes. We use the module and direction of the gray-scale gradient vector at a pixel to represent the rate of change and direction. Obviously, when the module of gradient vector at a pixel is greater than a certain range, the pixel is on the boundary, and the direction of gradient vector will help us connect the boundary pixels into a point sequence. The classic edge detection algorithm is used to examine the gray changes in a certain neighborhood of each pixel of the image, using the variation of the adjacent first or second order directional derivative of the edge. This is called the local operator edge detection method.

Roberts operator

Roberts's edge detection operator, as shown in Fig. 6.3, is an operator to find the edge with the use of a partial differential operator. It is defined by the following formula:

0	1
−1	0

1	0
0	−1

Fig. 6.3 Convolution kernel of Roberts operator.

$$g(x,y) = \{[\sqrt{f(x,y)} - \sqrt{f(x+1,y+1)}]^2 + [\sqrt{f(x+1,y)} - \sqrt{f(x,y+1)}]^2\}^{\frac{1}{2}} \tag{6.1}$$

where $f(x, y)$ is the input image with the integer pixel coordinate. The process here is similar to the process in the human visual system using the operation of square root. Roberts operator is more accurate in positioning the edge, and has the best response of the steep low-noise images. The template is shown in Fig. 6.3.

Sobel operator

Sobel operator (see Fig. 6.4) consists of two convolution kernels. The rate of vertical change of gray-scale is calculated using h_x, and the rate of horizontal change of gray-scale is calculated using h_y. By the calculation of the two convolution kernels, g_x and g_y, the vectors of x and y of the gradient, of each pixel can derived. Then we can calculate the gradient vector [3]. If the output value is the module of the gradient of the pixel, we can get an edge strength map. The corresponding boundary can be achieved by threshold processing for the image.

-1	0	1
-2	0	2
-1	0	1

(a) *hx* convolution kernels

-1	-2	-1
0	0	0
1	2	1

(b) *hy* convolution kernels

Fig. 6.4 Sobel operator.

Prewitt operator

Prewitt operator (see Fig. 6.5) is similar to Sobel operator. Prewitt operator also consists of two convolution kernels, and convolution of each pixel in the image is done with the use of the two kernels. The output is the maximum value, which will create an edge margined image [4].

-1	0	1
-1	0	1
-1	0	1

(a) *hx* convolution kernels

-1	-1	-1
0	0	0
1	1	1

(b) *hy* convolution kernels

Fig. 6.5 Prewitt operator.

Kirsch operator

The typical Kirsch operator consists of four or eight convolution kernels, which are used to calculate the rate of change of gray in four or eight directions [5]. Figure 6.6 represents a Kirsch operator of four convolution kernels.

-1	0	1
-1	0	1
-1	0	1

1	1	1
0	0	0
-1	-1	-1

0	1	1
-1	0	1
-1	-1	0

1	1	0
1	0	-1
0	-1	-1

Fig. 6.6 Kirsch operator of four convolution kernels.

Each pixel in the image is a convolution with eight masks; each mask makes the maximum response against a particular edge direction. The output of marginal rate of the image is the maximum value of all the four directions. The serial numbers of the maximum respond of the masks constitute the codes of edge direction.

Using the three edge detection operators described above (Sobel operator, Prewitt operator, and Krisch operator), we can get similar edges of the image. The border of the image is always not a single pixel, and not continuous. The 3×3 convolution kernel cannot avoid the influence of high frequency noise. In this case, edge detection operator base on gradient often cannot get the best edge.

6.2.2 Restoration of Damaged Region

The approach of image restoration can be divided into a partial differential equation, texture synthesis technique, fast image restoration technique, and image decomposition techniques.

Structure-based restoration method suits patching defects in small-scale of digital image. There are two main methods: one is based on PDE, the main idea of which is to use heat diffusion equation in physics to disseminate information from around the restoration area to the restoration area. The pattern of dissemination is determined by the diffusion equation. On the contrary, we may also establish appropriate diffusion equation according to the mode of dissemination. The typical methods include the BSCB model [6], using the third-order PDE to simulate the smooth transfer process, and CDD model [7]. The other method is based on the principle of Best Guess [8], which is a variational restoration technique. The method refers to the basic principles of restoration the artists used, who believe that resoration of a defect image depends on two factors. The first one is how to use the existing information of the image (data model) and the second one is which type the original image belongs to (Prior model of the image). That is, we may convert the problem of restoration to a variational problem of functional extremum by establishing a prior model and data model of the image. Such algorithms include the TV model [7, 9], Euler's elastic (Euler's elastica) model [10], Mumford-Shah model [11], and Mumford-Shah-Euler model [12]. By means of the variational principle, partial differential equations and calculus of variations can be equivalent to each other, so they can be together as an image restoration algorithm based on variational PDE [13]. This method focuses on analyzing the microstructure of the image (such as gradient or curvature), and thus we can get the pattern of the information diffusion to implement the restoration. Because the analysis is regional, a blurring effect will appear when we restore a larger area. This method is appropriate for repair the nontexture image and texture image with small scale defaced area.

Block-based texture synthesis for an image is suitable for a chunk loss of information in the image, which is known as image inpainting technique. The main idea of this algorithm is to solve the problem according to the similarity of the blocks. Above all, select a pixel on the boundary of the region to be restored, ensuring the image block with suitable size taking the pixel as the center. Then find the matching block with the biggest similarity in the region to replace the defaced texture block. The main idea of the restoration technique based on image decomposition is to decompose the image into structure part and texture part, then to restore the structural part using the restoration algorithms, and to fill the texture part using the texture synthesis methods [14]. A number of related algorithms have been put forward, and have achieved good results.

Restoration of paintings based on BSCB model

BSCB image restoration model was proposed by Bertalmio et al. in the SIGGRAPH conference in 2000 [6]. The definition of image restoration, the intended purpose, and the classification of application are clearly proposed. The model made use of analytical methods based on partial differential equations. This model laid the basis for PDE image restoration and promoted the research in this area. As the BSCB model was built on the basis of manual restoration, the basic principles of manual patching summarized by Bertalmio et al. will be introduced firstly before the discussion of model.

The basic principles of manual restoration

In Fig. 6.7 Ω stands for the stained area, and $\partial\Omega$ stands for the edge of the stained area.

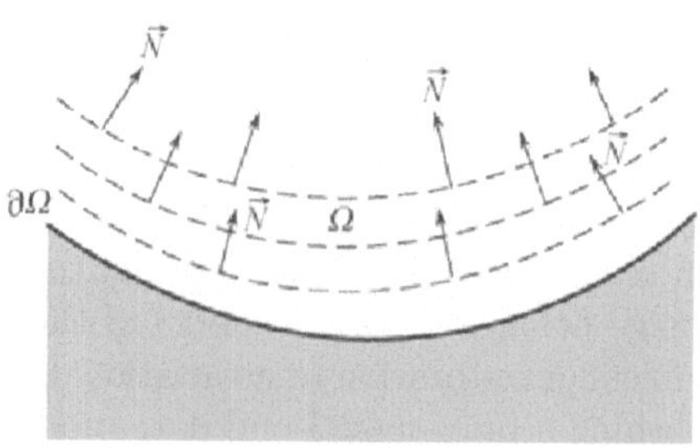

Fig. 6.7 Information diffused to the region to be restored through the edge of the region (with perimission from Bertalmio) [6].

The basic principle of manual restoration includes:

(1) The entire information of the image determines how to fill the cracks in the image, and the purpose of restoration is to rebuild the unity and integrity of the image.

(2) The image information of area surrounding the stained area Ω will be extended to the inner part of stained one, so the image can be restored by extending the isophote deriving from the boundary curve $\partial\Omega$.

(3) The inner parts of stained area Ω are still distinguished by the isophote, so we can fill the various part with the appropriate color in order to match the information of boundary curve $\partial\Omega$.

Combining the above restoration principles summaried by professional experts, Bertalmio proposed the BSCB restoration model. In this model, repeate step (2) and step (3) to disseminate gradually the information progressively into the stained area to reduce the stained region in order to implement the restoration.

Basic principles of BSCB

Assuming $I^0(i,j)$ is the patched image, the size of which is $M \times N$. The process of image restoration is a continuous iteration of the defaced image. A series of intermediate results will be produced during the iterative process and then they consist of a set of sequences $I(i,j,n)$, defining $I^0(i,j) = I(i,j,0)$, then the equation $I^R(i,j) = \lim_{n\to\infty} I(i,j,n)$ defines the final restoration image.

The iterative process can be described in mathematical language as follows:

$$I^{n+1}(i,j) = I^n(i,j) + \Delta t I_t^n(i,j), \qquad \forall (i,j) \in \Omega. \tag{6.2}$$

The superscript n defines the iteration number of the current patch, (i,j) defines the coordinates of the pixel, Δt is the rate of iteration, and $I_t^n(i,j)$ defines the updated capacity of the image for each time. Pay attention that the iterative process is only for the pixels within the region Ω to be restored and does not work on the pixels in other regions. With the progress of iterative process, the effect of image restoration is improving and the next iteration of image is the result of the update to the current image with the corresponding update capacity. Therefore, it is very vital in how to design the updated capacity.

According to the principles of manual patching, we need to extend the outside boundary line of Ω (the region to be restored) to the interior of Ω. We need to transmit useful information smoothly from the external of Ω to the internal of Ω. $L^n(i,j)$ indicates the information to be transmitted, and $N^n(i,j)$ indicates the direction of transmission, then we will get the following formula:

$$I_t^n(i,j) = \delta L^n(i,j) \cdot N^n(i,j), \tag{6.3}$$

where $\delta L^n(i,j)$ indicates the variation of transmission capacity $L^n(i,j)$, and $L^n(i,j)$ is calculated according to Laplace equation:

$$L^n(i,j) = I_{xx}^n(i,j) + I_{yy}^n(i,j).$$

The transmission capacity $L^n(i,j)$ and the variation along the direction of $N^n(i,j)$ of the original image are calculated according to Eq. (6.3). With the increase of iterations n, the transmission capacity $L^n(i,j)$ will gradually transmit into the region to be restored along the direction of $N^n(i,j)$. The iteration will continue until the two adjacent restoration effects are similar, and at this moment $I_t^{n+1}(i,j) = I_t^n(i,j)$, that is $\delta L^n(i,j) \cdot N^n(i,j) = 0$.

Then the direction of transmission $N^n(i,j)$ will be ascertained. In this model, the direction of transmission takes the direction of an isophote. The gradient $\nabla I^n(i,j)$ corresponds to the direction of maximum changes in gray-scale images, while the direction perpendicular to the gradient corresponds to the direction of minimal changes in gray-scale images. Therefore, $\nabla^{\perp} I^n(i,j)$, the 90° rotation of gradient direction, is taken as the direction of the isophote.

In order to guarantee correct evolution during the image restoration, diffusion should be monitored. To maintain the sharpness of the edges, nonlinear isotropic equation should be adopted during the diffusion process [15, 16].

$$\frac{\partial I}{\partial t}(x,y,t) = g_\varepsilon(x,y)\kappa(x,y,t)|\nabla I(x,y,t)|, \qquad \forall (x,y) \in \Omega^\varepsilon. \tag{6.4}$$

Ω^ε indicates the region that delivers morphological expansion according to the structuring element of Ω region with the radius of ε. $\kappa(x,y,t)$ indicates Euclidean curvature of isophote.

BSCB numerical discretization scheme

The iterative equation is as follows,

$$I^{n+1}(i,j) = I^n(i,j) + \Delta t I_t^n(i,j), \qquad \forall (i,j) \in \Omega. \tag{6.5}$$

In this equation, the transmission capacity is

$$\begin{aligned} I_t^n(i,j) &= \delta L^n(i,j) \cdot N^n(i,j) \\ &= \left(\delta L^n(i,j) \cdot \frac{N^n(i,j)}{|N^n(i,j)|}\right) |\nabla I^n(i,j)| \\ &= \left(\delta L^n(i,j) \cdot \frac{N(i,j,n)}{|N(i,j,n)|}\right) |\nabla I^n(i,j)|, \end{aligned} \tag{6.6}$$

$$\delta L^n(i,j) = (L^n(i+1,j) - L^n(i-1,j), L^n(i,j+1) - L^n(i,j-1)), \tag{6.7}$$

$$L^n(i,j) = I_{xx}^n(i,j) + I_{yy}^n(i,j). \tag{6.8}$$

The unit direction vector of isophote is

$$\frac{N^n(i,j)}{|N^n(i,j)|} := \frac{(-I_y^n(i,j), I_x^n(i,j))}{\sqrt{(I_x^n(i,j))^2 + (I_y^n(i,j))^2}}. \tag{6.9}$$

In the procedure of calculating the value of the gradient mode, if the central difference is used directly, it may lead to instability in the iteration

[17, 18]. Bertalmio used the Slope-limited method [6], which is defined as follows:

$$\beta^n(i,j) = \delta L^n(i,j) \cdot \frac{N(i,j,n)}{|N(i,j,n)|} \tag{6.10}$$

$$|\nabla I^n(i,j)| = \begin{cases} \sqrt{(I^n_{xbm})^2 + (I^n_{xfM})^2 + (I^n_{ybm})^2 + (I^n_{yfM})^2} & \beta^n > 0 \\ \sqrt{(I^n_{xbM})^2 + (I^n_{xfm})^2 + (I^n_{ybM})^2 + (I^n_{yfm})^2} & \beta^n < 0 \end{cases}. \tag{6.11}$$

For simplicity, the coordinates on the formula are omitted, where the subscripts b and f respectively indicate the backward difference, forward difference, and subscript m and M indicate the minimum comparing partial derivatives and zero, and the maximum comparing partial derivatives and zero separately. That is to say:

$$\begin{cases} I^n_{xbm}(i,j) = \min(I^n(i,j) - I^n(i-1,j), 0) \\ I^n_{yfM}(i,j) = \max(I^n(i,j+1) - I^n(i,j), 0) \end{cases}. \tag{6.12}$$

Although the BSCB method is very suitable for image inpainting, this method is very complex and sensitive for the selection of the initial value. Improper values will fall into an exception so that an algorithm maybe unstable and result in erroneous results. To some extent, this problem affected the BSCB method in practical applications.

Calligraphy and painting restoration based on TV model

TV theory

As shown in Fig. 6.8, D indicates the region to be restored, and the boundary of the region ∂D is a piecewise smooth, E is a ring region close to D. TV image restoration is the best guess to the pixel values in the stained region D by the overall variation of the region $E \bigcup D$ under the condition of noise constraints in the region.

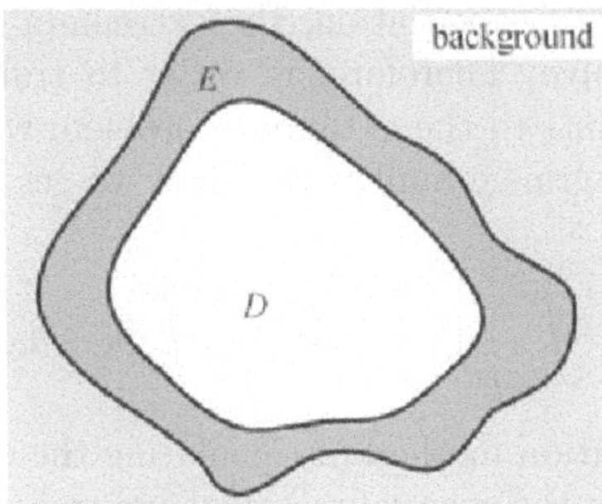

Fig. 6.8 Stain area and neighbor area.

The purpose of image restoration is to repair the image with the information of the neighborhood of the region, and to make the image more lifelike after the restoration. TV model is used to find a cost function on the region of $E \bigcup D$, and then to achieve the restoration of the image by minimizing the cost function.

u_0 is the original image, u is the restored image and the cost function is defined as following:

$$R[u] := \int_{E \cup D} r(|\nabla u|) dx dy. \tag{6.13}$$

The equation must be completed with the following noise constraints:

$$\frac{1}{A(E)} \int_E |u - u_0|^2 dx dy = \sigma^2, \tag{6.14}$$

where $A(E)$ is the area of the region E, the initial image value u_0 in D is polluted by Gaussian noise, and σ is the standard deviation of the white noise. The purpose of Eq. (6.13) is to make the region to be restored and its boundary smoother, and Eq. (6.14) ensures the robustness to noise.

In order to ensure that the broken edges can be repaired, we need to select the appropriate functional form $r(\cdot)$. On the edge of the image, ∇u is a one-dimensional impulse function δ, thus the required cost function $R[u]$ is limited, that is

$$\int_{E \cup D} r(\delta) dx dy < \infty. \tag{6.15}$$

This means that the function r(s) is unfolded as follows:

$$r(s) = s^\alpha + o(s). \tag{6.16}$$

When $\alpha = 1$, Eq. 6.13 is the TV model:

$$R[u] := \int_{E \cup D} |\nabla u| dx dy. \tag{6.17}$$

Equation (6.17) is also subject to the noise constraint of Eq. (6.14). According to the theory of variation, the extremum problem without constraint is easier to solve. Therefore, in order to transform the extremum problem with constraints to the extremum problem without constraint conditions, we use the Lagrange multiplier. Then we get the new cost function as follows:

$$J_\lambda(u) = \int_{E \cup D} |\nabla u| dx dy + \frac{\lambda}{2} \int_E |u - u_0|^2 dx dy. \tag{6.18}$$

According to the variation method of calculating the extremum of the function, the problem to get the energy functional extreme value can be attributed to solving the corresponding Euler equations.

The energy functional of a two-dimensional case can be expressed as follows:

$$E = \iint_{\Omega} F(x, y, u, u_x, u_y)\mathrm{d}x\mathrm{d}y, \tag{6.19}$$

where F is a two-dimensional function, and E is the energy functional solution. The Euler equation is as follows

$$\frac{\partial F}{\partial u} - \frac{\mathrm{d}}{\mathrm{d}x}\left(\frac{\partial F}{\partial u_x}\right) - \frac{\mathrm{d}}{\mathrm{d}y}\left(\frac{\partial F}{\partial u_y}\right) = 0. \tag{6.20}$$

The first item in Eq. (6.18) is denoted as follows:

$$J(u(x, y)) = \int |\nabla u|\mathrm{d}x\mathrm{d}y. \tag{6.21}$$

Refer to Eq. (6.19), that is $F = |\nabla u|$, we can obtain the following expression according to Euler equation (6.20):

$$\frac{\mathrm{d}}{\mathrm{d}x}\left(\frac{\partial F}{\partial u_x}\right) + \frac{\mathrm{d}}{\mathrm{d}y}\left(\frac{\partial F}{\partial u_y}\right) = 0. \tag{6.22}$$

Take $F = |\nabla u|$ into Eq. (6.22), and ultimately make E match the minimum u under the conditions of the following expressions:

$$-\nabla \cdot \left(\frac{\nabla u}{|\nabla u|}\right) + \lambda_e(u - u_0) = 0, \qquad \lambda_e = \begin{cases} \lambda, & (x, y) \in E \\ 0, & (x, y) \in D \end{cases}. \tag{6.23}$$

This is the total variation model of image restoration.

TV numerical discretization scheme

Discretize the equation of TV image restoration in Eq. (6.23) using the scheme of half-point central difference, which is described as: O is the target pixel, $\Lambda_O = \{N, S, W, E\}$ is the single pixel neighborhood point of O, and $\Lambda' = \{n, s, w, e\}$ is the half-point of O as shown in Fig. 6.9. Denote $v = (v^1, v^2) = \dfrac{\nabla u}{|\nabla u|}$, the divergence can be approximately indicated using the half-point central difference as following:

$$\nabla \cdot v = \frac{\partial v^1}{\partial x} + \frac{\partial v^2}{\partial y} \approx \frac{v_e^1 - v_w^1}{h} + \frac{v_s^2 - v_n^2}{h}, \tag{6.24}$$

where h indicates the size of the grid (here h takes one). The gradient of the half-point needs to be recalculated, such as point e:

$$v_e^1 = \frac{1}{|\nabla u_e|}\left[\frac{\partial u}{\partial x}\right]_e \approx \frac{1}{|\nabla u_e|}\frac{u_E - u_O}{h}, \tag{6.25}$$

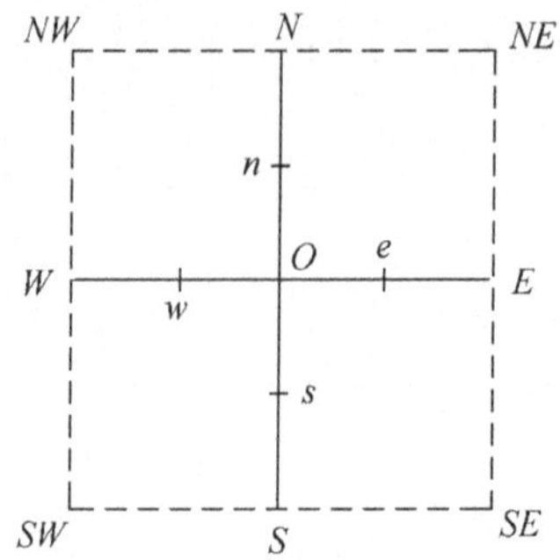

Fig. 6.9 Target pixel and neighborhood point diagram [19].

$$|\nabla u_e| \approx \frac{1}{h}\sqrt{(u_E - u_O)^2 + [(u_{NE} - u_{SE})/2]^2}$$

To the other points n, s, w take a similar manner to expand. Substitute the points into Eq. (6.24), we obtain the discrete expression against the target point O:

$$\sum_{P \in \Lambda_O} \frac{1}{|\nabla u_p|}(u_O - u_P) + \lambda_e(O) \cdot (u_O - u_O^0) = 0. \tag{6.26}$$

P represents 4-neighbors point $\{N, S, W, E\}$ of the current pixel; Accordingly, p represents half-pixel neighborhood point $\{n, s, w, e\}$, as shown in Fig. 6.9.

Next, expressions are defined as follows:

$$w_P = \frac{1}{|\nabla u_p|_\alpha} = \frac{1}{\sqrt{|\nabla u_p|^2 + \alpha^2}}, \qquad P \in \Lambda_O, \tag{6.27}$$

$$h_{OP} = \frac{w_P}{\sum\limits_{P \in \Lambda_O} w_P + \lambda_e(O)}, \tag{6.28}$$

$$h_{OO} = \frac{\lambda_e(O)}{\sum\limits_{P \in \Lambda_O} w_P + \lambda_e(O)}, \tag{6.29}$$

where α is the factor of weight in Eq. (6.27), the general value of α is among $0.1 - 0.5$, and the problem of gradient $|\nabla u_p|$ is equal to 0 in the smooth region that can be prevented. Simplify Eq. (6.26) using Eqs. (6.27)–(6.29):

$$u_O = \sum_{P \in \Lambda_O} h_{OP} u_P + h_{OO} u_O^0, \tag{6.30}$$

where $\sum\limits_{P \in \Lambda_O} h_{OP} + h_{OO} = 1$.

Expression (6.30) is equivalent to a low-pass filter. It is a nonlinear filtering system because its filter coefficients depend entirely on the value of the target point O. Freeze the filter coefficients (to get the linear equations), then solve the iterative equation using numerical iterative algorithm of Gauss-Jacobi. The value of point O can be calculated by Eq. (3.31):

$$u_O^{(n)} = \sum_{P\in\Lambda_O} h_{OP}^{(n-1)} u_P^{(n-1)} + h_{OO}^{(n-1)} u_O^{(n-1)}. \tag{6.31}$$

Information from the results of a previous restoraton u^{n-1} is used to update to u^n, where $h^{(n-1)} = h(u^{(n-1)})$. Because h is a low-pass filter, the iterative algorithm is stable.

Image restoration based on CDD model

The basic principles of CDD model

Chan et al. proposed the CDD model by means of the introduction of curvature control in the TV model. In this model, the conductivity is affected not only by the gradient but also by the curvature of isophote. This can accelerate the diffusion in order to meet the “connectivity standards”. The CDD model can restore an image with a large stained region.

The CDD model evolved on the basis of TV model. In the TV model, the diffusion is along the direction of the gradient (vertical to the direction of isophote), and the intensity of diffusion is determined by the conductivity:

$$\widehat{D} = \frac{1}{|\nabla u|}.$$

The diffusion is not along the direction of the geometric information of isophote. The geometrical information of the plane curve is described by the curvature of its isophote.

The CDD model adjusts the conductivity by considering a curvature. During the process of restoration, we have to take into account not only the length of the whole isophote, but also the changes of curvature. This model is also appropriate for the restoration of slender defaced area.

The coefficient of conductivity of CDD model is as follows:

$$\widehat{D} = \frac{g(|\kappa|)}{|\nabla u|}, \tag{6.32}$$

where $g(s)$ is a monotonic increasing function of s:

$$g(s) = \begin{cases} 0, & s = 0 \\ \infty, & s = \infty \\ 0 \sim \infty, & 0 < s < \infty \end{cases}. \tag{6.33}$$

Usually the value of $g(s)$ is as follows:

$$g(s) = s^p, \quad s > 0, p \geqslant 1.$$

Here, the intensity of the diffusion is influenced by both the gradient and curvature of isophote. Because the function $g(s)$ is a monotonic increasing function, the coefficient of conductivity is large at the place with the large curvature, and the coefficient of conductibity is small at the place with low curvature when performing restoration. This function makes the influence of the large curvature area reduction and the influence of small curvature area stability to guarantee the restoration image smoother.

Curvature is defined as follows:

$$\kappa = \operatorname{div}\left(\frac{\nabla u}{|\nabla u|}\right) = \nabla \cdot \left[\frac{\nabla u}{|\nabla u|}\right]. \tag{6.34}$$

CDD restoration model is as follows:

$$\begin{cases} \dfrac{\partial u}{\partial t} = \operatorname{div}\left[\dfrac{g(|\kappa|)}{|\nabla u|}\nabla u\right], & x \in D \\ u = u^0, & x \in D^c \end{cases}, \tag{6.35}$$

where u^0 is the original image, D is the region to be restored, and D^c is the normal region.

In normal circumstances, the original image u^0 is with noise. Denoising is required in the model. Because the topology of the region to be restored is usually more complex and the denoising results are generally not good before the restoration, the model itself needs to have a denoising function. The TV model is good at denoising, so at the peripheral regions the TV model is adopted. At the region to be restored the CDD model is adopted to perform denoising. The restoration and denoising construct a unified model:

$$\frac{\partial u}{\partial t} = \nabla \cdot \left[\frac{G(\mathrm{x}, |\kappa|)}{|\nabla u|}\nabla u\right] + \lambda_e(x)(u - u^0). \tag{6.36}$$

The conduction coefficient $G(\mathrm{x}, \kappa)$ and Lagrange multiplier must satisfy the following formula:

$$G(\mathrm{x}, s) = \begin{cases} 1, & \mathrm{x} \in D^c \\ g(s), & \mathrm{x} \in D \end{cases}, \quad \lambda_\mathrm{e}(\mathrm{x}) = \begin{cases} \lambda, & \mathrm{x} \in D^c \\ 0, & \mathrm{x} \in D \end{cases}. \tag{6.37}$$

Outside the restoration region, the value of $G(\mathrm{x}, |\kappa|)$ is 1, and Eq. (6.36) changes to the TV model, which can achieve denoising.

Numerical discretization of CDD

In restoration region, without considering the effect of noise, Eq. (6.36) changes to ($\lambda_\mathrm{e} = 0$):

$$\frac{\partial u}{\partial t} = \operatorname{div}(j) = \nabla \cdot j, \tag{6.38}$$

$$j = \frac{g(|\kappa|)}{|\nabla u|}\nabla u.$$

For convenience, the vector j is expressed as $j = (j^1, j^2)$ and j^1 is the horizontal component, j^2 is the vertical component.

$$\nabla \cdot j = \frac{j^1_{(\mathrm{d},0)} - j^1_{(-\mathrm{d},0)}}{h} + \frac{j^2_{(0,\mathrm{d})} - j^2_{(0,-\mathrm{d})}}{h}, \tag{6.39}$$

where d is the length of the grid, and h is the distance between the two grids.

The iteration scheme of Eq. (6.38) is shown as follows:

$$u^{(n+1)} = u^{(n)} + \Delta t \nabla \cdot j^{(n)}. \tag{6.40}$$

Δt is the time step. In order to ensure the stability of iterations, it is generally equal to 0.1. $u^{(n)}$is the value of the point to be restored at the time of $n \cdot \Delta t$. The discrete process in Eq. (6.40) uses the slightest restoration program explicitly, as shown in Fig. 6.10.

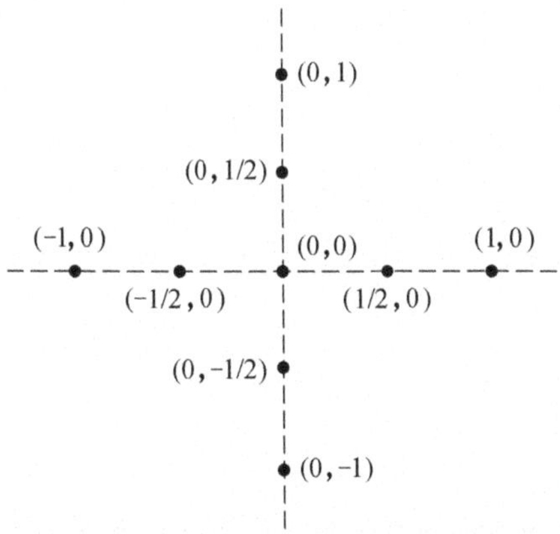

Fig. 6.10 Numerical implementation [7].

In Eq. (6.39), $d = \dfrac{1}{2}$, $h = 1$, as follows:

$$\nabla \cdot j = \frac{j^1_{(\frac{1}{2},0)} - j^1_{(-\frac{1}{2},0)}}{1} + \frac{j^2_{(0,\frac{1}{2})} - j^2_{(0,-\frac{1}{2})}}{1}. \tag{6.41}$$

Slightest gradient $|\nabla u|$ and slightest curvature κ should be calculated.

(1) $\nabla u_{(\frac{1}{2},0)}$ as an example:

$$\nabla u_{(\frac{1}{2},0)} = \left(\left.\frac{\partial u}{\partial x}\right|_{(\frac{1}{2},0)}, \left.\frac{\partial u}{\partial y}\right|_{(\frac{1}{2},0)} \right)$$

$$= \left(\frac{u_{(1,0)} - u_{(0,0)}}{1}, \frac{u_{(\frac{1}{2},1)} - u_{(\frac{1}{2},-1)}}{2} \right)$$

$$= \left(\frac{u_{(1,0)} - u_{(0,0)}}{1}, \frac{\frac{1}{2}(u_{(0,1)} + u_{(1,1)}) - \frac{1}{2}(u_{(0,-1)} + u_{(1,-1)})}{2} \right)$$
$$= \left(\frac{u_{(1,0)} - u_{(0,0)}}{1}, \frac{(u_{(0,1)} + u_{(1,1)}) - (u_{(0,-1)} + u_{(1,-1)})}{4} \right) \tag{6.42}$$

(2) $\kappa_{(\frac{1}{2},0)}$ as an example:

$$\kappa_{(\frac{1}{2},0)} = \nabla \cdot \left[\frac{\nabla u}{|\nabla u|}\right]_{(\frac{1}{2},0)} = \frac{\partial}{\partial x}\left[\frac{u_x}{|\nabla u|}\right]_{(\frac{1}{2},0)} + \frac{\partial}{\partial y}\left[\frac{u_y}{|\nabla u|}\right]_{(\frac{1}{2},0)} \tag{6.43}$$

Among the formula, the methods to get $\frac{\partial}{\partial x}\left[\frac{u_x}{|\nabla u|}\right]_{(\frac{1}{2},0)}$ and $\frac{\partial}{\partial y}\left[\frac{u_y}{|\nabla u|}\right]_{(\frac{1}{2},0)}$ are the same as Eq. (6.42). The values of $\left[\frac{u_x}{|\nabla u|}\right]_{(1,0)}$ and $\left[\frac{u_y}{|\nabla u|}\right]_{(0,1)}$ are achieved by central difference calculation.

References

[1] Jin F (2008) Restoration of Silk Painting of Wu Zhuo in Qing Dynasty. Cultural Relics of Central China, (6): 103 – 106

[2] He B, Ma T, Wang Y, et al (2002) Visual C++ Digital Image Processing (the Second Edition). Posts & Telecom Press, Beijing

[3] Davis L (1975) A Survey of Edge Detection Techniques. Computer Graphics and Image Processing, 4(3): 248 – 270

[4] Prewitt J (1970) Object Enhancement and Extraction. In: Lipkin BS, Rosenfeld A (eds) Picture Processing and Psychopictories, pp 75 – 149, Academic Press, New York

[5] Kirsch R (1971) Computer Determination of the Constituent Structure of Biological Images. Computers and Biomedical Research, 4(3): 315 – 328

[6] Bertalmio M, Sapiro G, Caselles V, et al (2000) Image Inpainting. In: Proceedings of the 27th Annual Conference on Computer Graphics and Interactive Techniques, pp 417 – 424, New Orleans, Louisiana, USA, 23 – 28 July 2000

[7] Chan T, Shen J (2001) Non-texture Inpainting by Curvature-Driven Diffusions (CDD). Journal of Visual Communication and Image Representation, 12(4): 436 – 449

[8] Geman S, Geman D (1984) Stochastic Relaxation, Gibbs Distributions, and the Bayesian Restoration of Images. IEEE Transactions on Pattern Analysis and Machine Intelligence, PAMI – 6(6): 721 – 741

[9] Rudin L, Osher S, Fatemi E (1992) Nonlinear Total Variation Based Noise Removal Algorithms. Physica D, 60(1–4): 259–268

[10] Chan T, Kang S, Shen J (2002) Euler's Elastica and Curvature-based Inpainting. SIAM Journal on Applied Mathematics, 63(2): 564–592

[11] Tsai A, Yezzi A Jr, et al (2001) Curve Evolution Implementation of the Mumford-Shah Functional for Image Segmentation, Denoising, Interpolation and Magnification. IEEE Transactions on Image Processing, 10(8): 1169–1186

[12] Esedoglu S, Shen J (2002) Digital Inpainting Based on the Mumford-Shah-Euler Image Model. European Journal of Applied Mathematics, 13(4): 353–370

[13] Zhang H, Peng Q (2007) A Survey on Digital Image Inpainting. Journal of Image and Graphics, 12(1): 1–10

[14] Tian Y (2008) Research of Image Inpainting Models Based on PDE. Dissertation, Northwest University, Xi'an, China

[15] Perona P, Malik J (1990) Scale-Space and Edge Detection Using Anisotropic Diffusion. IEEE Transactions on Pattern Analysis and Machine Intelligence, 12(7): 629–639

[16] CatteF, Lions P, Morel J, et al (1992) Image Selective Smoothing and Edge Detection by Nonlinear Diffusion. SIAM Journal on Numerical Analysis, 29(1): 182–193

[17] Stanley O, Sethian J (1988) Fronts Propagating with Curvature-Dependent Speed: Algorithms Based on Hamilton-Jacobi Formulations. Journal of Computational Physics, 79(1): 12–49

[18] Marquina A, Osher S (2000) Explicit Algorithms for a New Time Dependent Model Based on Level Set Motion for Nonlinear Deblurring and Noise Removal. Journal on Scientific Computing 22(2): 387–405

[19] Chan T, Shen J (2002) Mathematical Models for Local Non-texture Inpaintings. SIAM Journal on Applied Mathematics, 62(3): 1019–1043

7 Digital Museum

Digital Museum utilizes computer and network techniques to provide a rich experience. Compared with a traditional museum, a digital museum has some unique characteristics, such as storage digitization, networking capabilities, and resource sharing.

A digital museum breaks through many bottleneck issues of a traditional museum, through utilizing some advanced technologies such as computer graphics, emulation technology, multimedia technology, artificial intelligence (AI), computer networking technology (CNT), parallel processing technology and multi-sensors input, to simulate a human's vision, sense of hearing and tactile senses. A digital museum is able to immerse someone in the virtual experience. A person can appreciate the charm of an ancient culture legacy with freedom and at their own pace. By means of diversified media methods, such as one-dimensional character information, two-dimension images, three-dimensional model and video a digital museum can demonstrate the contents of an actual museum and give an expansion in the visual sense. Also, it offers content-oriented searching technology method to seek and pinpoint cultural relic documentation quickly. This provides outstanding services better than a traditional museum. A digital museum offers various methods of digital watermarking technology to protect digital cultural relic material's copyright infringement. With this method, it can provide cyber security to protect rare cultural relic's material and to provide effective means for spreading numerical data efficaciously.

A digital museum is free from the constraints of building, an exhibition hall and standard visiting times of a traditional museum [1]. It has changed the features of a traditional museum which demonstrates a cultural relic statically. It has realized stereoscopic color displays, multimedia access, telecommunication network transmission, intelligential retrieval, and virtual reality platforms.

The development of digital museum is increasingly attracting attention. People can learn about culture relic information indoors via digital museum [2]. At present, studies towards the digital museums have achieved some results. There are many digital museums on the internet for people to view, and lots of famous museums in China and abroad have set up websites. Currently eighteen university digital museums in China that are supported by the Nation Ministry of Education have opened.

7.1 Foundation of Digital Museum

In this section, definition of digital museum, functionality of digital museum, digital museum's model type, digital museum's framework and software, exhibit database and management are introduced.

7.1.1 Definition of Digital Museum

A museum is a place which collects, protects, and demonstrates all kinds of important culture relics and it is a significant component of social infrastructure. The personal computer and network technologies have had a major impact on modern lives. Digitization and virtual reality are now a reality and this new insight has allowed us to look beyond the traditional building as a meeting place. Along with the development of information technology, network technology, and the rise of network-oriented education, it is important for us to build a network based digital museum to upgrade and digitalize our college and national museums for the sake of resource sharing and protection as well. The tide of Chinese museums digitization construction offer chances for museum teaming on the Internet.

In recent years, the idea of digital museum has emerged along with the development of information technology and expanding applications on cultural relics in the domain of museums. In academic circles it has not reached a common name but "digital museum", is also called a "digitizing museum", "virtual museum", "on line museum", "electronic museum", etc. [3].

A digital museum can be interpreted as a platform dealing with the storage and management of both natural and cultural heritage information through the use of digitalization. It utilizes information technologies such as computer network technology, database technology, multimedia technology, virtual reality techniques, AI, and human computer interaction technology (HCI). It applies these technologies to tasks of sampling, custody, research, exhibition, and management of real museum's collections. It offers permanent digitization storage, repair, and management with demonstration methods for cultural relics.

The design of a digital museum needs to meet the requirements for a digital museum server to run robustly while a relatively large number of users access the site simultaneously. The design of a digital museum needs to meet the following traits:

(1) Because the number of digital museum system's users can be high the hardware system design needs to account for a surge of clients requests.

(2) Due to the authority of a digital museum, cyber security and reliability should be taken into account during the design process.

(3) Designs also need to pay attention to the diversity of software system components, in order to make digital museum system with many uses.

(4) The development of management software must follow the open system principle, ensuring the platform's generality, and follow common international standard for the purpose of upgrading and maintenance in the future.

(5) Users' communication with digital museum varies due to their different internet connection speed. Since this communication is multimedia information-oriented, it can require a high demand of network bandwidth. In addition, the site will be frequently visited by some experts, while at the same time, it also provides services to those people who occasionally view the site.

7.1.2 Functionality of Digital Museum

Compared with traditional museums, digital museums have the following advantages:

(1) Exhibit infinite replicability reduces the frequent of real show, protects the cultural relics, and reduces the possibility of exhibits' damage or theft.

(2) With the help of various demonstration methods, a digital museum transmits numerous information experiences to users. This allows various kinds of multimedia information to present users and to immerse the users into the experiences.

(3) People can visit freely without restriction by time and visiting routes, which makes contribution for enhancing a nation's scientific and cultural level.

(4) In the digital museum, people can use computer technologies to recover a cultural relic's intrinsic environment, to add to the exhibit demonstration's atmosphere and demonstrate cultural background which adheres to the exhibit. It is difficult to recover cultural relic's intrinsic environment in traditional museums.

(5) The application of digital museums enhances the management levels of a museum exhibit. It adds convenience for retrieval and research.

For carrying out public education activities, a digital museum can launch effective education activities in interactive ways. Several restrictions should be taken into consideration such as time and budget. A digital museum breaks these restrictions and allows cooperations between museums and school education. A digital museum is composed of various kinds of databases. It uses a figure document format to save and modify a museum's information accurately. A digital museum could be used as an information storage center and a historical data's storage base. Its information database contains the entire museum's information. Retrieval and classification access to this database allows visitors or staffs to search relevant information they need. A digital museum can simulate real scenes through virtual technology so that an audience can pay a visit to exhibition without leaving their home. It allows browsing of the digital museum with voices and images to achieve a sense of reality and deliver interaction between digital museum and the audience.

Traditional museums and digital museums cannot replace each other, but they can complement each other. A digital museum is a traditional museum's representation in digital domain, and its role is to assist a traditional museum to realize its function. The "Digital Museum" is a site of realizing cultural education function in the virtual cyber world, based on traditional museum's digitized information. In the construction idea of a digital museum, "virtual" is helping people build up relevant cultural knowledge's framework through information online. It leads the audience to come back to a traditional museum, through their own experience to build up their own knowledge. The construction of "digital museum" or "virtual museum" and traditional museum bring out the best in each other.

7.1.3 Digital Museum's Model Type

Due to several differences of expression, contents, and sustainability technologies, a digital museum can be presented in various modes. A digital museum's development model has a simple website mode, an exhibit and exhibition hall's three-dimensional virtual demonstration mode. The third mode is exhibition hall's or scene's wander and three-dimensional mode. The finally mode is through some virtual reality equipment to accomplish virtual wander and simulation mode.

Simple website mode

A simple website is through the use of print media's (picture, characters, video, etc.) integrated. This mode is adopted by many civil museums. It can be created simply with low cost, low technical requirements, and quick access speed. Its major role is to publicize and announce museum information data. Using this mode, it can add digital watermarking in a picture to protect the copyright.

Exhibit and exhibition hall's three-dimensional virtual demonstration

This mode can use environmental technology to realize three-dimensional demonstration of exhibits, using many two-dimensional photos and gluing (image combination). For three-dimensional relics, shooting photos around them continuously with different angles, merged they will be later. Panoramic camera technology can take a picture in a full circle (360°). For a more complicated three-dimensional demonstration, one can use digital three-dimensional capturing device or 3Ds Max for modeling. In case there is no three-dimensional capturing device available, one can still use 3Ds Max to model the cultural relic, then take a 2D photo of the cultural relic. Next, capture the texture information and capturing map onto the sculpture of the cultural relic. After using popular software such as WEB 3D format to store the image the user can post online.

Realizing exhibition hall or scene's wandering and three-dimensional simulation

Modeling software makes elaborate modeling and rendering for a scene. 3Ds Max format can be used to store it. The model can realize user's virtual wandering and three-dimensional simulation after defining a certain route. Users can use the direction key on the keyboard, walking freely in a museum, and watching particular content by clicking a hotkey which is defined in the virtual scene. But this method cannot accomplish complicated user interaction. After modeling, the placement pattern and route of the cultural relic cannot be changed. This method can restrict users' ability to understand cultural relics.

Accomplishing virtual wander and emulation mode through some virtual reality equipment

Users can wear virtual reality equipment (three-dimensional glasses etc.) to explore in a virtual museum, which adds to the user's immersive sense. However, virtual equipment has yet to be popularized in this stage, so normal users at home cannot browse and wander in a virtual museum by virtual reality equipment.

7.1.4 Digital Museum's Framework and Software

A digital museum is divided into three parts: hardware platform, software platform, and resource platform. The hardware platform contains servers, various kinds input and output devices, and network equipment. It is the foundation of a digital museum framework. The resource platform contains all kinds of media information resources, such as text, sounds, images, animations and three-dimensional virtual demonstrations. These are the soul and core of the digital museum and store the data in a digital museum's system. The software platform is divided into system software and utility software. The constitution of a digital museum is showed in Table 7.1.

The digital museum software platform is further divided into three parts: digital museum sustain system, digital museum exhibit resource library, and digital museum management system which are showed in Fig. 7.1. Detailed system constitution is showed in Fig. 7.2.

Table 7.1 Digital museum system constitution

Digital Museum	
System Sustain Software Platform	
Web Server	Multimedia Database

(to be continued)

(Table 7.1)

Operation System (OS)	
System Hardware Platform	System Resource Platform
Digital Museum Hardware (high-performance server, network equipment and high bandwidth Internet connection)	Digital Museum Resource (characters, sound, image, multi-media and three-dimensional virtual exhibition)

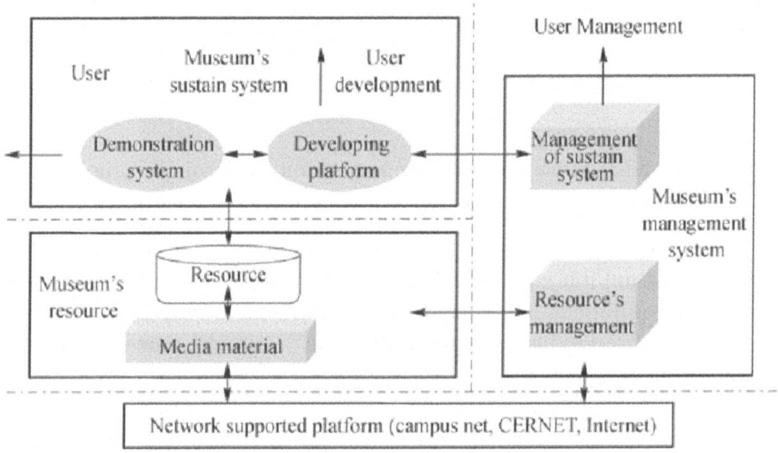

Fig. 7.1 Picture of software platform constitution.

Four-layer function structures of the software platform.

An early digital museum design mainly applied to the management of cultural relic's text and simple picture information, utilizing Client/Server (C/S) or Browser/Server (B/S) structure. Along with the development of information technology and the Internet, a digital museum began to cover more content. The frame work of the digital museum consists of four-layers:

The first layer is the browser presentation layer. It accomplishes the function of a user interface. It may have several applications from client-side to AS (application server) which is specified by URL, conveying needed file materials to user through HTTP. The client-side may just accept file materials which are displayed in a browser.

The second layer is AS layer, which is in the charge of integrating functions of each Web service. This will shape the museum's business logic to provide invocation to a visitor. A web service accepts a user application by first finding the needed Web service according to a Universal Description, Discovery and Integration (UDDI) registration center, then it sends out an application to a Web service with the result which is returned from Web service, then uses HTTP to provide feedback to the client-side.

The third layer is the Web service layer. This layer offers the final Web service to the browser. Each Web service can be on different physical equipment, reflecting the demand of distributed system. It offers certain Web services which are registered in the UDDI registration center to the application service.

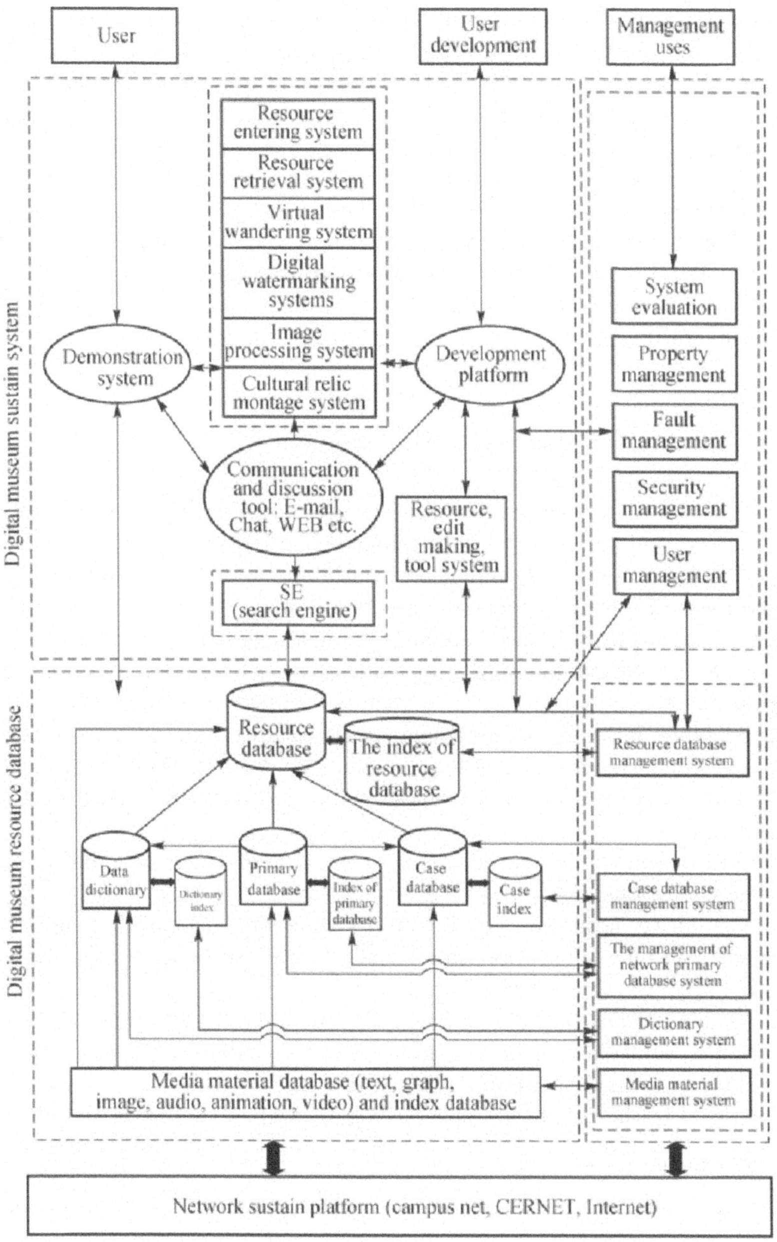

Fig. 7.2 Detailed software platform constitution.

The fourth layer is the database service layer. It processes inputs according to a user's requests. Because of the existence of Web services, each independent Web service can use a certain database service, which truly implements data's distributed storage and allows adaption in a large scale application.

Employing Web service technology can sustain all kinds of the digital museum resource's inter communication and sharing between isomerism and heterogeneous platforms. It also can describe system service functions by the machine reading format. Using the HTTP method to convey between objects through the Web Service Description Language Protocol (WSDLP) allows other systems to know of the system services. Web Service technology can place an interlayer before the existing subassembly and code. This can set up a new business solution to provide an effective integration of technology for reusing and integrating current available system resources. By means of a Web service a digital museum can deliver cross-platform functionality, gather data system information to establish an information portal, and achieve system demand requirements which span multiple platforms.

7.1.5 Exhibit Database and Management

According to a digital museum's data features, the database is generally divided into several parts, such as the management database, image resource's image database, video and animation's database, and three-dimensional entity database. Their main functions are as follows:

(1) Management database: manage the holdings management task. It is responsible for maintaining and coordinating other databases and providing retrieval interfaces.

(2) Holding database: saves document literatures, relevant introductions and researching essays that belong to various kinds of exhibits.

(3) Image resource database: saves exhibit and relevant history's photos and pictures.

(4) Video demonstration database: saves relevant video data and animation demonstrations.

(5) 3D entity database: saves exhibit's three-dimensional data information which can offer vivid representations to the corresponding exhibits and can provide materials for virtual reality.

In combination of the several parts discussed above the related database management solution can have a hierarchical distributed cluster database system that is formed as follows, showed in Fig. 7.3.

Each part of the database's specific organization structure is as follows:

Management database

The Management database manages the holding of goods' day-to-day management, such as storage, archives maintenance operations, and the manage-

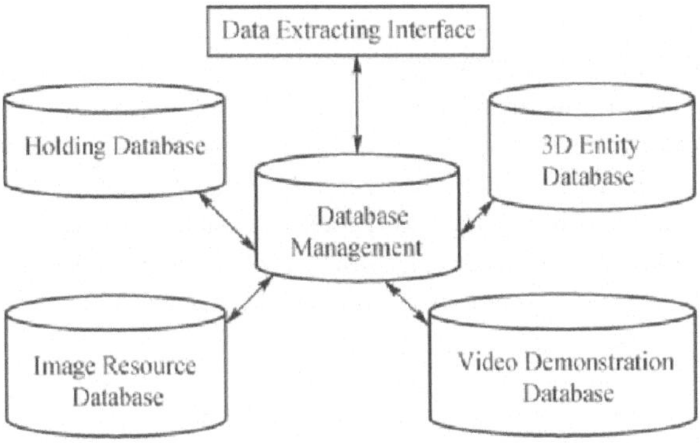

Fig. 7.3 Distributed cluster database system.

ment of the other four parts of the database with operational authority. The management database is the place in which the holding goods inventory and other information is stored. Specific content includes the exhibit inventory. All holding goods have unique tabs, while using a classification system to organize the holding goods in the museum. In addition, it also includes the time when holding goods are being put in storage and the time of entering into museum of holding goods. It also includes the information of maintenance personnel and limits of authority, to guarantee holding information security. It also has relevant photo, data, three-dimensional entity, and video and audio data, so as to abstract pertinent data and holding goods information into the relevant database.

Museum database

An article collected by a museum has high material and scientific research value, accompanied by relevant historical materials. These contents include holding goods' document materials and relevant introductions, for instance, the genus information of specimen and relevant habit introductions. This part of material is the core data of holding goods, possessing a high usage value. Taking document material as the principal component makes it easy to retrieve the result from a classified index.

Holding goods image database

The holding goods image database is a database where effective storage, management, organization, and the retrieval of image data of the holdings takes place. On account of an image as multimedia information, it also has content clues which are related to human sensory system (vision and hearing) that are relatively explicit but are not effectively described in the data. Content-oriented retrieval, which fits a human's sensory experience, is apt to acceptance, yet becomes a significant feature of an image database.

Image data has some content clues which can be hard to describe by character and numeric values, for instance, a certain object's shape, color, and texture of the image. When users want to use these clues to retrieve data, they first have to translate it into text and performa keyword search. However, this transformation has certain subjectivity and is extremely time-consuming. Constructing a holding image database will have enormous data volume. If doing this task by keyboard entry it will require a huge amount of work as well as difficulties in proceeding effectively. Content based retrieval (CBR) will be of urgent demand. CBR, as a technology of information retrieval will quickly fetch inquired cultural relic information from a large-scale distribution database in a response time can be accepted by users.

Video and audio demonstration database

Video and audio demonstration database contains rich information and can demonstrate relative data in a digital museum, such as relevant activities or the documentary of an event. Due to their traits that can express real world intuitively, vividly and efficiently, this database can store additional information content. Video and audio data have huge amount of information and complicated structures. Performing effective management and retrieval with it present tremendous difficulty. Structuring the video database reasonably is the key of a success. Video data consists of a set of related image frames according to the interdependency of frames. Thus a video is separated into several fragments, and multiple video fragments compose a video. It also has video shot change situation, image character, and domain knowledge. The storage of video and audio should adopt standard compression formats which are convenient for retrieval and storage space optimization. At present, International Organization for Standards (ISO) MPEG4 is the norm that is widely applied. MPEG7 and MPEG12 as a norm will provide the standard based on content-oriented compression storage standard.

Video annotation bank deposits a few descriptive pieces of information to the corresponding video that is needed to for an annotation-oriented index. It takes full advantage of the abundant information included in video and audio. In the light of semantics content in the video database, the annotation via HCI (Human-computer Interaction) is automated.

An annotation language includes character annotation and icon annotation origin annotation.

The character annotation contains statement annotation and critical annotation. The icon annotation utilizes an icon to indicate the time domain character of video. The origin annotation takes advantage of a digital video camera to add relevant information in the video data stream server in accordance of the video annotation, including a video camera's motion, angle, camera lens range or the acoustic information of video.

Three-dimensional entity bank

Three-dimensional entity bank is used for depositing the three-dimensional information of Museum's holding goods. It is used to realize goods' sense of reality, reproduce damaged goods and can be used in the component bank of virtual reality. Its data types can be as abstract as dot-line-face data and the museum's holding three-dimensional scanning data. Because of the huge data volume of a three-dimensional entity database and certain three-dimensional space structures, it adopts an object-oriented hierarchy group possessing prodigious superiority.

Three-dimensional point data or data which deposits museum's holding goods can be used for an entity's display. It can include the material's quality information so as to reveal an entity factually.

For three-dimensional point data, we can use a layered structure to manage through multilayer stacking to turn it into an entity. The dot-line-face abstract model uses dot-line-face as objects by means of object combination composes entity. These data that are saved in the database should provide multi-resolution to show its features. This is convenient for different browsing demands. A uniformed storage format provides easy presentation, browsing and search capabilities.

The fundamental management demand of the media material bank contains:

(1) providing the make function;
(2) providing a compilation function;
(3) providing an editing function;
(4) providing an inquiry function;
(5) providing a preview function.

For inquiry functions, the text database's inquiry technologies and multimedia data's inquiry strategies are significant technologies to a digital museum. As with traditional museums, plenty of information needs to be classified, indexed, organized, and combined for browsing and use in a digital museum. Without specific tools, people cannot fulfill these tasks by hand. A digital museum's platform can offer automatic tools to produce visiting indicators to direct text or multimedia information. This is infeasible using a manual indexing process. An ample information processing ability can offer indexing, filing, relevancy construction, intellectual and a baseline foundation to be used by administrators. Managers have access to file organizations and screening device. These devices provide certain customized information and manages large amounts of information. A hotspot of current research is how to establish an index toward multimedia information to make a user inquiry effective. Using an index, the image can be found according to color, shape, and texture that is located in an image. To retrieve the information's attributes in a digital museum, a text search tool can provide full-text search capability. Beyond text searching, the search tool also needs to offer advanced digitization-oriented image, vision, or voice content's inquiry technologies.

The specifications needs are discussed in the following. The system should guarantee the security and reliability of the content. The system should establish media material based on the facing of the visit-oriented metadata model. The system should provide a search function of various media material efficiently. The system should provide a structural model that has different demonstration content which is constructed by relevant media material and an effective design method. The system should provide downloadable or a compressed download function to allow built demonstration content. The system should sustain maximum concurrence and visiting capability to ensure the system's expand ability. The facing content transmission management includes: sustain multimedia upload and download function; ensure the security, stability, and confidentiality of multimedia transmission; integrate existing practical, mature technologies and products; guarantee the reliability and the upper bound of transmission delay.

7.2 Standards and Norms of Exhibition Digitization

In this section, content classification and index system, metadata norm of a digitalize exhibition, and content and type of media material bank are introduced.

7.2.1 Content Classification and Index System

The features of object properties and the basic requirements of management allow confirmation of the museum exhibition's information category. The norm adopts a stratum level taxonomy to divide museum exhibition information into three layers, which are index group, index set and index item. Its architecture is showed in Table 7.2.

Table 7.2 Index system architecture chart

<table>
<tr><td rowspan="4">index group</td><td rowspan="2">index set</td><td>index item</td></tr>
<tr><td>index item</td></tr>
<tr><td rowspan="2">index set</td><td>index item</td></tr>
<tr><td>index item</td></tr>
</table>

The Exhibition information index system includes three index groups, thirty-three index sets, and one hundred and thirty-nine index items [4].

Index coding method:

This norm's index category code is an alphanumeric mixed type layer code. Each integrated code is divided into 3 layers, whose length is 5 bits. Its architecture is shown in Fig. 7.4.

Index group is indicated by a 1 bit capital Latin letter.

For instance:

A Exhibition information index group

B Exhibition management information index group

C Exhibition document and acoustic image material information index group

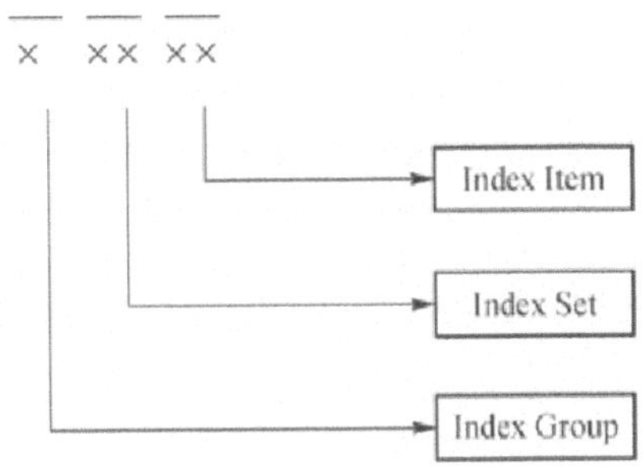

Fig. 7.4 Alphanumeric mixed type layer code structure.

Index set indicate by 2 bits Arabic numerals.

For instance:

A01 Name index set

A02 Classification index set

A03 Age index set

Index itemsare indicated by 2 bit Arabic numerals.

For instance:

A01 Name index set

A0101 Original name

A0102 Name

Note: specific information classification code of museum exhibition is not listed here.

Correlative standard:

The description of relevant index items of a digital museum exhibition's information index system reference the following standards:

GB2260–1995 PRC (The People's Republic of China) administrative division code

GB2659–1994 The world name code

GB3100–1993 SI (The International System of Units) and its application

GB3304–1991 China ethnicity name code

GB7156–1987 Literature security classification code

GB/T7408–1994 Data element and exchange format's information interchange

Date and time's notation:

GB2261–1991 Human's gender code

GB9649–1998 Geology mineral products term's classification code

Aerolitics, petrology and paleontology:

GB9649.9–1998 geology mineral products terminology's classification code—mineral products

GB/T14467–1993 Chinese plant classification and its code

GB/T156281–1995 Chinese animal classification code—vertebrate

ZB40–94/CBLB The form of publication of works category code

7.2.2 Metadata Specification of Digitalized Exhibitions

In the management process of various digitalized information, the metadata method is the most widely adopted method. Metadata is data which describe other data, and it can be used for describing and managing digital information resources generally. The amount of digitalized cultural relic resources is enormous, so we must take a normalized management approach.

Metadata is data which describes the attributes of a piece of data. Metadata in the process of resource's storage, management, and exchange is widely applied to a data set attribute's structure description. Metadata possesses the trait of abstractness, and is the description of structuring, abstraction, and summarization for an information set. It is able to depict substantive characteristics digitalized resources and data.

Metadata is an effective means and prerequisite to ensure digitalized resource sharing and exchange. It is generally used on a normalized description of a digitalize resource and overall information. This kind of description scope contains: the feature of resource's content, quality, expression method, storage format, and management method. This allows its use in normalizing the task of digitalize resource's storage, searching, checkout, evaluation, and selection.

The application of metadata in a digital museum, is the ability to manage the digital information resource of tangible holding goods in a museum with respect to the digitalize resource's generation, description, annotation, retrieval, management, application, and sharing that is of significantly important meaning. Among the application of a digital museum both domestic and abroad there is not yet an agreed upon metadata standard directed at digital museums. The choice is usually to adopt a relative mature digital museum's metadata standard. Commonly used metadata standards in digital museum include Dublin core (DC) metadata, Categories for the Description of Works of Art (CDWA) metadata, and VRA core metadata.

The DC (Dublin core) metadata is a metadata standard which has the most influence at present. This standard is an international and interdisciplinary research achievement, and has already formed an international factual application standard. The DC metadata roots have had project achievement and were organized by Online Computer Library Center (OCLC). The Dobin Core Metadata Initiative (DCMI) takes charge of maintenance, fundamental norm aggregation to include 15 "core elements", and is used for restraining the organization and description method of digitalize information. It is also widely applied to the digital library domain. The DC metadata standard is exploited by an informal group that is made up of computer, network, and library experts. Its purpose is to set up an extensive metadata element set and use it to describe any network information resource as simply as possible. This ensures that any author can set up his/her own metadata. The DC metadata standard has the following traits: simple establishment and maintenance, easily comprehended sentence structure, system inter operability, and expand ability. It also supports expansion which can be expanded to an element by using TYPE and SCHEME definitive and LINK reference.

The CDWA metadata standard uses categories for the description of works of art and was exploited by the AITF (Art Information Task Force) in 1996. The AITF offers a structuring tool for the group (such as museum and archive) that uses art information to describe works of a piece of art (include image). The design of this metadata is aimed at the demand of describing works of a piece of art. The main points of the description lies in "movable" objects and images that include oil painting, carving, pottery, metal work, furniture, and design performing arts that come from different periods and geographic ranges. This metadata has 27 core element categories, and each core element's category contains a layer or multilayer subcategory element that includes theme, record, management, and other attributes. A museum's digitalized holding goods have corresponding physical forms and they also have digital multimedia's material resources and background knowledge which correspond to space-time, figure, historical culture, and other attributes. The elements of CDWA can effectively reflect peculiar characters of digitalized holding goods, which fit for the description of digital museum's holding goods and digital resources.

The Visual Resources Association (VAR) core, visual resource association core is the standard established by the United States Visual Resource Association, and is used for regulating the description of visual works of culture and its image resource. This standard has already been published to the third edition in June 2000. It describes visual arts including painting, carving, performance, music, literary and artistic works, architecture and their design, or other goods which describe the cultural meaning. The objects that are described by this metadata include goods' reproduction or representation. It can be a material object's information, relevant slide show, photograph, picture recording, or all kinds of digital forms. The work described by this metadata method can have multiple digitalize forms. This standard contains 17 core elements.

7.2.3 Content and Type of Media Material Bank

The media material is a basic material unit which conveys a museum's resource information. According to the media form, it can be divided into text material, graph (image) material, acoustic material, animation material, and video material. According to its content, it can be divided into noun conception, symbol, name, background material, introduction, history material, relevant research achievement, or other material.

A media material library is the basic unit of a digital museum. It includes all kinds of material objects and specimens that are collected in the museum and information resources which explains and introduces objects or specimens. The material in the material library should have material objects and its relevant data and script. The chart, image, voice, animation, and video within the library should be compressed through advanced, efficient methods complying with international standard's compression technology. To be satisfied with the demands of storage and network transmission, a media material bank ought to set up index information so as to inquire, browse, and provide storage quickly.

Text material

The main type of text material is reference material that considers characters as the medium, including exhibit introduction, figure explanation, history material, and relevant research achievements.

Two-dimensional graph and image material

Owing to the nature of a museum, large quantities of material objects should be displayed on the network via graph or an image's forms. Two-dimensional graph or image material should adopt GIF (graphics interchange format) or JPEG (joint photographic experts group) format commonly used in a network for processing and storage. Color image's color depth should not under 256. A gray level image's gray-scale should not lower than 128. Scanning image's resolution ratio should not be lower than 150 dpi.

The main types of materials to include are symbol, apparatus, scenery, character, botany, animal, architecture, electrical equipment, computer, transportation, sign, advertisement, microorganism, crop, geology and explanation.

Audio material

A characteristic of visiting a museum is that they can at the same time get live commentary and guidance from staff while visitors are appreciating exhibitions in a museum. Some subjects have information resources with acoustic information in the material libary. Digital voice sampling frequency cannot be under 1 kHz, quantization digit should be at least 8 bits, and the number of sound track is at least a single track.

The main formats of voice data storage are WAV, MP3, and MIDI. Digital voice uses the WAV format. Music has adopted the MP3 format. Music that is recorded by MIDI equipment uses the MIDI format set for live interactive audio adopt streaming media format. All audio data needs to be converted into a streaming media format, if it has other format's audio (WAV, MP3, MIDI etc.). Therefore, there is the need of two sorting formats to put in the storage, one is original format, the other is streaming media format which has original data transformed. The speech which is used for commentary dubbed by male and female adopts standard Mandarin, English or native host language.

The main types of audio have music, natural sound, and speech.

Video material

Due to the disadvantage that some museums' material objects cannot clearly exhibit through the form of graph or image, and in order to further visualize explanation of parts of material object, we need to use video material to illustrate the idea.

Video materials have four storage formats, AVI format, Quick Time format, MPEG format, and streaming media format.

The AVI format is preferred on a PC platform, while Apple (Mac OS) series should use the Quick Time format. The video material which is used for appreciation should use the MPEG format. An audio material which is real time transmitted on the Internet should use a streaming media format. All video data need to be made into the ASF streaming media format, if it has another video format (AVI, MPGE, MOV etc.). Therefore two sorts of the formats need to be submitted. One is original format and the other is AFS streaming media format which has transformed. The color of an image of each frame should not be under 256 colors or the gray level should not lower than 128 levels. The audio and video in given multimedia data should be perfectly synchronized. The sampling of video uses Y, U, V component sampling mode. The sampling reference frequency is 13.5 MHz. It should include three sampling formats, 4:1:1, 4:2:2, and 4:4:4.

Animation material

Sometimes, a few illustrative materials need to be performed by way of animation. Animation material uses formats including GIF format, Flash format, AVI animation format, FLI/FLC animation format, or Quick Time animation format. All animation data needs to be made into a GIF format or Flash format, and if it has other format's animation data (AVI, FLI/FLC, MOV etc.), two sorts of formats need to be submitted, one is original format, the other is GIF format or Flash format which has been transformed. The color and modeling of animation should be harmonious, and inter-frames should be strongly related.

3D model material

The main types of 3D model material are three-dimensional scanning point cloud of an exhibit or meshes data, exhibit's 3D artificial modeling data, relevant geometrical characteristic and model's attribute and its grouped data.

7.3 Virtual Exhibition of Digital Museum

In this section, the two-dimensional technology of exhibition and 3D technology of exhibition are introduced for virtual exhibition.

7.3.1 Two-dimensional Technology of Exhibition

The two-dimensional demonstration of an exhibit is the most basic means of an exhibit's demonstration [5]. Each cultural relic is displayed by a high-quality two-dimensional picture and accompanied with detailed comments and clear three-view drawing. The three-view drawing can ensure the detail of cultural relics from multiple angles, such as seal cutting, inscriptions and modeling. It also can develop the special effect system of pictures of a cultural relic, utilizing special effects technology to fulfill special effect aimed at the pictures of a cultural relic. An example is adding illumination, varying background, zooming in/out, increasing rain or snow effect, so as to enhance the effect of demonstration.

7.3.2 3D Display Technology of Exhibitions

The pattern of an object movie

The object movie is a technology proceeding goods' demonstration. By means of photographing an object 360 degrees around a fixed angle, if we can ensure picture's exposure in an identical level, the image can give people a panoramic illusion when the image is processed in a loop playback. People regard it as appreciating a real object. Users can appreciate objects from multiple angles in front of a computer. To an exhibit about to be shown, photographing many photos of a cultural relic in 360°, each photo should have obvious repetitive parts. It uses flash or special montage software to accomplish the montage of many two-dimensional photos.

VRML visual demonstration

For advanced and complicated three-dimensional demonstrations, modeling utilizes some digital three-dimensional collection device or the use of 3Ds Max to add a texture's information. The use of WEB3D technology is implemented for demonstration on a web page. For example, we use a three-dimensional camera which is produced by Inspect Company of Canada by the use of multiangle photography of a cultural relic, to collect three-dimensional information and texture's information of an object to form a whole object with textures to output various WEB3D formats. This can be saved as a .wrl file. In this manner, installing a VRML plug-in on a browser, users can browse three-dimensional cultural relic. Users can see a virtual cultural relic through any angle and any size according to the user's own will. The modeling and texture of a cultural relic is lifelike, so it can fully reflect a cultural relic's original appearance, such as size scale, damaged degree, and engraved character. If we do not have a three-dimensional collection device, one can use 3Ds Max to model artificially this cultural relic, then photograph a two-dimensional picture to the cultural relic. The next step is to collect the texture's information of the photos. After proceeding with the input model the cultural relic is saved into WEB3D format. The product allows the user to browse on the Internet. A cultural relic's modeling and texture's information is unable to coincide with the real cultural relic completely using this method.

Cult3D virtual demonstration

To demonstrate a virtual cultural relic it needs to emphasize its interactive function. The interactive function of a VRML virtual demonstration is relative simple. It can simply rotate and zoom to the surface information of three-dimensional virtual cultural relic. However, due to the high craftsmanship of an ancient cultural relic and its skillful internal structure's design, if we want to show its internal structure, operating principles or some skills, only using VRML virtual demonstration is not enough. The Cuoory Company's Cult3D is a network 3D technology which is brand-new and of promising potential. It is produced by a company in Sweden, and is mainly used for setting up interactive three-dimensional entities on a webpage. It has a cross-platform's three-dimensional engine that belongs to Cult3D, which is known as the fastest three-dimensional image engine currently. For practical applications, we found that Cult3D not only draws quickly but also has outstanding effects of drawing. In addition, Cult3D is without the need of support by a particular graphic accelerator, which is controlled by the software. The core of Cult3D is based on JAVA and can be implanted into JAVA. Thus it can sustain all main streaming browsers cross-platform. Its excellent interactivity is the reason why the use of Cult3D to demonstrate virtual cultural relic is popular.

Virtual demonstration of an exhibition hall

To display the three-dimensional demonstration of an exhibition hall, two methods are adopted. One method is to use many consecutive photos' montage technology, the 360° panoramic montage. Its essence is using a quantity of overlapping photos which were took at different moments and different orientations in the same place to combine a whole picture (horizontal direction and vertical direction) seamlessly, meanwhile, making the binding area's color or gray level transit even. Panorama technology can make wide-field wide-angle holograms and panoramas. If the number and angle of photos relatively is high, we can piece into sphere-form exhibition halls with three-dimensional effect. The other method is to use modeling software, such as 3Ds Max, MultiGen Creator, etc. to model and render scenes, then save in a popular WEB3D format. After defining a certain route, we can realize a virtual walkthrough and three-dimensional simulation, while users can roam in the museum freely by using interactive equipment. Also, we can define some hot spots and set inter-linkage in virtual scenes, users can watch some content after clicking buttons. The biggest defect of this method is that an exhibition hall's model including cultural relic's data, the pattern of disposal and route's information is fixed. After modeling, the model cannot be changed, so it cannot fulfill complicated user's interactivity.

7.4 Copyright Protection of Digitizing Collection

The copyright protection is very important for digital museum. In this section, we focus on digital watermarking technology, image watermarking technology and 3D watermarking technology.

7.4.1 Digital Watermarking Technology

Digital watermarking technology directly implants some sign information (watermarking) into a digital carrier (include multimedia, document, software, etc.). This does not influence the use or value of the original carrier. It is not perceived by a human's conscious system (vision system or hearing system) easily. The information is hidden in a carrier. The purpose of affirming the content's creator or buyer is to convey covert information or judging whether the carrier has been tampered. Watermarking is an important research orientation of information technology security.

Digital watermarking technology has several traits:

(1) Security: Watermark's information should be safe and difficult to tamper or forge. At the same time, it should have a low error detection rate. When its original contents have changed, watermarking should change along with contents. It can detect the changing of the initial data. Watermarking has strong resistance to repeated addition;

(2) Invisibility: Watermarking should not be perceptible and cannot influence the normal use of data which it is protecting; the quality cannot be degraded;

(3) Robustness: After a series of unintentional or intentional signal processing, a watermarking can still maintain a certain degree of integrity and can be identified accurately. Possible signal processes includes the channel noise introduced by transmission, filtering, D/A (digital/analog) or A/D (analog/digital) conversion, resampling, cutting, displacement, change of size, and bad compression code. It is used in digital watermarking and fragile watermarking of copyright protection and protects integrity. This type of watermarking also implants invisible information into content data. When contents have changed, watermarking should change correspondingly, as a result specialists can identify if initial data has been tampered.

(4) The payload of data: It means that watermarking code's bit number in unit time or in a piece of work. Different application may need different payloads of data. Plenty of applications ask for a detector executing two functions. It must first judge whether watermarking exists. If watermarking exists, the second step is it can identify which information is encrypted.

(5) False positive rate: False positive means, detecting watermarking in works which actually do not include watermarking. False positive rate is the number of times of false-positive occurrence which is given in the number of detection. We have two appreciably different ways to define the false positive rate. This often is confusing in the two ways in watermarking works. The difference between them lies in regarding a watermark as a random variable or regarding carrier's works as a random variable.

In the second definition, a false positive rate means assuming watermarking is certain and picks the exhibit randomly. The detector can detect the probability of watermarking in the works. The distribution should be tightly related to an application. The false positive rate of first definition and second definition have distinct differences, so in most applications, people still pay more attention to the second definition of the false positive rate.

The classification of watermarking:

Classified by character

According to the characteristics of watermarking, it can be divided into robust digital watermarking and fragile digital watermarking. The robust watermarking is mainly used to identify the copyright's information in digital works to implant creator and owner's marking information into multimedia content's data, and to implant the mark of the buyer (serial number). When violations of copyright occurs, the creator or owner's information is used for indicating information which belongs to the copyright's owner, as well as, a serial number that is used for tracking users who violated the agreement and offered multimedia data to pirates. Protecting copyright's digital watermarking requires strong robustness and security. Besides survival in ordinary image processing (such as filtering, adding noise, replacing, compressing etc.), it also need to resist some malicious attack.

The fragile watermarking is contrary to robust watermarking. It is mainly used for protecting integrity, by implanting invisible information into the content data. When contents have been changed, watermarking should change correspondingly. As a result specialized persons can identify if initial data has been tampered. The fragile watermarking has strong immunity (robustness) when coping with ordinary image processing (such as filtering, adding noise, replacing, compressing, etc.). Meanwhile, it also asks for a strong sensibility, allowing distortion of a certain degree and can detect a distorted condition. It must be sensitive to an alteration of signal. According to the status of fragile watermarking, people can judge the data whether if or not it has been tampered.

Classified by different media attached by watermarking

According to the media which attached by watermarking, digital watermarking can be divided into image watermarking, audio watermarking, video watermarking, text watermarking and meshes watermarking which is used for the 3D mesh model. Along with the development of digital technology, it will appear in more kinds of digital media and the emergent corresponding watermarking technology simultaneously.

Classified by the process of detection

According to the process of detection of watermarking, digital watermarking can be divided into plaintext watermarking and blind watermarking. The Plaintext watermarking needs initial data in the detection process, while blind watermarking only needs the secret key, not the initial data. Generally speaking, the robustness of plaintext watermarking is strong, but its application suffers from restriction of the cost of storage. At present, watermarking research by academic circles is mainly focused on blind watermarking.

Classified by content

According to the content of watermarking, it can be divided into meaningful watermarking and meaningless watermarking. The meaningful watermarking means watermarking itself is a code which belongs to certain digital image (such as brand image) or a fragment of digital audio. Meaningless watermarking copes with only one serial number. The superiority of meaningful watermarking lies in if watermarking which has been decoded has damage because of an attack or other reasons. People can still affirm watermarking and whether it exists by means of optical observation. But for meaningless watermarking, if watermarking sequence which is recoded has some errors of code element, users only can use statistical decision to confirm watermarking and whether it exists in signal.

Classified by purpose

The demand of different applications brings up different watermarking technologies. According to the purpose of watermarking, it can be divided into ticket anti-counterfeiting watermarking, copyright protecting watermarking, tamper prompting watermarking, and hiding identification watermarking.

The ticket anti-counterfeiting watermarking is a kind of watermarking, mainly used for anti-counterfeiting of printed tickets, electronic tickets, and certificates. Generally speaking, the maker of fake money cannot make much modification to the ticket's image, so an operation likes the change of scale needs not to be considered. But on the other hand, people have to consider some situations such as damaged tickets and vague patterns. In consideration of the demand for rapid detection, the digital watermarking algorithm is used for a ticket's anti-counterfeiting and cannot be too complicated.

At present, the copyright identification watermarking is a research area of digital watermarking that has been highly explored. Digital works area commodity as well as intellectual works, and the dual nature decides copyright identification watermarking that mainly emphasizes invisibility and robustness, and have less demand for data amount.

Tamper prompt watermarking is a kind of fragile watermarking. Its purpose is to identify original document information's integrity and authenticity.

The purpose of hiding identification watermarking is to hide an important label of secretive data and to restrict illegal users to use the secretive data.

Division by the hidden location of watermarking

According to the hidden location of watermarking, it can be divided into time domain watermarking, frequent domain watermarking, time/frequent domain, and time/scale domain digital watermarking.

Time domain digital watermarking is adding watermarking information directly into the signal, while frequent domain watermarking, time/frequent domain, as well as the time/scale domain watermarking is by adding a watermark into the discrete cosine transform (DCT) transformed domain, time/frequent transformed domain and wavelet transformed domain respectively.

Along with the development of digital watermarking technology, various kinds watermarking algorithms have emerged, and the hidden location of watermarking is no longer restricted to the four kinds mentioned above. So long as constituting a kind of signal transformation, we might hide watermarking in its transformation space.

7.4.2 Image Watermarking Technology

Following the development of multimedia technology, digital media has become more important in people's life. It is widely used in various domains, such as education, scientific research, projects, and other faucets of everyday life. However, the digital media (mainly including digital picture, video, and audio) provides a great quantity of convenience, and has a serious defect in that is it is easily modified illegally, copied and transmitted. The rapid development and popularity of the Internet makes safety a problem. If intellectual property cannot be protected effectively, it will cause tremendous economic loss.

In order to protect the intellectual property of digital media, people adopted the method of encryption. One method of encrypting data is to allow deciphering only by an authorized user that possesses a secret key allowing use of a digital media production. But the method of encryption only controls users whether they are able to access data. It has no direct relation between the base data. In case of being deciphered, the data will be easily modified, copied, and transmitted. To solve this hidden danger, people put forward the new method of intellectual property protection (IPR), that is a digital watermark. It is implanted into the information (such as a pseudorandom sequence or a processed mark media) which marks the copyright's owner into media productions which need protection. However, in this process, implanted information cannot be perceived by using a specific technology, only the owner of intellectual property can confirm the digital watermark existing through a detector.

The application areas of digital picture watermarking:

Copyright protection

Watermarking information which is implanted into the image can be used for marking a copyright's owner. In the legal dispute related to a copyright, if the copyright's owner of an image has added watermarking in advance, we can use a secret key to pick up the watermarking from an image, hereby proving owner's intellectual property and protecting owner's interest effectively.

Adding fingerprints

Watermarking (fingerprint) is used for marking users who make use of an image generated from user's information and then implanted when release. In case of discovering an unauthorized illegal copy, we can ensure its source in accordance with watermarking (fingerprint) which is detected. It can be used for tracking illegal copies and illegal usage.

Content checking

Digital images can be easily modified. In order to verify the integrity of the image's content, we must add some corresponding content checking measure. Traditional methods use a digital signature, but because a digital signature is very sensitive to the change of an image's content, so it greatly restricted its application. After having digital watermarking technology, it can judge an image and if it has been modified by watermarking detection.

Information hide out

Information hide out is one of most important applications of watermarking. It is putting communication information implanted into images by the form of watermarking, then delivering it to opposite side, which can accomplish communication with opposite side through a form which is difficult to perceive.

7.4.3 3D Watermarking Technology

Digital museums are established for the well-being of research, exploration, and appreciation of cultural relic's experts and enthusiasts. The contents are placed on the internet, and allow more persons to freely visit, browse, or download museums' information without the restrictions of time and place. People who download information from digital museums can be divided into two groups. One group uses the information for collection and appreciation. The other group utilizes museums' information on the internet for other purposes (such as people use the information in another place and give clear indication that they are originator or people use the information which is modified partly as commercial data). If we want to protect copyright infringement effectively, a challenge is in front of us. We need to take some measures to cope with the infringement act, so we can devise and achieve a digital watermarking system.

A digital museum ordinarily includes text information, 2D still images, audio, video, and meshes model information. The system which is introduced here is mainly a study on 3D meshes digital watermarking. We put forward three kinds of mesh watermarking algorithms which can be used in digital museums, testing and watermarking attacks have been finished. The functions of the system are shown in Fig. 7.5.

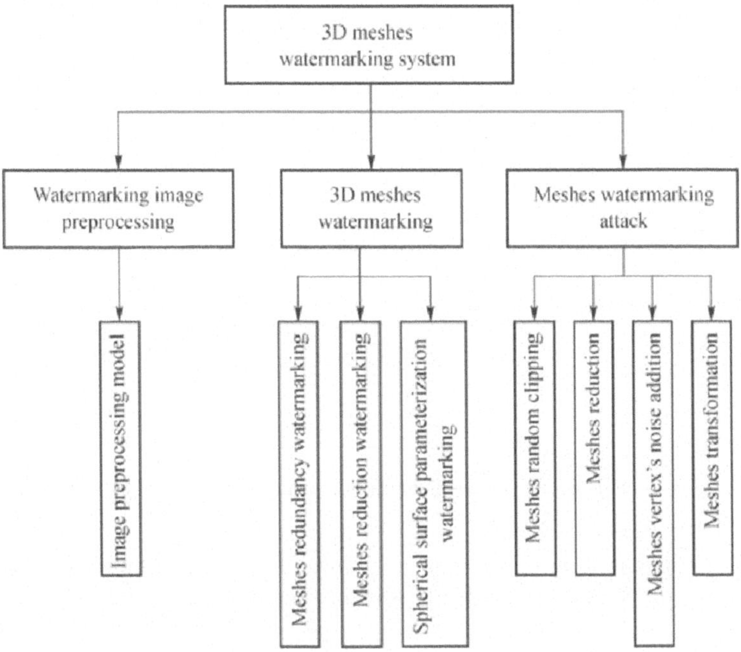

Fig. 7.5 3D meshes watermarking system.

In consideration of the features of a three-dimensional data model, it cannot be the same as two-dimensional digital watermarking algorithms. To process an image's pixel and implant and extract watermarking the use of changing the triangular patch's vertex coordinates among a three-dimensional data model to achieve the implanting operation of watermarking is applied. In the three-dimensional space, a little change to a vertex coordinate would not influence the visual effect of a three-dimensional data display. We can also change the relationship between vertices to implant watermarking. If we mishandle the major relation, we will cause a large change in its vision. We can also change its texture mapping information in three-dimensional data to implant watermarking, but this method has defects. For a 3D scanner or self-reconstructed initial three-dimensional data, which are not embodied with texture information, watermarking information cannot be implanted.

The texture is only the additional information of three-dimensional data and it is easily damaged or replaced. The supreme advantage of this algorithm introduced below is it is simple and practical.

Implanting watermarking algorithm:

(1) Read three-dimensional data. Processed three-dimensional data of the system is restricted to universal 3Ds Max format data, extracting its vertex coordinate from three-dimensional data.

(2) Divide watermarking information into binary code streams. In this system, we still adopt two-dimensional colored image signs as watermarking information to protect three-dimensional cultural relic's data.

(3) Implant watermarking operation. Implanting binary code streams into vertex coordinate which have been extracted.

The specific procedure indicated in Fig. 7.6.

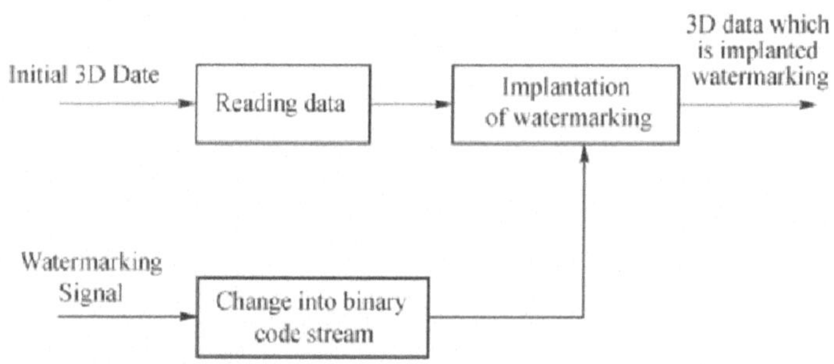

Fig. 7.6 Flow chart of 3D geometrical model implanted watermarking information.

The watermarking extraction procedure of this algorithm is simple. The extraction procedure has no need for involvement of initial three-dimensional data:

(1) Reading three-dimensional geometrical model data: to extract vertex coordinate information from numerous three-dimensional data information.

(2) Watermarking extraction. Extracting watermarking from the vertex coordinate information as extracted before.

(3) Byte recovery to binary code stream which has been extracted for the process recovery byte operations. Revert to two-dimensional colored image information when it is implanted.

The specific procedure is indicated in Fig. 7.7.

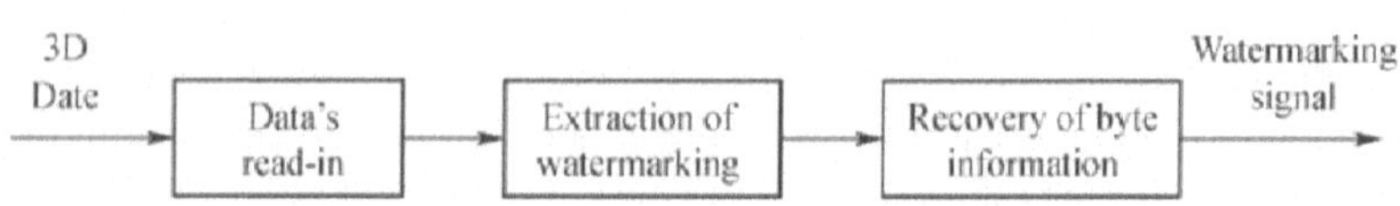

Fig. 7.7 Flow chart of 3D geometrical model watermarking extraction.

References

[1] Xu S, Chen H, Dong S (2007) The Introduction of Digital Museum. Shanghai Science and Technology Press, Shanghai

[2] Beijing Association of Science and Technology Information Center (2009) The Research and Practice of Digital Museum. Communication University of China Press, Beijing

[3] Liu Y, Zhang H (2007) The Vitality of Digital Museum: The Research of Beijing Digital Museum in 2007. Beijing Broadcasting Institute Press, Beijing

[4] Chen H, Wu Q (2006) The Norm and Method of Digital Museum's Resource Construction. Shanghai Science and Technology Press, Shanghai

[5] Qi Y, Shen X (2008) The Management and Demonstration of Museum's Digital Resource. Shanghai Science and Technology Press, Shanghai

8 Application Examples of Cultural Heritage Digitization Protection

This chapter introduces the key technologies of digital protection successfully applied at the third excavation of Pit One of Terracotta Warriors and Horses of Qi Shihuang. Also the virtual exhibition of Tang Paradise and other digital protection of cultural heritage will be discussed. These applications also raised new requirements for digitization protection technology of cultural heritage.

8.1 Digitization of Terracotta Warriors and Horses of Qin Shihuang

The Terracotta archaeological team of the Institute of Archaeology of Shanxi Province carried out excavation of pit one during 1978 – 1984. They excavated an area of 2,000 square meters and unearthed 1087 figurines. Part of the figurines were repaired and reset. In 1985, the archaeological team started a second exploration area of 2,000 square meters. Unfortunately, because of inadequate technical equipment, the second excavation was stopped in 1986 to better protect the cultural relics. On 13 June 2009, the third excavation of Pit One of Terracotta Warriors and Horses of Qin Shihuang was started as the first independent excavation. Currently, the heritage accumulation layer has been emptied and has unearthed 114 soldiers, 12 horses, and a large number of bronze and lacquered devices. Figure 8.1 (a) shows the famous Pit One panorama of Terracotta Warriors and Horses of Qin Shihuang. Figure 8.1 (b) shows the G:9 and G:10 dig sites through the location of the third excavation. Figure 8.1 (c) shows the panorama of the G:9 and G:10 dig sites through holes. Figure 8.1 (d) details of the portion of the G:9 dig site (G:9 and G:10 represent the index dig site of Pit One respectively).

The third excavation of Pit One of Terracotta Warriors and Horses of Qin Shihuang is of great significance in academic research and heritage preservation. But with the excavation, monuments, and weather exposure of the relics, the traditional means of recording the information became too stretched to be completed. The Visualization Research Institute of Northwest University of China in September 2009 along with the Pit One archaeological team began to explore digitalization of the third excavation of Pit One of Terracotta

Fig. 8.1 Terracotta Warriors and Horses of Qin Shihuang (with permission from Weihong Xu).

Warriors and Horses of Qin Shihuang. Digital technologies with three-dimensional capabilities are used to scan, perform virtual recovery, virtual extraction, provide multi-angles, profile, and produce a three-dimensional map to model the excavation sites. This laid the groundwork for preparation of the excavation report that included collection data, a three-dimensional model, monuments, and relics to establish an information database of the site. Report writing and other written materials about the classification, statistics, query, and display was performed. The collection of figurines pieces for the virtual figurines recovery phase was an output. The preparation of a database to provide real-time recovery graph, preparation vertical and horizontal angles of figurines profiles, data sheets and other forms of information for report was achieved.

8.1.1 Fragment Assembly and Virtual Restoration of Pottery

In the third excavation of Pit One of Terracotta Warriors and Horses of Qin Shihuang Horses, more than 100 pieces of pottery were unearthed along with some figurines. The question arose of how to manage the burnt charcoal, and over a thousand pieces of figurines and pottery horses that were smashed. To transform this debris into a virtual recovery, excavations of the terracotta figurines were needed to solve the problem

Data capture and preprocessing

Data collection is a digitization process that contains steps of obtaining some kind of surface, texture, material and other discrete data information of debris using technical means. Next, converting this information into a certain format, and storing it in a computer for research. Figure 8.2 shows the data capture.

(a) Figurines defragmentation

(b) Marker positioning

(c) Data capture by 3D laser scanner

Fig. 8.2 Data capture.

The collected data usually includes a certain amount of noise, and often has some missing data. Therefore the preprocessing step is used to remove the noise and repair defects as necessary. Figure 8.3 shows the data pre-processing work on the figurines.

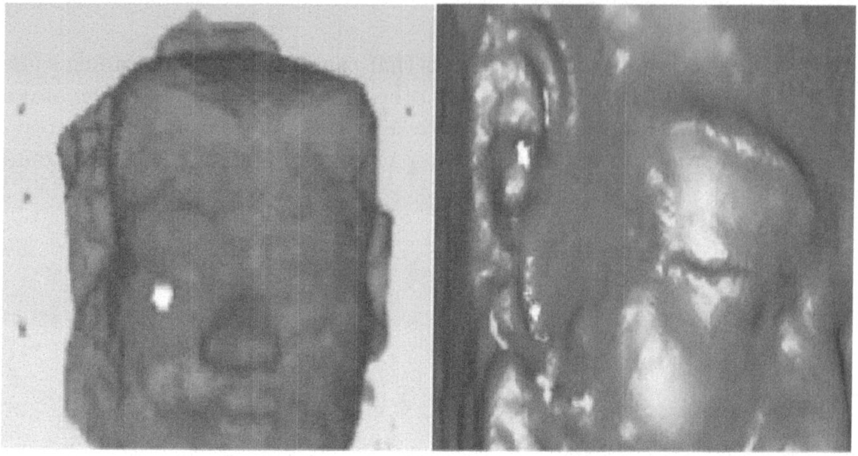

(a) Noise data (b) Model repair

Fig. 8.3 Data preprocessing.

Information management

The collection of the terracotta figures and unearthed information are imported into a database. 2D and 3D model information of each fragment is stored. Figure 8.4 shows the storage information.

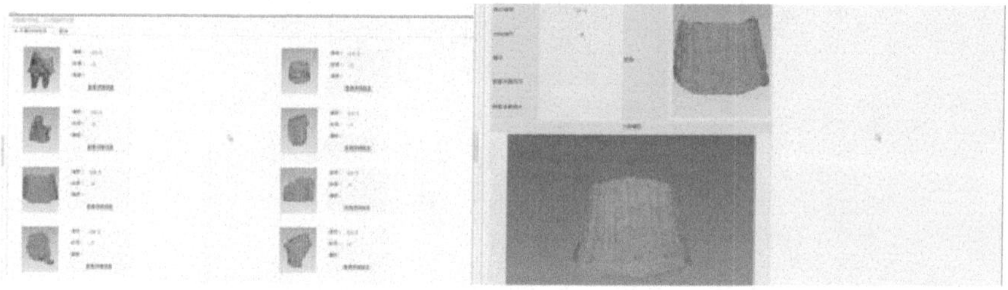

(a) 2D information storage (b) 3D information storage

Fig. 8.4 Information management.

Fragments assembly

After pre processing and the extraction of contour features of three-dimension data, we conduct inter active matching using feature matching to perform virtual recovery of the terracotta figures. Figure 8.5 shows the splicing process of the terracotta fragments.

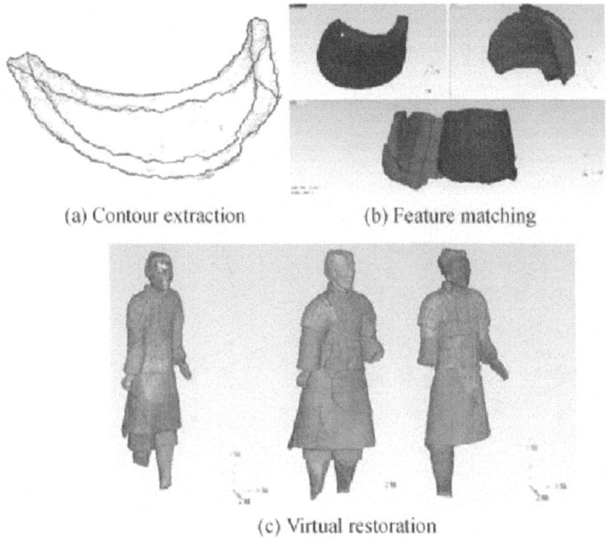

(a) Contour extraction (b) Feature matching

(c) Virtual restoration

Fig. 8.5 The splicing of terracotta fragments.

Digitization of archaeological data

According to the needs of the archaeological excavations report, we develop a computer-assisted automation system to extract an artifact's front view, rear view, left view, and right view, a line graph, cuts and quantitative dimensions in order for the archaeologists to understand the internal structure of the (cultural) characteristics. Figure 8.6 shows the front view of the fragment of G:9 – 36 figurines. Figure 8.7 shows a line drawing. Figure 8.8 shows three views and the quantitative dimensioning of fragments of G:10 – 37 figurines.

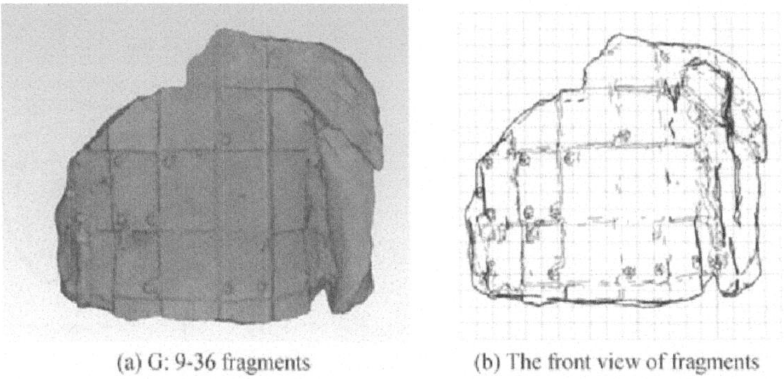

(a) G: 9-36 fragments (b) The front view of fragments

Fig. 8.6 The front view of fragments.

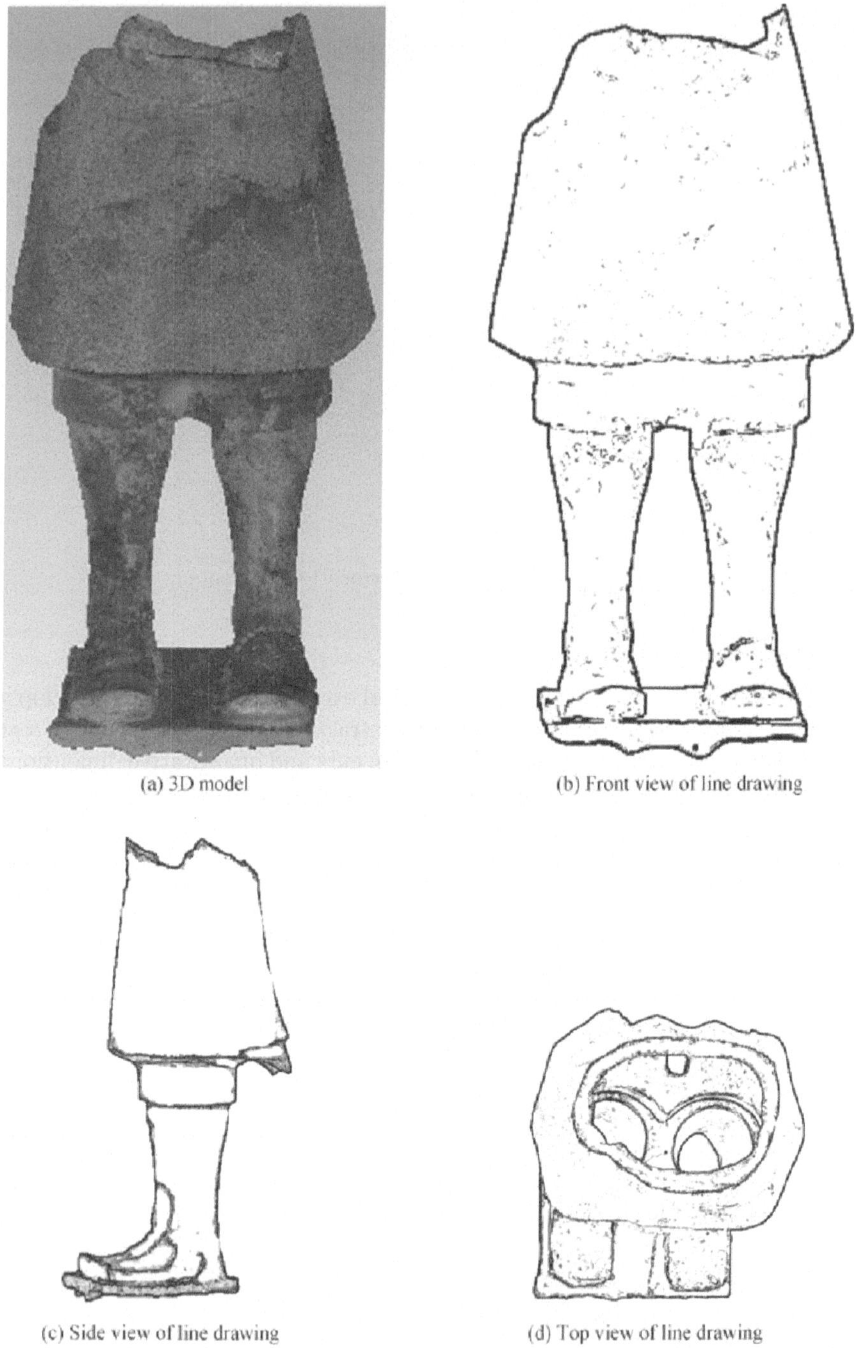

Fig. 8.7 Line drawing.

Fig. 8.8 Three views and the quantitative dimensioning of G:10–37.

8.1.2 Reconstruction and Display of Original Excavation Site

Data capture of scene

Using a 3D large scene laser scanner to obtain a more complete and high quality 3D scene data, we need to consider the viewpoint, laser scanner, resolution, the data format and other issues. In addition, we introduced a number of auxiliary equipment for the extraction of relevant data. In order to restore a large scale three-dimensional model of the scene, a GPS system to get the location information and a digital video camera was used to obtain texture information of buildings. Figure 8.9 is a large three-dimensional laser scanner.

Fig. 8.9 A 3D large laser scanner.

Data fusion

As the model data is based on many different viewpoints, the data obtained in each scan defines the current viewpoint as the origin of a co-ordinate system. Therefore, in order to obtain all the scan data in a common coordinate system, we first need to solve the problem of data fusion under different points of view. Figure 8.10 is the point cloud data of Terracotta

(a) Excavation site in March 2010 (b) Excavation sitein in June 2010 (c) Excavation site in March 2011

Fig. 8.10 The point cloud data of Terracotta Warriors and Horses of Qin Shihuang G:9 and G:10 indifferent periods after fusion.

Warriors and Horses of Qin Shihuang G:9 and G:10 in different periods after fusion.

Triangularion

The data is a discrete three-dimension point cloud after fusion. This cannot be a true and accurate representation the surface of excavation site, soa three-dimensional cloud point needs to be transformed into triangle mesh model. Figure 8.11 is the grid model of the the 3D model of Terracotta Warriors

(a) The first excavation

(b) The second excavation

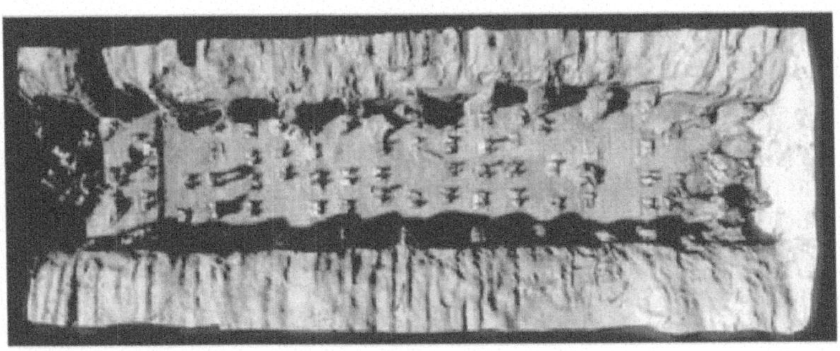

(c) The Third excavation

Fig. 8.11 Model of Terracotta Warriors and Horses of Qin Shihuang G:10 in different periods.

and Horses of Qin Shihuang Warriors G:10 in different periods. To achieve better visual effects, we need to provide further refinement of the grid model. Compared with the manual measurement method, the extracted cutaway view and dimensions directly from the 3D mesh model are time-saving and accurate options. Figure 8.12 is cutaway view of Terracotta Warriors and Horses of Qin Shihuang G:10 in different periods.

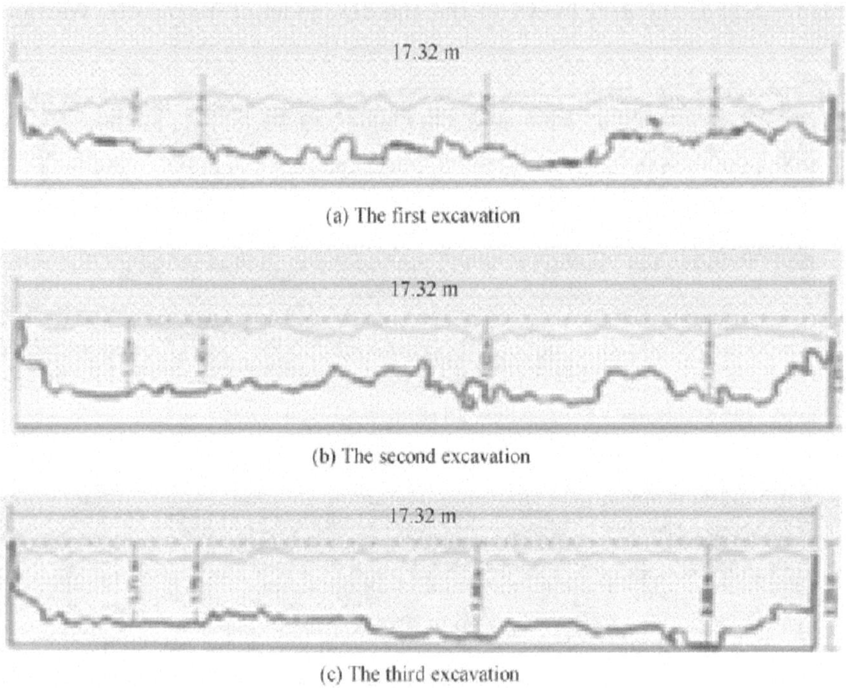

Fig. 8.12 Cutaway view of Terracotta Warriors and Horses of Qin Shihuang G:10 in different periods.

Texture mapping

After data fusion and grid stages, we derive a triangle mesh model with a certain geometric features but with complex accuracy. In order to better meet the visual requirements and restore a more realistic three-dimensional model, it must be transformed into a simple polygon mesh. To perform this step one must flat out the three-dimensional model in order to make a better match of texture photographs and three-dimensional models. Fig. 8.13 is the final renderings of Terracotta Warriors and Horses of Qin Shihuang G:10 after texture mapping.

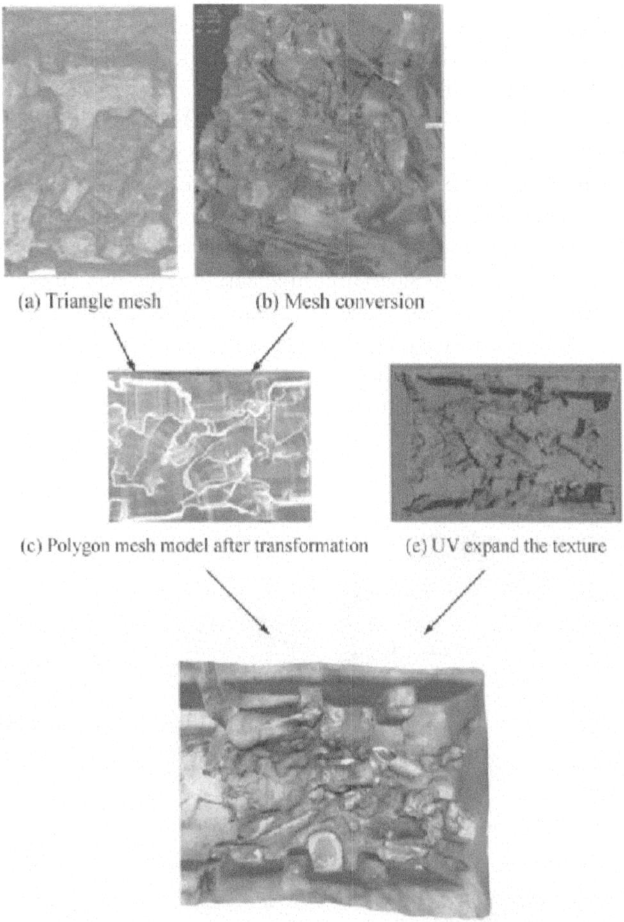

Fig. 8.13 Final renderings of Terracotta Warriors and Horses of Qin Shihuang G:10 after texture mapping.

8.2 Digitalization and Virtual Display of Tang Paradise

Tang Paradise is a cultural themed garden with a comprehensive display of China's large scale style of the Tang Dynasty. In history, the Hibiscus Park was a prestigious Royal Regency. Emperor Wen (AD 583) built "Paradise" on Tang Paradise. Today Tang Paradise was built at the original site of the Tang Dynasty Lotus Park. Tang Paradise has a total construction area of nearly 100,000 square meters, including Pavilion, Units Floor, Balconies, Bridges, Galleries, and other attractions. Garden pavilions are richly and ornamented

Ladies Pavilion, Royal Palace Banquet, Lim Court, Apricot garden, Luyu Teahousem, and many other city attractions. The background environment brings the visitor back into history, allows them to experience culture, life and shows the brilliant civilization of the Tang Dynasty.

Ancient buildings of the Tang Dynasty style garden are the first in the country on an architectural scale. Tang Paradise concentrates on all the architectural forms of the Tang period. The design and construction of Tang's architectural and park landscape inherit and develop China's classical architecture and classical garden style buildings. Its unique charm is unparalleled in Chinese history and is the spiritual home of the local descendants. It is known as the Chinese history garden, the spirit garden, nature garden, and humanities garden. It is a symbol of a great era in the rise of China and is a totem of China's prosperity in the new century. Fig. 8.14 shows the Tang Paradise Park building.

The main entrance

Apricot garden

Ladies hall

Thecorner of Tang Paradise Park

Fig. 8.14 The Tang Paradise park building.

Fig. 8.14 Continued.

Virtual Tour of Tang Paradise

The overall design ideas of Tang Paradise are inspired by architectural ideas and architectural forms of the Tang Dynasty. The layout of three triple door sign, the courtyard and use of the Tang Dynasty stratification and sub-system approach, provide the essence of ancient architecture conversion in the actual construction. In order to establish the three-dimensional digital files of the Tang Dynasty building reconstruction process, we need to get three-dimensional data of a single timber component through a variety of high-precision measurements. There has to be comprehensive quality control and supervision from wood processing to the whole building components assembly. The final step is using virtual reality technology to develop virtual building environments.

Data acquisition

Taking into account the requirements of the complex structure of Tang Paradise and the precision needed, a series of data acquisition methods are applied to the process. Steps include the manual measurement, measuring instruments, photogrammetry, and laser scanning. Their results complement each other and help to explore the best solution.

Three-dimensional modeling

Based on the above means to obtain the data, modeling of all of the building objects and components are executed as a unit. Figure 8.15 shows a complex house that is composed of different types and shapes of components. Three-dimensional modeling work is used in each component model.

Fig. 8.15 3D model of house

Texture mapping

A digital camera is used to produce digital images and photos hop software is used to correct, scale, and match the features. Due to the runtime of three-dimensional models, the modeling approach is very different with a shape-based model. Most of other technologies (such as texture) are increasing the complexity of geometric shapes to improve fidelity. Figure 8.16 is ancient buildings after texture mapping.

Fig. 8.16 Texture mapping.

Virtual tour

Application of a virtual reality development platform for secondary development is used to add sky boxes, sunlight, rain, snow and other scenes visual effects. The use of a fixed camera or walking in a VRP is used to generate a roaming camera system. Figure 8.17 is a virtual tour of Tang Paradise.

Fig. 8.17 Virtual tour of Tang Paradise.

This chapter shows the protection technologies of cultural heritage digitization by two application examples. One is the third excavation of Pit One of Terracotta Warriors and Horses of Qin Shihuang and the other is the virtual exhibition of Tang Paradise. From the applications, it should be said that the digital protection of cultural heritage is a complicated work. For the particularity of cultural heritage, it brings about some new challenges for digitization protection technologies such as data capturing and pre processing, 3D scenario modeling, data fusion. To a certain extent, massive archaeological data processing, large scale scene modelling and some new end-user applications such as interactive touring are the direction of future development.

References

[1] Information Center of Beijing Association for Science and Technology (2009) The Research and Practice of Digital Museum. Communication University of China Press, Beijing

[2] Chen H, Wu Q (2006) The Norm and Method of Digital Museum's Resource Construction. Shanghai Scientific and Technical Publishers, Shanghai

[3] Qi Y, Shen X (2008) The Management and Demonstration of Museum's Digital Resource. Shanghai Scientific and Technical Publishers, Shanghai

[4] Xu S, Chen H, Dong S(2007) The Introduction of Digital Museum. Shanghai Scientific and Technical Publishers, Shanghai

[5] Liu Y, Zhang H (2007) The Vitality of Digital Museum: The Research of Beijing Digital Museum in 2007. Communication University of China Press, Beijing

Appendix Demos of Cases Study

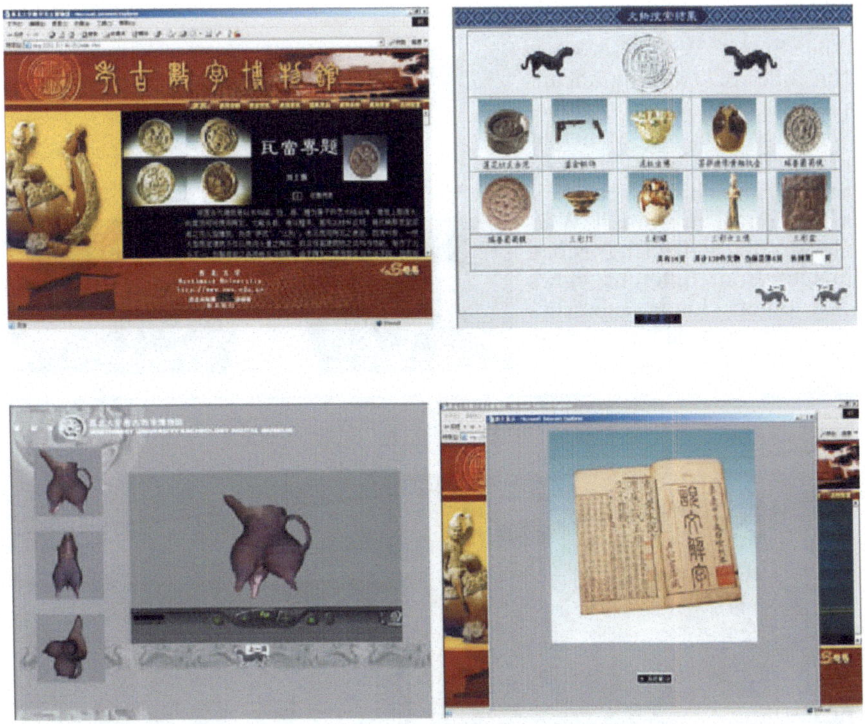

Digital museum utilizes computer and network techniques to provide an on-line museum visiting. We develop an archaeological digital museum based on Browser/Server (B/S) structure providing a content-based retrieval function for images and models (top). Visitors can access the website to see the artifacts with a various forms: 3D models, panoramic photography, images, videos, and text (bottom).

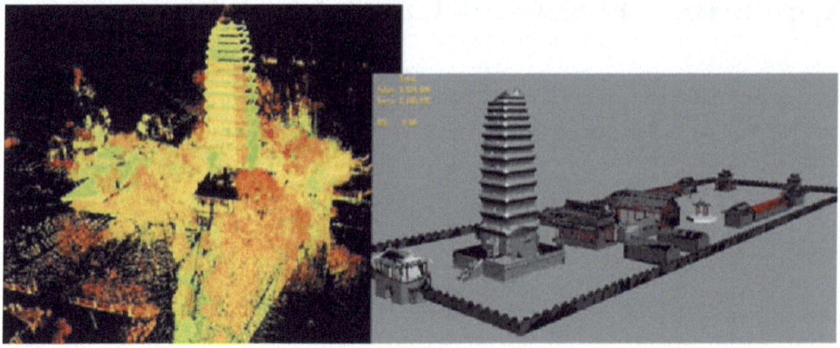

The Small Wild Goose is the one of two significant pagodas in Xi'an, China, which stands at a height of 43 meters with thirteen tiers. We achieve the digitalization of the Small Wild Goose by registering range images from different views and point clouds construction. The right is virtual tour of Small Wild Goose Pagoda.

Beijing Hutong is the most representative civil building of Beijing. We construct the Beijing Hutong digital scene and develop a system for virtual tour of Beijing Hutong in the virtual environment.

We develop a virtual recover system, which has been applied in the virtual restoration of fractures collected in the procedure of the third excavation of pit one of the Qin Terracotta Warriors and Horses. The top is the fractures assembly (the left shows the fractures of Terracotta Warriors and Horses and the right is the restoration result displayed from two views). The middle is another example of virtual restoration of fragments. The bottom is the digital model of pit one of Terra Cotta Warriors and Horses.

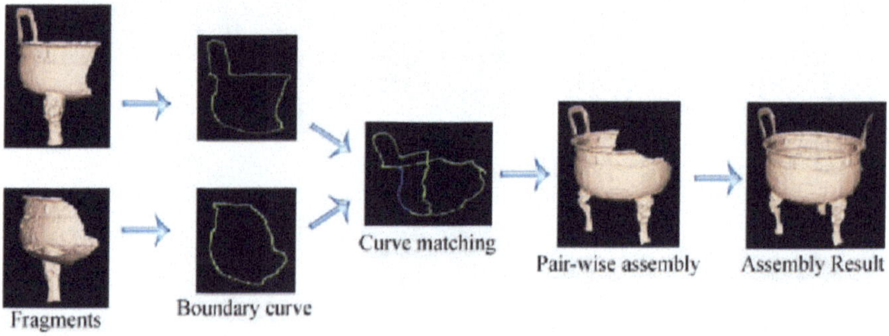

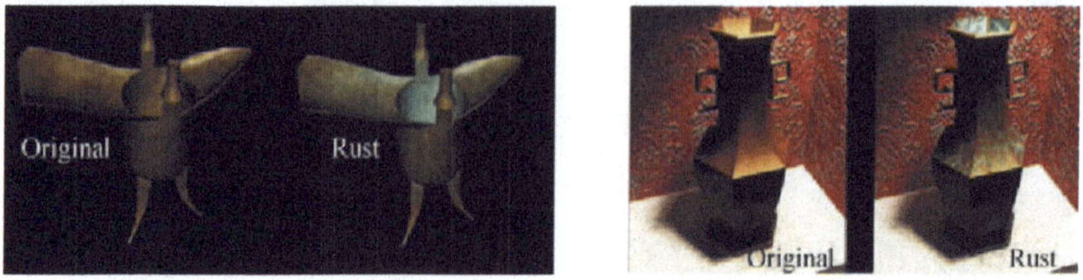

Bronze wares were used in ancestral rituals during the Shang and Zhou Dynasty. Aiming at Bronze ware digital preservation, we do some researches and develop a system on artifact modeling, fractures assembly, and reality rendering, and achieve the Bronze ware modeling by register multi-view range images (top). In order to recover the incomplete artifacts, we match the neighbor fragments by fracture surface and fracture curve. The middle is the procedure of virtual restoration by fracture curve. In order to improve the reality rendering of artifact, we simulate Bronze wares rust (bottom).

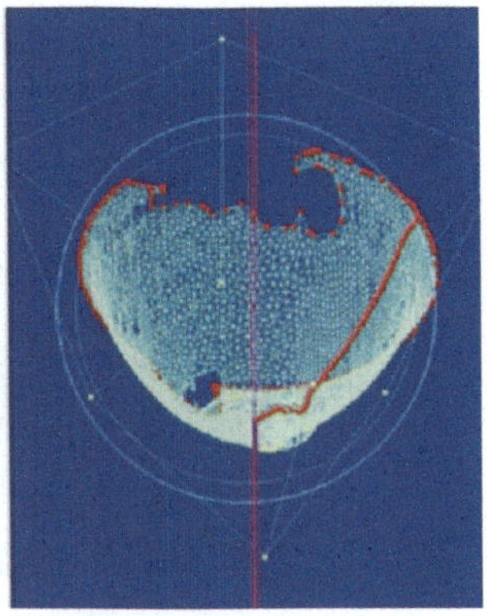

In China, most of porcelains are made by a potter's wheel. Aiming at restoring these incomplete pottery shape artifacts, we develop the virtual restoration system based on their two characteristics: symmetry axis and generatrix profile (top). The middle is the artifact reconstruction based on characteristics, and the texture mapping technology is applied to show the pottery more reality. The bottom is other examples of the recovery of Yao Zhou's porcelains.

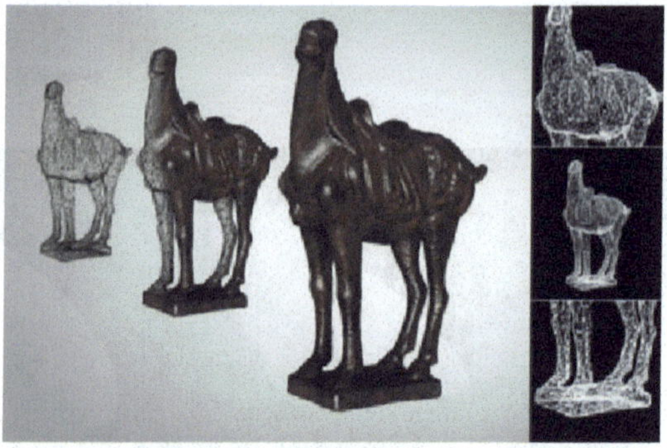

We use 3D laser scanners to capture the range images of artifact from different views and register all the range images to generate a complete digital model. The top is the 3D model of ancient stone horse more than three meters high. The middle is the 3D model of bronze copper clepsydra, which was excavated from one of the tombs of Han dynasty. The bottom is a stone horse less than 20 centimeters high.

Index

The manufacturer's authorised representative in the EU is Springer Nature Customer Service Centre GmbH, Europaplatz 3, 69115 Heidelberg, Germany. If you have any concerns regarding our products, please contact ProductSafety@springernature.com

Printed and bound by CPI Group (UK) Ltd, Croydon, CR0 4YY
22/09/2026
02221055-0010